Implementing Mentoring Schemes

Implementing Mentoring Schemes

A Practical Guide to Successful Programs

Nadine Klasen and David Clutterbuck

ELSEVIER
BUTTERWORTH
HEINEMANN

AMSTERDAM • BOSTON • HEIDELBERG • LONDON • NEW YORK • OXFORD
PARIS • SAN DIEGO • SAN FRANCISCO • SINGAPORE • SYDNEY • TOKYO

Elsevier Butterworth-Heinemann
Linacre House, Jordan Hill, Oxford OX2 8DP
200 Wheeler Road, Burlington, MA 01803

First published 2002
Reprinted 2003, 2004

British Library Cataloguing in Publication Data
Klasen, Nadine
   Implementing mentoring schemes: a practical guide to
   successful programs
   1. Mentoring in business 2. Employees — Training of
   I. Title II. Clutterbuck, David, 1947–
   658.3'12404

ISBN 0 7506 5430 9

For information on all Elsevier Butterworth-Heinemann publications
please visit our website at www.bh.com

Typeset by David Gregson Associates, Beccles, Suffolk
Printed and bound in Great Britain by MPG Books Ltd, Bodmin

Contents

Case studies

Foreword

A Chartered Institute of Personnel and Development (CIPD) Survey in 1999 suggested that 87 per cent of businesses in the UK utilized mentoring. However, both the definition and practice of mentoring varies enormously, as Nadine Klasen and David Clutterbuck testify in this helpful book. It is also true that mentoring, as a practice, is as old as the hills and indeed, as the authors show, has inevitable roots in Greek mythology!

If this is so, what now can be said? What this book contributes is a thorough and rigorous implementation manual for the enthusiastic champion of best practice mentoring in any twenty-first century organization. This knowledge is based on over 20 years' experience of putting mentoring into practice and is laced with a great variety of successful examples of mentoring schemes in both UK and international settings.

I have been 'menteed' and a 'mentor' over my career, and can instantly recall many of the lessons learnt – often the hard way! I smiled when I read the authors' specification for a mentor – characteristics that included 'having negative experiences in business knowledge and experience'. I remember a first failure at persuading a company board to embrace a radical change program some 20 years ago. I remember describing to my mentor, Ralph Cowan, then Managing Director of Wimpey PLC, that I wished the ground had opened up underneath me and I could have disappeared. He asked, 'Did you lobby anyone about these changes before the board meeting?'. His advice, shared from his own experience, was 'never go in cold'. This has stayed with me ever since – I have so often seen the sense of it in later opportunities. As a mentor, that, along with a lot of other positive and negative experiences, has, I hope, helped me to help others attain their goals.

Mentoring, it strikes me, is like a lot of other solutions to the complex nature of organizational survival and growth today – it can remain as another good idea or become part of the culture. No-one will say it is bad or redundant, but how many will see it as important enough to take priority over other seemingly important calls on management and employee time? Most organizations will have enthusiasts and champions for the concept and practice of mentoring. A few, the minority, of organizations have thoroughly embraced the best practice ideas and techniques described in this book and have made it part of their culture – the 'way we do things round here'. These organizations will have potentially reaped the benefit of the growth and development of the people they employ – both in mentor and mentee roles, as the authors demonstrate. Those organizations will have made mentoring part of the language, and created an expectation that mentoring will happen, that it is worth spending time on, and that the top of the organization supports and believes that business and personal results will be demonstrated. I was pleased to see the authors give due weight to the issues of evaluation and measurement.

I learnt a lot from this book, and I believe others keen on the subject will also gain. It contains helpful positioning concepts such as the integrating role of mentoring in bringing together for the mentor the roles of coach, guardian, networker, facilitator and counsellor (Chapter 1). At the other extreme, it gives detailed checklists for the mentoring scheme implementer to ensure that the pitfalls of experience are learned from. In fact, the volume is a mentoring experience by definition in its own right.

Professor Clive Morton OBE
Associate Professor of HRM and Business Strategy, Middlesex University
Chairman, Association of Management Education and Development
Former Vice President, CIPD PAGE

Preface

Mentoring as a process formally endorsed, encouraged and supported by an organization is a relatively new phenomenon. Until a few decades ago, mentoring happened informally, on an *ad hoc* basis, typically because a senior person in an organization – be it a company, politics or religion – was seized by the urge to share the secrets of his or her success. The instinct to help others to follow in one's footsteps, to pass on accumulated wisdom, to relive one's career vicariously, is a powerful one. Properly harnessed, with the best interests of the less experienced individual at heart and in an atmosphere of mutual respect and mutual listening, this instinct can be a power for great good. Used selfishly, without sufficient understanding of the needs of the recipient and without commitment to mutual learning, it can be suffocating, or the source of dysfunctional dependency.

Structured mentoring provides a framework where both parties in a relationship can be supported in clarifying their roles, their objectives and how they will behave towards each other. It enables mentoring to be focused on those who will most benefit from it, including groups who might otherwise be marginalized. It also provides the bedrock upon which informal, unsupported relationships can grow.

Views of what constitutes good practice have evolved significantly over the past three decades. The emphasis of mentoring in many countries has shifted away from sponsorship and career management to self-development and helping the individual tobecome self-reliant. The outcomes have become much more clearly linked to organizational goals. The degree of formality in the structure has been softened to allow much greater freedom for the mentoring pair to pursue their own goals in their own style, and mentees have been encouraged to use the mentoring relationship as the foundation for building a wide network of learning and supporting resources.

Of course, there are still many organizations that continue to apply mentoring in a more directive style (I recently encountered one that gave each mentoring pair a monthly guide on what to talk about when they met!). However, the trend is inexorably towards a more enabling process, which benefits both mentor and mentee, the organization, and other important third parties such as line managers.

This book attempts to capture some of the best practice in mentoring program design and management, based on research, observation and the experience of companies around the world. It also tries to reflect the diversity of application and perception of mentoring in different environments and cultures.

So what exactly is this phenomenon we are describing? The *core* of structured mentoring is that it is a relationship entered into willingly by the participants and supported by the organization. As a *role*, it requires a sense of purpose and must be off-line (i.e. the mentor must not be in a position of power over the mentee), even though line managers may often use mentoring behaviours. As a *skill set*, structured mentoring has much in common with other roles, notably coaching, counselling and career management, with all of which it shares specific developmental behaviours.

Beyond the core of structured mentoring, usual practice is that the relationship is one-to-one, involves a high degree of mutual challenge and has a limited time frame, after which it evolves into an informal relationship or gradually fades away, depending on the depth of friendship achieved and the perceived utility of the meetings. Most of the interactions will be face to face rather than by e-mail. None of these aspects is central to mentoring, however, and there are examples of successful mentoring where none of these is the case.

The business of mentoring program management is at one level straightforward – enthusiasm and commitment can overcome a lot of process failings – and at another highly complex. To design and manage a *sustainable* program demands a considerable investment in preparation, resourcing and continuous support for all the parties involved. However, the rewards, particularly for the organization, are usually well worth the effort.

The job of mentoring scheme co-ordinator is not particularly easy – far from it. It demands a deep understanding of the nature and dynamics of mentoring, and a remarkable store of patience, tenacity and political skill. Yet we have never encountered a scheme co-ordinator who did not enjoy the role and feel motivated to do more of it. As mentoring becomes a core competence of managers in learning organizations, experience in managing mentoring programs will increasingly become a core competence for ambitious HR professionals.

Nadine Klasen
David Clutterbuck

Acknowledgements

We would like to express our deepest gratitude to the following people whose time, effort, and commitment have contributed so substantially to this book:

Bushra Ashraff and Belinda McGann; Melynda Benlemlih; William Benn; Malin Boultwood; Adrienne Buchanan-Murphy; Paul Burns; Alan Bush; Ian Christians; Lindy Cozens and Keith Gulliver; Tony Hardwick; Amanda Harrison and Jill Johnson; Lin Kendrick; Trish Longdon and David Rowlands; David Megginson and Paul Stokes; Clive Morton; Kristen Nostrand and Jenny Zeilmann; Eny Osung; Bernard Wynne.

Introduction

This book is written mainly from the perspective of the person responsible for designing and implementing a structured mentoring scheme – whether the program champion, the scheme co-ordinator and/or an external consultant. That said, it will be of interest to *everyone* involved with a program – for example, sponsors will gain useful insights into the potential of mentoring schemes, and mentors and mentees can gather tips on how to create successful relationships within the framework of structured mentoring. Whatever your role within a mentoring scheme, you can gain value from the book either by reading it from front to back or by dipping into individual chapters or even sections within chapters.

The book is primarily but not solely intended for organizations wanting to set up an *internal* mentoring program. It is also going to be highly relevant if you are tasked with setting up a program for, say, one or several other companies or individuals. Included in this book you will find several case studies which describe just that situation – for example, BT helped to set up a mentoring scheme for schools, to which it contributed mentors (BT employees) and an overall program co-ordinator (also a BT employee).

Throughout the 11 chapters we have tried to provide you with a thorough understanding of both mentoring *per se* as well as the design, implementation and troubleshooting of structured programs. Thus, Chapter 1 is an introductory chapter: it familiarizes you with the topic of mentoring and the particular issues that will be covered in the book. For example, it defines relevant terms and outlines the origins of mentoring. The chapter places great emphasis on ensuring that readers will understand what mentoring is and how it differs from related approaches.

The purpose of Chapter 2 is to examine the multiple ways in which mentoring benefits organizations and their people. This topic is tackled from three different perspectives: the mentee's, the mentor's, and that of the organization. Potential risks and disadvantages as well as myths surrounding mentoring are also explored. Lastly, special attention is given to the way in which mentoring outperforms other training and development approaches.

Chapter 3 explores the different objectives of business mentoring schemes such as graduate and diversity programs. These 'variations' of schemes are illustrated with case studies from a number of companies.

Chapter 4 takes account of the factors that influence mentoring relationships (e.g. the different models of associations and the degree of formality imposed on the relationship). Ways to manage these are discussed.

Chapter 5 takes a close-up look at mentors and mentees – for example, it details the mentor and mentee characteristics and behaviours that support and hinder successful relationships. It also draws attention to the roles and responsibilities of mentors and mentees.

Chapter 6 considers mentoring techniques, the mentoring process and phases of the mentoring relationship.

Chapter 7 has two main aims: the first is to explain to you *why* and *how* to conduct organizational needs and readiness analyses, and the second is to provide practical advice on the elements and format of an implementation proposal. The role of the mentoring champion is also explored.

Chapter 8 gives a step-by-step guide to implementing mentoring schemes, including the illustration of a special kind of scheme: a globally implemented program. Issues such as founding an implementation team and marketing your program are discussed.

Chapter 9 is devoted to training for mentoring schemes. It explains the rationale for training, and makes suggestions regarding who should be trained, how and by whom. Account is taken of all parties involved with a mentoring scheme, including the program co-ordinator and mentees' managers. For each of these roles you will find a separate training agenda. Suggestions for practical exercises are also made.

The topic of Chapter 10 is evaluation, which focuses on measuring the processes and outcomes of the scheme, the individual relationships and the organization as a whole. We discuss methods and timing of evaluation as well as some of the more tricky issues, such as maintaining confidentiality during measurement.

The last chapter, Chapter 11, discusses mistakes and pitfalls of mentoring schemes. It also includes tips on how to avoid and/or resolve problems in order to maintain a healthy mentoring program.

Mentoring – introductions and definitions

Learning is crucial in enabling people to be successful. This applies to both our professional and personal lives. The learning process begins on the day we are born, and continues throughout our entire life. Mentoring is one of the best methods to enhance individuals' learning and development in all walks of life. It is increasingly used at work, in education and the community for the professional and personal development of learners, bringing enormous benefits to them, their mentors and their organizations alike.

Before moving on to broader issues of mentoring, it is necessary to explain the terms used in this book. Naming the person who is (at least initially) the most instrumental in stimulating the learning and development of another individual within a mentoring relationship is the easy part: such a person is unanimously referred to as the 'mentor'. However, in the case of the person receiving the mentoring, there is no common consensus. 'Mentee', 'mentoree', 'protégé' and 'student' are among the names that have been assigned to the learner, all of which terms hold a variety of connotations. In the North American literature, 'protégé' seems to be most frequently used. However, for the purpose of this book 'mentee' is most suitable, as it best reflects our understanding of the roles that both learner and mentor play within a mentoring relationship.

Why choose 'mentee' in favour of 'protégé'? Whilst the term 'mentee' seems fairly neutral, the term 'protégé' means 'the protected one', and suggests the existence of an unequal distribution of power between the mentor and the learner. In a mentoring context this should not be the case, and any differences in power should be 'parked' outside of the relationship. This statement holds true at least for most mentoring relationships in European organizations, although the North American conceptualization of mentoring, the mentee and the mentor is distinct from the European one – a topic that we shall return to later on in this section.

'Protégé' also seems to propose that the learner is somewhat naive and less knowledgeable and has not much to contribute to the relationship, which is clearly not the case. Learners may naturally not have much knowledge to contribute in relation to their own learning needs, but the mentor may be able to learn a lot from them in other respects!

So, from here on the learner in a mentoring relationship is referred to as the mentee.

One caveat before moving on to the next sections: this chapter will be dipping into many 'big' areas of mentoring. They are 'big' in the sense that they may be controversial or complicated or very interesting (or all of these), and therefore require a lot of explanation. However, since this is only the introductory chapter, it will merely be touching on these big issues to give you a good overview of mentoring. Detailed coverage of these topics will follow in later chapters of this book.

You may now wonder why an overview of mentoring's 'big issues' is at all necessary. The answer is that it will enable you to understand the contents of the forthcoming chapters much better. In particular, it will help you to see connections between topics and to build a comprehensive model of mentoring from early on. Without such an introduction, you might experience that well-known feeling of being unable to see 'the wood for the trees'.

The importance of learning

The importance of learning for our survival and continued well-being cannot be underestimated. For virtually everyone, the following statements hold true:

- Everything an individual knows has been learned.
- Everything an individual can do has been learned, apart from a few basic reflexes that are innate and functioning from the time a human being is born.
- All attitudes, assumptions, values and beliefs have been learned.
- Attitudes, assumptions, values and beliefs influence our thoughts and behaviour. Since these have been learned (see point above), the ways in which we think and behave are also the result of previous learning.

Taken together, the above statements imply that we are, literally, the sum of all that we have learned to date. According to Honey (1999), learning is the key to our effectiveness and fulfilment:

> there is general agreement that learning is of paramount importance to us all since it underpins every aspect of our existence and well-being ... learning is the central issue for the 21st century ...

Learning is important in all aspects of our lives: for example, it can be vital for our healthy social, emotional and indeed physical development! Within the context of professional development, there are a number of compelling reasons for continued emphasis on learning:

1. Formal education and induction training alone do not fully prepare individuals for the world of work; continuous learning by way of a variety of learning methods is the only way to achieve maximum performance.
2. Changes at work are occurring faster and are often more radical as well; learning is the only way to keep up and/or keep ahead.
3. Jobs for life have gone; learning is the way to develop and maintain your employability.
4. Global competition is increasing; individual and organization-wide learning is the way to sustain a competitive edge.
5. Increasing emphasis is being placed on the need for individuals to take on greater responsibilities, and for this learning is vital.
6. 'Learning to learn' is recognized as the highest life skill.

Whichever way you look at it, learning is the key to fostering and enhancing knowledge, skills and abilities. These qualities enable people to increase their effectiveness, and thus lead more successful and fulfilling lives.

Where and how do people learn?

Learning begins at the time we are born. The majority of learning stimuli are initially provided by the immediate environment, notably by the infant's family and/or guardian. With age, formal education comes to the fore, and this may be followed by activities and courses aimed at enhancing our professional competence, knowledge and skills. Some learning occurs almost accidentally – it is unplanned and may even go unnoticed. Such is the case when a person unexpectedly comes across relevant new information; when an experienced person recognizes and develops new talent in an individual; and when people ask for knowledge and/or advice from others and receive much more relevant information than they had expected.

However, for the vast majority of people, formal education in schools and colleges constitutes the most significant part of the learning process. By and large, formal schooling is (rightly or wrongly) considered as 'the' prerequisite for competence in the workplace, in the community, and in life in general. Yet it is clear that learning is not something that is confined to school and college only. In today's fast-changing climate, learning is for life – a notion that is emphasized by Wicks (1999) in the quotation below:

> No-one can afford to stop learning when they leave school. To maintain their employability, people will need to keep learning at different stages throughout their lives. There will be those who have been too busy to learn a language or to master Information Technology, skills which can improve our employability as well as being fun to do. ... But learning is not just about employability. New research ... show{s} that ... learning improved ... enjoyment of life ... self-confidence ... health.

Among the repertoire of learning and development methods, mentoring stands out as one of the most effective and powerful; one that can be highly satisfying for all individuals involved. Yet there is a proviso: mentoring is not suitable for addressing every possible learning and development need; sometimes coaching, training or simply reading a book might be more appropriate. Furthermore, it is unlikely to be an equally effective learning method for every single individual – the result of factors such as individual differences in personality and learning styles. We will consider all of these topics in more detail later on in the book. You will therefore soon have a firm understanding of the type of individual and the kinds of learning needs that render themselves suitable for mentoring. To return to the initial statement of this paragraph: if the conditions are right, mentoring can safely be said to be *one of* the *most* effective and powerful learning and development methods. Under certain circumstances, it is even the *most* effective and powerful one. And, according to a CIPD study (Pearn *et al.*, 1995), it is *always* the most intensive learning experience.

In the following sections we will begin to take a closer look at mentoring, starting with a brief outline of its origins.

History, definitions and prevalence of mentoring

Mentoring – its origins

Mentoring as a concept and practice is by no means new. Its origins date back to Greek mythology, with the story of Mentor in Homer's *Odyssey*. The story is as follows:

> When Odysseus, king of Ithaca, went to fight in the Trojan War, he entrusted the care of his household to Mentor, who served as teacher and overseer of his son, Telemachus. After the war, Odysseus was consigned to wander vainly for years in his attempt to return home. With age, the now grown Telemachus went in search of his father. Athena, the Goddess of War and patroness of the arts and industry, accompanied him on his quest and assumed the physical form of Mentor. Following a long search, Odysseus and Telemachus were finally reunited, and together they cast down pretenders to Odysseus' throne and to Telemachus' birthright.

> In time, the word 'mentor' became synonymous with trusted advisor, friend, teacher, and wise person. As you will see in the explanations to follow, much but not all of this conceptualization of the role of a mentor still prevails today.

Mentoring today

The use of mentoring and other one-to-one development methods reflects a widespread recognition of the limitations of formal classroom-based teaching and training. Both empirical research and anecdotal accounts suggest that the latter can be ineffective in various ways, notably the transferral of knowledge and skills from the training course to the workplace. The limitations of formal teaching methods in schools and training courses will be addressed in detail in Chapter 2, but to provide you at this stage with some concrete examples of their limitations, consider the following points:

- People typically forget as much as one-third of classroom-style learning before they leave the learning situation.
- Within a month, more than three-quarters of the learning is forgotten.
- In the long term, little if any of the learning is either remembered, or transferred.

In contrast to that, mentoring is seen as an effective method of enhancing the development of people, precisely because it typically improves both learning retention as well as the transfer of the learned information to real life situations (e.g. the workplace). Emphasizing the motivation for adopting mentoring, Jossi (1997) points out that:

today's protégés are better educated but still need a mentor's practical know-how and wisdom ('craft knowledge') that can be acquired only experientially. Therefore, many organizations are instituting formal mentoring programs as a cost-effective way to upgrade skills, enhance recruitment and retention, and increase job satisfaction.

Defining mentoring practice today

Many people continue to confuse mentoring with related concepts such as coaching and counselling, and there are significant variations in the practical guidelines on how to 'do' mentoring properly.

This persistent difficulty with defining mentoring can be explained in various ways. For example, never has a newly emerging management practice been accompanied by an entirely valid and robust definition from the very beginning. It will always take time to arrive at a definition that has its parameters fully worked out. Although mentoring is not a completely novel development method, it is only in the past few decades that it has taken on real significance in organizational settings as it has begun to be applied as a structured program. Since then, its use has spread rapidly whilst its definition still awaits a shared understanding.

Defining mentoring: development versus sponsorship

Another, and perhaps more important, explanation for the continued confusion surrounding mentoring is that the concept of mentoring has evolved differently in North America and Europe. In North America mentoring is still more closely associated with its roots, whereby the learner, who is a younger, less powerful and perhaps more naive person, is being guided by an older, more senior and more powerful individual. The French term 'protégé' could in this instance be used to describe accurately both the role of the learner and the power relationship between learner and mentor. The aim of a mentoring relationship in an American context is primarily that of sponsorship and advice on making the right career moves.

In contrast to that, mentoring in a European context has evolved in a somewhat different direction. First, the mentor is not necessarily a more senior person, nor is he or she supposed to be more powerful than the learner. This means, for example, that having a mentor who is your line manager is inconsistent with the European model of mentoring. Instead of more power, the mentor ought to have more *experience* in an area relevant to the mentee's needs. Secondly, the aim of the European mentoring relationship is also different to that of the North American one: it emphasizes learning and development (ultimately *self-managed*), and indeed *mutual* learning rather than sponsorship.

Figure 1.1 illustrates the four main goals of mentoring. In this respect it is important to note that developmental mentoring emphasizes self-reliance, learning and support more than sponsorship, whilst it is the other way round in sponsorship mentoring.

The statement that developmental mentoring emphasizes self-managed learning is not to say that mentoring in Europe is never

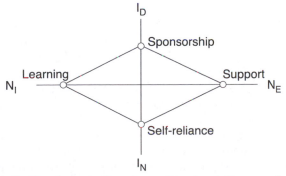

Figure 1.1 Goals of mentoring. I_D = directive influence; I_N = non-directive influence; N_E = emotional need; N_I = intellectual need.

supporting people with the advancement of their careers! It only means that sponsorship is not usually regarded as the primary purpose of mentoring relationships in Europe, but that it could well be made its objective if this was to be the mentee's explicit need and/or the emphasis of a corporation. Furthermore, improved career prospects and career management are likely to be the natural consequences of a mentoring relationship in which a great deal of learning and development takes place.

To complete the discussion regarding the American and European approaches to mentoring, we would like to introduce the terminology that shall from hereon be used to describe these; 'North American mentoring' will from now on be referred to as *sponsorship* mentoring, whilst 'European mentoring' will be called *developmental* mentoring.

What is mentoring to us?

Having discussed some explanations for the continued difficulty with defining mentoring, let us now take a look at a sample of definitions that have been put forward:

> Mentoring is a process which supports learning and development and thus performance improvements, either for an individual, team, or business.
>
> (Sutton Regeneration Partnership, 1999)

> The purpose of mentoring is to support and encourage people to manage their own learning in order that they may maximize their potential, develop their skills, improve their performance and become the person they want to be.
>
> (Parsloe, 2000)

The definition most endorsed by the authors of this book is that developmental mentoring is:

> off-line help by one person to another in making significant transitions in knowledge, work or thinking.
>
> (Megginson and Clutterbuck, 1998)

In saying that, it cannot be overemphasized that the mentors' task is merely to *assist* mentees in making these transitions – not to do the work for them! Mentors should enable mentees to learn from their past successes and failures, and encourage them to engage in self-determined learning and to find their own solutions – mentors unleash mentees' capacity to solve problems and arrive at high-quality decisions by being supportive, challenging and, above all, helping them to reflect on

Table 1.1 Developmental mentoring

Always	Sometimes	Never
✓ Listening with empathy	✓ Using coaching behaviours	✓ Discipline
✓ Sharing experience and learning	✓ Providing help and support	✓ Performance management
✓ Developing insight through reflection	✓ Opening doors	✓ Assessment for a third party
✓ Being a sounding board		✓ Supervision
✓ Professional friendship		
✓ Challenging		

events. Table 1.1 provides a concise summary of what developmental mentoring does and does not entail.

To further clarify what mentoring is, attention is drawn to a very good analogy for understanding the essence of mentoring practice today, written by Steve Torjussen (1999), a leading consultant, professional trainer and speaker on success strategies. He wrote as follows:

One of the first things a child or baby will learn is how to walk. Having spent the first nine or so months of its life sitting and crawling, probably watching adults walking around, the baby will soon have a go! On this first occasion the inevitable result is him or her falling, not succeeding in the task. I find it amazing that when this event is witnessed by a parent there is often huge excitement, enormous encouragement to the baby, and includes telephone calls to other members of the family describing the child's discovery, development and growth, despite its apparent failure. With all this positive activity, the baby is motivated to give it another go – and again the child falls!

This process continues over some time. With the parents' active support and positive praise despite the young child seemingly not achieving the results or outcomes that it has set itself. I have never yet met a parent who has said to the child: 'It is clear to me this walking lark is too difficult for you. Give it up!' I have also not met a child who gives up.

They constantly look to take action, constantly look to improve what they are doing so that they can refine the 'process' and perfect the art. After 3, 6 or sometimes 9 months hard work and effort the child succeeds. It walks across the room for the first time.

The mentor–mentee association is in many (although not all) respects similar to that of the parent–child relationship described above. The similarities include:

- The acceptance that mentees should set their own learning objectives.
- An appreciation that individuals have prior knowledge and experiences that are relevant to and should be used for the achievement of learning objectives.
- The acceptance that mentees' attempts at attaining their objectives will not always be successful.
- The understanding that mentees' experiences and developments, even in their apparent failure to achieve objectives, are positive – they are still learning experiences, even (or especially) mistakes!
- An understanding that mentees need to be motivated to continue to strive to achieve reasonable objectives and should never be given the impression that 'this lark is too difficult' for them.
- The understanding and belief that with hard work and effort, coupled with support and guidance by a mentor, mentees will have a better chance of success in achieving objectives.

Effective mentoring programs provide mentees with these conditions, thereby enhancing their development and potential to achieve personal and professional objectives.

Prevalence of mentoring

Arguably, the majority of mentoring experiences are informal and unplanned. Individuals may receive advice, insight, knowledge or support from people who have not been assigned specifically as their mentors. As a result, accurate data about the use of mentoring is difficult to obtain. A further limitation in accurately assessing the prevalence of mentoring concerns its widespread application in society. It is used both in business and in many other contexts such as education and social welfare. Thus far, little attempt has been made to collect and integrate statistics relating to the prevalence in all these mentoring situations.

One exception with regard to mentoring in business is a survey of 800 training managers conducted by the Institute of Personnel and Development (1999), which suggests that around 87 per cent of businesses in the UK utilize mentoring. This figure may be accurate considering its utilization on both a formal and an informal basis. It might, however, be inaccurate when taking into account the fact that many people do not distinguish clearly between mentoring and other forms of one-to-one development such as coaching. Respondents in the survey may therefore have claimed to be using mentoring in their organization when in fact they are really using a related development technique. (The distinction between mentoring and other learning and development approaches will shortly be addressed in more detail.)

Positioning mentoring within teaching and learning contexts

The transmission method

Traditionally, people acquired knowledge and skills through formal education and training, which was heavily influenced by behaviourist views and principles (Malderez and Bodoczky, 1999). In this context the following elements were true:

- The learner was considered a 'blank slate', with no previous experience, knowledge and skills – prior learning was not considered to be important.
- Information and knowledge was intended to be transmitted to the recipient learner.
- The learner was expected to receive external knowledge and information from the all-knowing teachers and trainers, supplemented by literature.
- The knowledge was to be stored in memory and perfected by practice.
- The received knowledge was considered to be relevant and sufficient for a lifetime.

The cognitive and constructivist teaching methods

The behaviourist approach was superseded in the 1950s and 60s by cognitive-based approaches to teaching and learning (Clutterbuck, 1998). These approaches saw learning as being less about behaviour and more about the individual's internal processes. In short, the important element was now 'what goes on in the person's mind'. From the constructivist viewpoint, for example:

- Learning is seen as a two-way process, with the learner interpreting and assimilating information and knowledge to their personal experiences and prior learning.
- Information from other people, books, personal experiences and/or practice is seen as new perspectives to be considered and possibly used to reconstruct the learner's existing internal knowledge – new information is no longer seen as information to be added to a store of knowledge.
- The individual's knowledge is seen as being personally created, in terms of schemata or constructs of understanding that can be added to, taken apart and reassembled in meaningful ways exclusive to the learner – the individual's knowledge is no longer about a store of transmitted information, nor a set of habits.
- Learning is seen as an assembly and reassembly of knowledge, which may or may not include new input – a process that can continue throughout the individual's lifetime.
- Knowledge is viewed as jointly and socially created through interaction with others.

Mentoring is firmly placed within the cognitive viewpoint:

- Mentoring utilizes the notion that the potential opportunities for learning include anything that enables mentees to consider or reconsider and possibly reassemble or expand their existing constructs; mentors facilitate this process.
- Mentoring utilizes the beneficial effects of knowledge being jointly and socially created through interaction with others; learning occurs in the mentor–mentee relationship.
- The objective is not for mentors to impress their knowledge on mentees and to expect them to store it unquestioningly; the aim is to provide opportunities for mentees to reflect on their mentor's input, assembling and assimilating it as is personally relevant.

Positioning mentoring among other employee training and development methods

Until recently, for the majority of organizations the most obvious and preferred solution to addressing employee needs was to design and run classroom-style training courses.

Approximately a decade or more ago, these began to be supplemented and in part superseded by other more intensive and sometimes more effective learning approaches, which can be grouped under the generic term of 'one-to-one learning and development'. Furthermore, the managerial role began to change as well. Whilst management used to be most strongly associated with work supervision, it is now about growing and nurturing talent. This development has further reduced the reliance on training courses as the sole means of development.

Let us now take a closer look at the most common roles in employee learning and development. These include:

- Managers.
- Counsellors.
- Guardians.
- Networkers/facilitators.
- Coaches.
- Trainers.
- Teachers/tutors.

As you will be able to see shortly, each of these learning sources is distinct from mentoring. In the following sections, we will take a brief look at the characteristics of each of those listed above, as well as *mentoring*, in order to highlight the differences between them.

Managers

The role of management can be described as follows:

- Organizing the elements of tasks and work processes to attain business objectives.
- Defining roles, priorities and processes with respect to achieving business objectives.
- Identifying and addressing deficits in employee knowledge, skills and abilities to enhance performance and to attain business objectives.

Counsellors

Counselling is the process that helps individuals to identify that they have a problem, to analyse it, establish a solution and commit to it. The counsellor role can be described as follows:

- Aiming to help individuals identify pathological, obstructive beliefs, feelings, thoughts and behaviours relating to personal issues.

- Assisting individuals in establishing desired outcomes in thoughts and behaviours.
- Establishing the methods to help individuals achieve the desired outcomes.
- Guiding individuals to the appropriate steps to achieve the outcomes.

Guardians

A guardian is typically a person who is more experienced, more senior and more powerful than another individual, and who has chosen to use this influence to sponsor the progress of this person's career. The behaviours a guardian might adopt include:

- Providing an individual with occasional advice on how to manage certain situations and how to advance their career; perhaps actively creating opportunities for them.
- Guiding individuals in setting objectives that would be beneficial to their career progression and advising on how to achieve these.

Networkers/facilitators

A networker/facilitator is someone who has access to an extensive number of people, the connections with whom may have been cultivated over a long period of time. Furthermore, networkers/facilitators are always looking to extend their networks by actively recruiting new people into them, even those who do not yet possess a lot of networking experience themselves. In the case of the latter, the networker/facilitator might make it his or her task to help people to acquire networking skills and to form their own connections. The role can further be described as follows:

- Sharing networks and (other) learning resources with the learner, exposing the said learner to different and wider networks.
- Perhaps establishing the learning needs of a chosen individual in the realm of networking (although these needs are not necessarily translated into specific objectives).
- Facilitating between the learner and the people in the network.
- Providing feedback and advice on networking skills.

Coaches

Coaching is the process whereby one person helps another to perform better than the latter would have done alone. The coach does so using various directive methods such as role modelling and guided reflection. Coaches typically deal with issues that require performance improvement rather than completely new knowledge or abilities, which the coachee is expected to possess already. The role of a coach includes:

- Determining and specifying an individual's learning needs and objectives in relation to work issues.
- Working out how the individual is going to improve performance deficits.
- Helping the individual to explore the problem, develop alternative solutions and decide which one to implement and how.
- Using appropriate and timely feedback.

Trainers

In the context of this book, the term 'trainer' is meant to refer to an individual who designs and delivers training courses in or for an organization, the objectives of which have been set by the organization (with or without the input of the trainer). The role of a trainer includes:

- Designing courses in a way that best supports the achievement of previously established objectives (typically, the development of a particular skill).
- Implementing the course with a view to achieving objectives involving instructing multiple learners in an appropriate way.
- Verifying that materials/skills have been learned and can be applied to an acceptable standard.

Teacher/tutor

A teacher/tutor is someone who engages a group of people or individuals in learning according to the guidelines of an external party. Thus, the learning topics are usually tied to a national curriculum and the teacher/tutor's role is to impose its contents upon the learner(s). Specifically, his/her role includes:

- Understanding the set curriculum.
- Structuring the learning experience according to the curriculum.
- Using methods such as lectures, videos, discussions and self-study to enable learning.
- Assessing the extent of people's learning through tests.

Mentors

The people development approaches described above can be contrasted with the role of a mentor.

Although we have previously attempted to define mentoring, we shall return to a similar endeavour in order to ease the comparison between mentoring and other learning methods. Mentoring is the process by which one person (the mentor) encourages another individual (the mentee) to manage his or her own learning so that the mentee becomes self-reliant in the acquisition of new knowledge, skills and abilities, and develops a continuous motivation to do so. Furthermore, mentoring is also a process by which the whole person, i.e. their work *and* personal life, is being developed, and which enables and supports (major) change within these areas.

Mentoring includes:

- Supporting individuals in discovering and defining their own development needs and setting their own objectives; fostering independent learners.
- Allowing individuals to raise and talk about *their* issues, occasionally clarifying, reflecting back, and challenging.
- Helping individuals to reflect on their beliefs, feelings, thoughts and behaviours, and to view issues from multiple perspectives.
- Guiding and encouraging individuals in the self-reliant analysis and solution of their problems and opportunities.
- Enabling people to become effective decision-makers.
- Supporting the solution of issues by embracing an integrated approach.

Mentoring – the integrated approach

The last point mentions the expression 'integrated approach', which is highly significant in the context of mentoring and warrants further explanation. According to David Clutterbuck (1998), mentoring derives its immense effectiveness in employee learning and development from being an integrated method that flexibly combines elements of four other one-to-one development approaches: coaching, counselling, networking/facilitation, and guardianship (see Figures 1.2, 1.3). It utilizes each of these at different points, the decision criterion for which one to use being the mentee's needs at the time. The view of mentoring as an integrated approach that draws on a variety of different learning methods is more in line with the European concept of mentoring than with the American one,

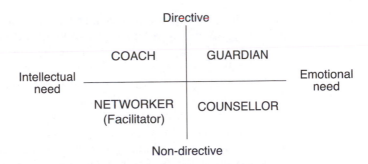

Figure 1.2 Mentoring – the integrating role.

both of which were discussed earlier. The reason for this is that the European view of mentoring focuses on enhancing learning and development in mentees, the vehicle for which is the utilization of an integrated approach. Since the North American view of mentoring, however, tends to be aimed mainly at sponsoring and assisting mentees with their career moves, using an integrated approach would be inefficient, and espousing a directive style would be more appropriate.

In Figure 1.3, the behaviours associated with sponsorship mentoring are mainly located in the upper right-hand quarter. The behaviours associated with developmental mentoring are more evenly spread across all four quarters of the axes.

Being a 'European' mentor and therefore using the integrated approach means having to be very flexible. It might require you to be directive and address intellectual needs in one situation,

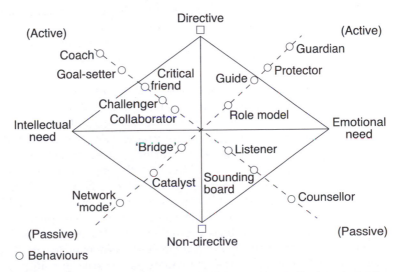

Figure 1.3 The integrating role – a corresponding behavioural matrix.

whilst being non-directive and addressing emotional needs in another. Being able to adapt one's style according to situational requirements demands great skill on the part of the mentor. Not only does he or she have to master any one of the underlying developmental approaches, the mentor also has to be acutely sensitive towards the mentee's needs and the appropriateness of a particular learning method in any given situation.

It is this integrated approach embraced by mentoring that, combined with the fact that mentoring is tailored to an individual's specific needs (as established by the individual), makes it so well suited to developing the *whole* person. Mentoring fosters within mentees the ability and desire for independence and self-reliance in the management of their own learning thereby creating individuals who are keen and capable of improving their performance independently. Coincidentally, these areas (i.e. achieving the development of the whole person and effecting continuous and independent learning) are also the main ones in which mentoring differentiates itself from other one-to-one development methods!

To further clarify how mentoring differs from training, management and other one-to-one development approaches, take a look at Table 1.2. This also illustrates the circumstances under which mentoring should be chosen as an employee learning method as opposed to any of the other ones.

Characteristics of mentoring relationships

Mentoring relationships provide an effective method of learning by avoiding the limitations of traditional teaching and learning methods. The unique positive characteristics associated with mentoring as a development method are as follows:

- It facilitates the application of the contents of learning in real life contexts, thus enabling the evaluation of its effectiveness with respect to achieving desired outcomes.
- It induces purposeful change and maximizes the return on the investment in learning. This is achieved by applying methods such as helping the mentee to analyse and reflect on 'what happened' and to compare this to 'what was intended'. This, in turn, equips individuals with the ability to learn how to learn, a skill that will prove forever useful.
- It fully utilizes the notion that learning can be a uniting and mutually beneficial process: 'Whoever learns together, grows together. The statement is as true for individuals, teams, whole organizations, businesses, academic establishments or

Table 1.2 Developmental mentoring

	Learning objectives	Power balance	Motivation to instruct	Direction of learning	Style	Dependency
Manager	Working in line with business goals; objectives specified by manager	One-sided – in favour of manager	High	One-way – to learner	Mainly directive	Varies between managers: some create autonomous learners and some do not
Counsellor	Changes in thoughts, beliefs and behaviours related to personal life issues; objectives specified by both parties but strongly influenced by counsellor	One-sided – in favour of counsellor	High	One-way – to learner	Mainly hands-off	High dependency on counsellor for learning (what to learn, when and how)
Guardian	Development of knowledge, skills and abilities that help individual to advance their career; objectives specified by guardian	One-sided – in favour of guardian	High (although some may accept that they can also learn from the relationship)	Typically one-way – to learner – but depends on individuals involved	Mainly directive – but learner has choice of whether or not to accept advice	High dependency on guardian for learning since s/he is the more experienced and powerful
Networker/ facilitator	Learning objectives related to networking skills; objectives set by both parties	Initially one-sided (in favour of networking) but later becoming more balanced	Initially high since n/f more experienced but later willingness to learn from one another	Initially one way (to learner) but can later be both ways	Initially directive and later hands-off	Creates independent self-managing learners

Table 1.2 (cont.)

	Learning objectives	Power balance	Motivation to instruct	Direction of learning	Style	Dependency
Coach	Changes in beliefs, thoughts, behaviours and skills acquisition related to work performance; objectives specified by coach	One-sided – in favour of coach	High	One-way – to learner	Mainly directive	High dependency on coach for learning
Trainer	Development of specific skills; objectives specified by company	One-sided – in favour of trainer	High	One-way – to learner	Directive	High dependency on trainer for learning
Teacher/ tutor	Learning the contents of a national curriculum; objectives set by external agency and teacher/ tutor	One-sided – in favour of teacher/tutor	High	One-way	Directive	High dependency on teacher/tutor for learning although self-investment has to be made to maximize learning
Mentor	Mentee's own objectives	Equal – mentor can provide guidance but mentee has choice in whether or not to utilize the input	Low – willingness to learn from one another	Two-way – learner and mentor both learn	Both directive and hands-off depending on individual's needs	Creates independent, self-managing learners

nations' (Oxtoby, 1999). Mentoring has the potential to enhance the learning and thinking, not just for the mentee, but also for the mentor, the organization and society.

- It optimizes learning through grounding itself in the cognitive and constructivist approaches to learning. This is in contrast to the classroom-style teaching that is characterized by the transmission method.
- It customizes the learning experience fully to the mentee, who ought to determine both the subject and the type/style of learning.

Mentoring environments

In addition to mentors helping learners within their own organization, mentoring programs can help people develop in a wide range of situations:

- Education – providing mentoring for teachers, administrators and students. Sometimes this responsibility is taken on by peers, i.e. students mentor other students or teachers mentor their colleagues.
- Business to welfare – mentoring people on Welfare to Work (US) and New Deal (UK) schemes.
- Special needs – people who are members of minority groups (the physically disabled, for example) are mentored by people from similar situations who understand their difficulties.
- Business start-ups – mentors are provided and their usage is often mandatory. The mentors are supposed to help the start-up business to whom money has been loaned in order to safeguard that investment and to guide the business through its initial growth period.
- Business-to-business – mentors with corporate managerial expertise are matched to the needs of owner-managers of small and medium-sized enterprises. Typically, the mentors focus on supporting mentees to enhance clarity and effectiveness in business.

Types of mentoring relationships

Not only do mentoring relationships differ because they are placed in varying environments, they also differ for a variety of other reasons – including the mentee's objectives and the personalities of mentor and mentee. A number of additional factors have a significant bearing on the nature of a mentoring relationship:

1. The formality of the program and the relationships within the program. Formal programs/relationships are planned,

implemented and managed by the organization in a highly structured manner involving various control mechanisms. This contrasts with a very informal program, and equally informal relationships, which 'grow organically'.

2. The extent to which mentoring schemes encourage line or off-line mentoring relationships.

3. The type of mentoring that a mentor and mentee engage in, such as:

- One-to-one mentoring – a mentor is allocated to one mentee and the relationship can be very strong; this is the most prevalent type of mentoring.
- Circles mentoring – a mentor is assigned to several mentees; this is typically used when there are fewer mentors than mentees.
- Needs-based mentoring – a pool of mentors is available for individuals to call on occasionally, i.e. when information or assistance is required.

Due to the immense importance of the issue of choosing between line and off-line mentoring relationships, as well as between an informal and formal approach for your mentoring scheme, these issues will be discussed in detail in Chapter 3.

Multiple learning through mentoring schemes

Mentoring possesses an enormous capacity for promoting individual learning and development. Mentees are encouraged to engage in self-determined and continuous learning throughout the relationship and into the future. You will also be aware by now that it is not only the mentee who learns, but the mentor and the organization as well. How this occurs is what we will explore in the last sections of this chapter. We will first consider how the mentee's learning is facilitated, before doing the same for mentors and organizations.

Enabling mentee learning

An individual learns through mentoring in a variety of ways – for example, by virtue of the various roles that mentors adopt. The following list, based in part on an analysis by Kathy Kram (1983), depicts some of these functions, but it is by no means exhaustive. The mentor's assumption of any one of these roles is largely guided by the mentee's needs, and this means that the mentor is unlikely to adopt all of these roles for every mentee.

Mentor functions include:

- To support mentees in managing their own learning.
- To encourage self-directed reflection, analysis and problem-solving.
- To promote effective, high-quality decision-making.
- To be a sounding board – to challenge assumptions, ideas and behaviours.
- To motivate the mentee to achieve objectives.
- To inspire.
- To 'open doors' by, for example, introducing the mentee to the 'right' people or by creating opportunities.
- To be there.
- To provide a safe, objective, non-judgmental, and confidential space for the mentee.
- To provide guidance and advice, particularly when the mentee has become unstuck or is about to make a mistake that will do long-term damage to his or her career.
- To be a credible role model.

Mentors further facilitate a mentee's learning and development by enabling mentees to:

- Practice, evaluate and adapt their ideas and processes in a sheltered way so that they emerge as confident and competent individuals within their profession.
- Develop and enhance the self-awareness and interpersonal skills that will enable them to function better in the world of work.
- Develop a professional perspective that will enable them to locate their work performance in the wider context of the work place and the community.
- Develop powers of self-evaluation and a capacity for autonomous learning, which together enable mentees to maximize their gain from all learning events and to seek out future learning opportunities on their own.

However, mentoring relationships can only achieve these positive outcomes if the mentee's learning objectives are clearly established. The objectives set the tone and focus for the mentoring association. They also enable the mentee's progress to be evaluated. Two of the many effective techniques that mentors use in order to enhance mentees' learning and development are formal learning objectives, and reviewing the development plan.

Formal learning objectives

Learning plans or personal development plans (PDP) detail mentees' goals and objectives, and the actions necessary to achieve them. In formal programs, mentees either come to a mentoring relationship equipped with a PDP that they previously set up with their line-manager, or devise one together with their mentor. Even if mentees already have a PDP when they enter the association, the mentor will help them to think it through, perhaps amending, adding to or clarifying the learning objectives. The plan may contain the following elements:

- What do I want to do?
- What do I want to achieve in my work or job?
- Where do I want to be in 3 years' time?
- What type of learning do I have to do to achieve that?

The answers to these questions as detailed in the plan, however, are not set in stone. To the contrary, both mentor and mentee should make a conscious effort to realize that the relevance of both objectives and actions may change over time. This also explains why it is important to review the PDP periodically.

Reviewing the development plan

The relevancy of PDPs should be checked at regular intervals, as agreed by both parties. Regardless of the outcomes of mentees' actions – whether they succeed or fail – the review encourages taking a critical stance towards the continued appropriateness of these in relation to achieving objectives. Asking oneself about the continued relevancy of goals and objectives is also part of reviewing a development plan. In this way, self-knowledge, self-learning and professional development are enhanced.

Mentor learning

Mentoring relationships are *mutually* beneficial associations. Mentors can, for example, earn greater respect from colleagues and superiors from engaging in these relationships. They can also gain a good deal of personal satisfaction by genuinely committing to a mentee. First and foremost, however, mentors learn. The type of learning that occurs in mentoring relationships will, if applied, benefit the mentor's work performance. In addition, mentoring relationships are also likely to promote learning relevant for a mentor's personal life.

Extensive learning is the result of having to guide and support others in reflecting on and handling situations. By doing so, mentors acquire new knowledge and skills and update existing ones. For example, throughout a mentoring relationship, mentors will repeatedly be confronted with novel situations. Furthermore, they will be required to (help the mentee) view these from multiple perspectives in order to arrive at new ways of thinking. These activities, in turn, tend to enhance creativity.

Organizational learning

Organizational learning is triggered by the individual learning that occurs in mentoring relationships. To understand this, we must remember that organizations are composed of individuals. The more these individuals learn and develop, the greater the organizational pool of competence becomes. Mentoring not only helps people to grow individually, it also inspires a learning culture. It stimulates people to see learning and development as continuous, and it encourages them to share knowledge, skills and abilities. Herein lies the secret of organizational learning as a consequence of mentoring schemes: the schemes draw attention to the importance of learning. They depict it as a core value. They promote knowledge to be passed on. In essence, mentoring schemes have the potential of creating a *learning organization*.

Summary

This introductory chapter is a foundation comprising the basics of mentoring, and has covered a broad range of topics, including the history, prevalence and definitions of mentoring. The chapter also considered the characteristics of mentoring relationships and looked at the ways in which mentors, mentees *and* organizations learn as a result of mentoring.

A crucial part of this introduction involved distinguishing mentoring from related learning and development methods, notably coaching, counselling, networking/facilitating and guardianship. Developmental mentoring is more than any one of these because it integrates all four approaches. This difference cannot be overemphasized. It is vital because it will impact on your ability to practise mentoring authoritatively and ethically. This in turn will determine the benefits any one mentoring relationship will bring to you, the mentee and the organization.

Business mentoring is regarded and practised somewhat differently in Europe and North America; whilst sponsorship mentoring is embraced in many American companies, European firms tend to embrace developmental mentoring, the latter also being the concept endorsed by the authors of this book. That said, we are presently witnessing an increasing use of developmental mentoring in the USA too. Furthermore, Australia and some practitioners in Canada are working along developmental lines.

The existing discrepancy between mentoring concepts and definitions is probably the result of its rapidly growing application. Its growth has been too fast for such aspects to be unified, a situation that practitioners and academics are working to correct. Having read through this preparatory chapter, it is now time to take a closer look at each of the 'big issues' of mentoring that were covered here. We will begin this by considering the advantages and disadvantages (or risks) that mentoring holds for mentors, mentees and organizations.

References

Honey, P. (1999). A declaration on learning – one year on. At: http://www.learningbuzz.com/ph017.cfm

Wicks, M. (1999). UK Minister for Lifelong Learning. Quoted at http://www.lifelonglearning.co.uk/

Jossi, F. (1997). Mentoring in changing times. *Training*, **34**, 50–53.

Clutterbuck, D. (1998). *Learning Alliances*. CIPD.

Institute of Personnel and Development (1999). *Training and Development in Britain 1999*, April, 1–4.

Kram, K. (1983). Phases of mentoring relationships. *Acad. Man. J.*, **26**, 608–25.

Malderez, A. and Bodoczky, C. (1999). *Mentor Courses: A Resource Book for Trainer-Trainers*. Cambridge University Press.

Oxtoby, B. (1999). United by learning. At http:/www.learningbuzz.com/bo001/cfm

Parsloe, E. (2000). In: *Mentoring – Draft Occupational Standards* (D. Wood and A. Reynard, eds), University of North London.

Pearn, M., Honey, P. and Clutterbuck, D. (1995). Training in action. *People Management*, November, 43.

Sutton Regeneration Partnership (1999). *Mentoring – an interactive guide to theory and practice*, CD-ROM.

Torjussen, S. (1999). Learning like a baby. At http://www.learningbuzz.com/st001/cfm

Drivers for mentoring

In this chapter we will look at the advantages of mentoring over other forms of learning, and establish why mentoring is rapidly becoming a growth area for organizations and employees. We explore the psychological as well as the practical benefits that mentoring brings to mentors, mentees and organizations. Potential risks or disadvantages of mentoring will also be identified.

The advantages of mentoring over other forms of employee training and development

Today's work environment demands that employees are ready and able to adapt to an ever-increasing pace of change. Managers are under continuous pressure to find new ways to obtain results; working methods that are cost-effective and efficient, yet do not compromise quality. To achieve this three-fold outcome, many companies have realized that substantial investment in employee development is vital. This investment, too, must be cost-effective, speedy, and produce high quality performance – both now and in the longer-term. Under certain circumstances (for example, depending on the employee's development needs), mentoring can meet these criteria better than any other training and development method such as coaching and conventional classroom-based training courses. The reasons for this will become clear over the following pages.

How mentoring outperforms other one-to-one development methods

There is no doubt that one-to-one development approaches such as coaching, networking/facilitation, counselling and guardianship all have their place in the world of employee learning. However, one significant advantage that mentoring holds over any one of these lies in its *integrated* approach (explained in Chapter 1). A second is its capacity for creating individuals capable of and motivated by managing their own learning on a continuous basis. These two factors enable mentoring to achieve an impact and effectiveness that goes far beyond that of other one-to-one development methods. But how exactly do they achieve this impact? To answer this question, let us look at both factors (i.e. the 'integrated approach' one and the one relating to 'continuous self-managed learning') separately, starting with the former.

The integrated approach

In spite of the fact that other one-to-one development methods can also be customized to individuals' needs, the integrated mentoring approach is capable of personalization on a substantially broader scale. Mentoring is tailored to a very wide range of learning needs that might arise from a learner's personal and work life. This broad scope means that mentees may be developed as a *whole* person and that change may be promoted in all areas of their lives. However, such breadth of change is not always the objective of the relationship. When the mentee's needs and the program objectives are narrower, the skills portfolio of the mentor need not be so demanding.

Continuous self-managed learning

In terms of continuous self-managed learning, effective mentoring fosters within the mentee the ability and desire for independence and self-reliance in the management of their own learning. This creates individuals who are self-sufficient as well as keen and capable of improving their performance independently and continuously.

It is precisely on these two counts – achieving the development of the whole person and effecting continuous and independent learning – that mentoring excels and other one-to-one development methods fail. That said, not every human being will benefit from mentoring in the same way; the most gain can only be achieved if a person is both *committed* to as well as *compatible with* the developmental mentoring process.

Additional advantages

Another key advantage of mentoring over other learning approaches is the speed with which performance changes can be effected. Mentoring can trigger changes faster because it is not simply tailored to some (very few) of the individual's needs but to many, causing more changes to happen in a shorter period of time. Lastly, mentoring also outperforms coaching and counselling in terms of cost. Coaching and counselling, if done professionally (i.e. by someone who is well-trained and is employed purely to focus on a particular individual's development needs at regular intervals), can cost a substantial amount of money. Internal mentors, on the other hand, are expected to invest the amount of time and effort required for the mentoring relationship as part of their core job responsibilities.

The key advantages of mentoring over other one-to-one development approaches are therefore that:

- It is an integrated approach that allows for customized development on a substantially broader scale.
- It encourages continuous self-managed learning, inspiring employees consistently to improve their performance.
- It is faster and frequently also more cost-efficient than other approaches.

How mentoring outperforms classroom training

Mentoring has also provided a practical alternative to conventional training courses, which are typically run in a manner resembling school classes (i.e. with one active player, the teacher/trainer, lecturing numerous passive recipients, the pupils/trainees). Until recently, training courses have been the main route for employees to acquire the knowledge and skills required in the workplace.

Most of us have been through formal education, later supplemented by professional training courses. However, these types of learning methods are not appropriate for all learning objectives. In particular, training courses have repeatedly been found to be ineffective since more than a quarter of the information taught has left us even before we have left the classroom. In addition, organizations tend increasingly to outsource training. Unfortunately, however, external tutors can never fully appreciate the operational processes and in-house challenges that an employee may have. This means that the training design is unlikely to be completely relevant for all employees. Furthermore, the chances of facilitating trainees' learning transfer in an ideal way are also minimized. In relation to all of these issues, i.e. embedding learning over a long period and transferring the learning to real life settings, mentoring has a clear advantage.

We will now look at the specific limitations of formal education and professional training courses.

The limitations of training courses

Undoubtedly, there are some very good training courses. Perhaps you have had some personal experience of them and you may be interested in attending more. However, most employees do not have a lot of control over which courses to attend and when, and neither do they have any influence over the quality of the course. Your ability to attend a training course at a *particular time* is often at the discretion of your company, and the *pitch* of the course the responsibility of the trainer. Timing and pitch are important determinants in making training effective or otherwise. *Timing* relates to whether a training course meets your needs on a 'just-in-time' basis or 'just-in-case'? Pitch relates to the appropriateness of the level of training for your current status of knowledge, experience and commitment. The content of a training course is unlikely to be customized to your specific needs. However, in today's volatile and no-more-careers-for-life age, our development and learning is too important to leave to anyone else.

The good news is that mentoring enables individuals to take charge of their learning and development by tailoring the relationship to their needs and experiences. The mentor merely encourages them on that journey. The bad news is that, in the process of formal education, many people have lost the ability to engage in self-determined learning. And herein often lies the main task of the mentor: he or she has to enable individuals to re-acquire this ability; mentees must learn to develop their own solutions. Since the mentee's learning is self-determined, it will also be more relevant than that which occurs on training courses. Furthermore, learning will *continue* to be relevant, since the contents and orientation of a mentoring relationship can be adjusted whenever necessary.

At this stage, you may begin to feel a little uneasy. You may think that focusing on the mentee's needs is all very nice, but what about the company's needs? What about the intention for the mentoring scheme to support *business* objectives? What if mentees simply use the mentoring program to enhance their market value with a view to changing companies? Although these fears are understandable, they are not really justified. This is because offering mentoring to employees is typically genuinely appreciated. Employees feel valued and satisfied (see, for example, Higgins, 2000). What is more, their commitment to the company increases, including a commitment to business objectives and an enhanced commitment to stay with your company – mentoring is known to increase retention substantially! If the purpose of the mentoring scheme has been clearly articulated to participants, mentees are likely to work within this given framework. However, it is also good to be flexible and to strike a balance between individual and organizational objectives. Imagine that the program/organizational objectives are the house, and the mentee objectives are the different rooms within the house. As long as mentees remain within the house, it should be up to them to choose which rooms they want to spend most time in. It should also be up to them how to spend their time in each room.

Let us now return to the main purpose of this section and consider the limitations of training courses when compared to mentoring (Oxtoby, 1999). Training courses:

- Adopt a dictatorial approach to learning; self-managed learning is discouraged.
- Happen only occasionally (e.g. every 6 months or once per year).
- If offered only occasionally, do not encourage, continuous and self-managed learning.
- Often do not enable the transfer of learning to the workplace; there may be gaps between what was taught on a training course and what is needed on the job.
- Typically lack customization and therefore *relevance* for many individuals.

- Are often chosen *for* employees, lowering the motivation to learn.

Advantages and disadvantages of mentoring

Because mentoring is a person-to-person, interactive developmental approach, it complements other methods of learning and is the best integrator of learning experiences. Mentoring fosters greater learning and work performance in a variety of ways, which we will consider by looking at the advantages mentoring brings to the mentee. When reading about each of these advantages, you should bear in mind that these are *potential* benefits. They will neither materialize necessarily nor automatically in every mentoring relationship. These benefits are the result of a lot of effort and commitment invested by both the mentor and the mentee.

Advantages for mentees

- *Competence*. Through thoroughly identifying development needs, through action planning, and through supporting and enabling problem solving, mentors can help mentees to enhance their competence substantially. Furthermore, because the development is tailored to mentees' individual needs, mentoring helps them to acquire knowledge, skills and attitudes that are *directly* relevant to their job and will improve job performance.
- *Goal setting*. A mentor can often assist mentees to clarify their goals. There is little point in having drive and ambition if you have no idea what to focus these qualities on or how to achieve a certain goal.
- *Motivation and satisfaction*. A mentor can be a source of motivation and satisfaction, and can assist mentees to keep up the momentum in their career path. Mentees have more confidence in the knowledge that there is someone backing their corner.
- *Employability*. Because mentoring enhances mentees' competence and inspires them to engage in life-long learning and development, they will improve their attractiveness to their employer.
- *Psychosocial support*. In addition to providing technical/professional guidance, mentors also provide help in psychosocial terms. Given that mind and body are intricately linked (i.e. thoughts and beliefs influence behaviour including work performance), this mentor function is vital. To fulfil this function,

mentors do not have to possess a master's degree in counselling, although some basic counselling skills are desirable. Most of the time, however, it suffices if they act as a confidential sounding board where mentees can offload professional and personal worries such as feelings of low self-confidence and anxiety.

- *Creativity*. Apart from supporting mentees in the acquisition of knowledge and skills that bear direct relevance to their job, mentoring fosters a range of skills that are useful in every job even though not directly required. Bouncing ideas off the mentor, learning to view issues from multiple perspectives, and acquiring new ways of solving problems all promote the enhancement of creativity (and, of course, the improvement of problem-solving skills!).

- *Networking opportunities*. The presence of a mentor can enable better networking opportunities, thereby opening doors that would not normally be easily accessible to mentees.

- *Organizational change*. In an age of rapid change and diversity within the workplace, a mentor can support mentees during times of insecurity and can enable them to thrive on change, to not be afraid of it and to keep ahead.

- *Personal change*. Mentors can be instrumental in supporting, enabling, and even triggering major changes in mentees. This is typically achieved through applying various mentoring techniques. Furthermore, personal change can be accelerated if mentees hold their mentor in particularly high regard and adopt the mentor as a role model. Through emulating the mentor and learning from their experience, mentees can pick up new qualities and enhance their chances of professional excellence.

- *Time-effectiveness*. Mentoring produces time savings on various counts. First, by addressing mentees' needs on a one-to-one and customized basis, objectives can be met faster than through training courses. For the organization, mentoring is also time-effective because it minimizes time spent away from work. As mentioned above, mentors and mentees are expected to hold their mentoring sessions outside of their regular jobs. Moreover, no time spent travelling to a venue for teaching/learning is required.

Advantages for mentors

- *Value and satisfaction*. Mentors tend to gain immense personal satisfaction from knowing that they have contributed greatly to another individual's growth and development. Some also find it satisfying to know that their knowledge and experience is handed down to someone else and continues to benefit a company through this person.

- *Learning experience.* A good mentoring relationship is power-free and allows for a mutually beneficial relationship. There is often much that mentors can learn from mentees, including fresh ideas, insights, feedback and social contact. Learning often also emanates from the fact that mentors reflect on mentees' problems and realize that they actually face similar issues in their own life. Furthermore, in espousing best practice to mentees, mentors also have to ensure that they are up-to-date with their own professional and technical knowledge.

Another learning experience for the mentor lies in the fact that they have to acquire new skills and abilities prior to and during a mentoring relationship. Becoming a mentor is equivalent to assuming a new job role: learning is urgently required. With regard to mentoring, this involves mentors attending to their own self-development throughout the course of a mentoring relationship and consists of two aspects: first, mentors should develop a *strategy* for such self-development, and secondly, they should evaluate and adapt their own mentoring practice where appropriate. Although the self-development described here emphasizes learning in relation to mentoring, it will automatically stimulate development in other areas of a mentor's career and personal life.

- *Credit.* A mentoring relationship can help mentors to gain credibility for their own professional progression. Mentors are considered talented and knowledgeable individuals and are highly respected for their ability to facilitate learning and development in others. This can greatly enhance mentors' future career opportunities and shows a commitment to the profession as well as to the mentee.

Benefits to the organization

- *Organizational effectiveness.* Improving organizational effectiveness is, of course, the main objective of mentoring schemes. Mentoring can realize this objective in a variety of ways, including enhancing individual and organizational performance, increasing motivation, supporting change, and ensuring the retention of key staff. Mentoring is also often a way of identifying high potential individuals, the discovery and nurturing of whom is central to organizational effectiveness. Furthermore, it helps organizations to bring out into the open issues the culture has ignored because they were too difficult to confront – e.g. work–life balance.

- *Performance.* Mentoring helps people to take responsibility for their learning. Through this they can acquire new skills and knowledge, thereby enhancing their overall competence. Furthermore, mentoring stimulates mentees to view learning as an *ongoing* process, reinforcing in their mind the importance of continued professional development. Where employees embrace this concept, they will continue to grow and develop themselves even after a mentoring relationship has ended. Naturally, greater individual competence will benefit the performance of the organization that they are part of. This has clearly been demonstrated in an informal interview with Belinda McGann, the training manager at British American Tobacco (BAT). BAT has been running a graduate mentoring scheme for the past 5 years, and is so convinced of its ability to enhance individual and organizational performance that it intends to extend the scheme to the whole of the organization. BAT feels strongly that the improvement in employees' competence as a result of mentoring has direct business benefits (see Case study 3.5).

Furthermore, if 'productivity' is considered as a measure of performance, mentoring can also add to this component. Consider, for example, the experience of Tegwin Pulley, director of diversity and staffing services for Texas Instruments (TI) in Texas. He maintains that TI's mentoring for new hires initiative has substantially improved the productivity amongst this employee group because mentoring enables them to understand more quickly how to go about their jobs (Tyler, 1998).

Employees who have experienced successful mentoring relationships are often filled by a desire to pass on this experience and act as mentors to other corporate members, helping them to improve their performance. Organizational performance is improved through mentoring in other ways, too – for example, its ability to encourage networking, communication and the sharing of resources across departments, teams and global units. In essence, mentoring can be a powerful way of linking disparate organizational sections and establishing co-ordination.

- *Motivation and satisfaction.* Mentors enhance satisfaction in an individual by providing support, friendship and guidance. The mere realization that an organization cares and invests in an employee is generally regarded as resulting in higher motivation. It is as if the employee wishes to 'give something back' to the company. In fact, investment in employee training and development is much more likely to increase motivation than are other methods such as remuneration and benefits (Herzberg, 1987).

- *Organizational change.* Mentoring relationships are excellent catalysts and support mechanisms for organizational change, be this a change of processes, culture, strategy or structure. This is because mentoring encourages performance in line with business strategy and vision – it regularly reinforces the desirable new behaviours and mindsets. Furthermore, employees' fear of change and the resistance associated with it is one of the biggest obstacles to change. Mentoring can help to make people feel safer and actually to welcome change. Time and again, evaluations of mentoring schemes show that mentors are a rich source of psycho-emotional support. An evaluation of the mentoring practice of Lex, for example, showed that their mentees regularly reported that their mentors acted as counsellors to them, helping them to cope with stress and pressure (see Case study 3.6).

Another example of mentoring and change is a mentoring scheme initiated by David Megginson and Paul Stokes from Sheffield Hallam University (see Case study 3.1). The program is intended to help local businesses who have traditionally only traded nationally and who wish to diversify into the export market to undergo this change. Although the scheme is still fairly young, anecdotal evidence suggests that the businesses undergoing the changes do find their mentors invaluable during this process.

- *Retention.* Time and again, this is shown to be both a very common as well as an extremely vital effect of mentoring. Given that organizational success frequently depends on a fairly small number of people, it is important for organizations to retain these key staff. For example, for SmithKline Beecham's finance division, staff turnover used to be a very big problem. However, upon the introduction of a mentoring scheme, turnover was substantially reduced. Thus, within the period from October 1998 until September 1999, turnover for non-mentored individuals totalled 27.6 per cent, contrasting with a 2 per cent turnover rate for mentored employees within the same period. Similarly, at Allied Irish Bank, mentoring reduced the turnover of graduate recruits by two-thirds within the first year of the scheme. This experience is echoed in a diverse range of organizations, including Proctor and Gamble, who had a particular problem with retaining talented women managers (see Case study 3.11). The main reason that mentoring enhances retention is that employees feel more valued and cared for by their company. Employees also often feel that mentoring has clarified their role in the organization and the goals to aspire to, which has a motivating effect. Feeling more valued and more motivated in turn tends to enhance organizational commitment.

- *Recruitment.* More and more talented potential employees are interested in whether or not an organization offers mentoring support. In fact, Gregg (1999) reports that 70 per cent of executives polled in a survey commissioned by RHI Management Resources said that job applicants nowadays make as many inquiries about corporate culture and benefits as they do about salary. Furthermore, some City of London companies suggest that MBA students are reluctant to join an organization that does not have a mentoring scheme. An organization that is seen to be supportive and committed to its employees will be more attractive than one that is not. Offering mentorships to potential new recruits has a strong positive impact on their decision to join a company because new employees do not just want to be thrown in at the deep end; they demand training and development, and mentoring seems to be highly appealing to them.
- *High-flyers.* Not only can mentoring schemes help to discover high-flyers, they can also help to develop their skills, influence their career path and, of course, retain them once they have been developed. Allianz Insurance's mentoring scheme, which is targeted at developing international management high-flyers and has been running since 1997, has been highly influential in developing more competent, motivated and committed international managers (see Case study 3.8).
- *Organizational learning.* With its emphasis on learning and its capacity to share knowledge, ideas and experience between mentor and mentee, the mentoring relationship is a powerful tool for promoting organization-wide learning. Mentors and mentees tend to learn from one another, and pass this on to other parties as well. This effect has been well demonstrated in ABB Sweden's mentoring scheme, where mentoring has become integrated into competence development. Carl Eric Gestberg of ABB believes that mentoring has supported the company's general process of knowledge recirculation – it is clearly seen as an effective way of disseminating knowledge across the organization.

- *Cost-effectiveness*. The vast majority of organizations with mentoring schemes report its cost-effectiveness to be one of its main advantages. Mentoring as a cost-effective method of individual, team and organizational development is the result of mentors typically being required to fulfil this role on a voluntary basis in addition to their core job. Even if mentors were to be paid, the professional and personal insights that a mentor may share with a mentee can be priceless for the organization (for example, the mentor may prevent the mentee from committing mistakes which might have otherwise harmed the company). The only expensive exception in mentoring might be executive mentoring, as executive mentors are often recruited from outside a company. In most cases, these people are professional experts who will charge accordingly. However, even this need not be the case, depending on the size of your company: ABB Sweden, for example, which consists of 130 companies, did not find it difficult to find internal mentors for its executive mentoring program.
- *Organizational culture*. Provided that the organization selects its mentors on the basis of their identification with its values and beliefs, mentoring is a powerful way of reinforcing corporate culture. By role-modelling a deep internalization of company purpose, values and strategy, the mentee will feel compelled to understand and embrace these as well. For example, Travis Wolff, an accounting firm in Dallas, implemented a mentoring program that is specifically aimed at integrating new recruits into the organization's culture (Gregg, 1999). The ability of mentoring to reinforce organizational culture amongst new recruits was also something reported by Allianz Insurance. During the scheme's evaluation, mentees reported an enhanced understanding of Allianz and of their role within it. Nowadays, mentoring is also a means of *changing* culture as well as *merging* different cultures following an acquisition.
- *National and cultural diversity*. As organizations become increasingly complex and global in scope, the face of the workforce is changing too. It is moving away from being homogenous to embracing many cultures and nationalities. Mentoring programs provide a powerful mechanism to support and promote cultural diversity within the corporation so that associated conflicts can be managed and the full benefits reaped.
- *Development*. Mentoring relationships are assumed to offer reciprocal benefits for mentors and mentees. Many corporations believe that mentoring programs may offer the optimal

mechanism for providing developmental job experiences for new managers. The very introduction of a mentoring scheme will promote greater awareness of the existence and benefits of employee development. It may also help to nurture an organization-wide development culture.

- *Time efficiency.* Mentoring expedites learning, particularly compared to other learning methods such as training. The worry about time spent away from work is also obviated in most cases, as mentors and mentees often work at the same company location. This also means that there will not be any, or only little, travelling time associated with meetings.

- *Internal and external communication.* Mentoring encourages networking both internally and externally to the organization. External networking provides valuable insights into the strategy of other organizations. Internal networking, for example across departments, improves organizational communication channels. This enhances mutual understanding and benefits organizational processes. For example, the sharing of corporate resources (e.g. people, knowledge, facilities) is made easier, as is inter-unit co-ordination. Furthermore, awareness of 'local' issues (meaning unique to a particular team, department, subsidiary etc.) is increased, and discrepancies in values and beliefs are uncovered. For the District Audit Scheme, for example, improved communication between field and head-office was a key benefit (see Case study 3.2). Lastly, mentoring pairs in which the mentor is more senior than the mentee can also support competitiveness. Mentoring provides a channel through which innovative, high-value business ideas can be communicated directly from junior to senior levels, skipping the unwieldy procedures often associated with bringing ideas to top management.

- *Strategic succession planning.* Mentoring can be a great vehicle for strategic succession planning. It can develop people for higher-level roles that they have recently assumed or are intended to assume in the near future. Examples of schemes that illustrate this use include District Audit, Allianz Insurance, and Ericsson (see Case studies 3.2, 3.8 and 8.1). Mentoring can also serve to identify high-potential employees who might then be considered for filling projected vacancies.

Summary

The advantages of mentoring for mentees, mentors and the organization are summarized in Table 2.1.

Table 2.1 Summary of the advantages of mentoring for mentors, mentees and the organization

Mentors	Mentees	Organization
✓ Value and satisfaction	✓ Competence	✓ Organizational effectiveness
✓ Learning experience	✓ Goal setting	✓ Performance
✓ Credit	✓ Motivation and satisfaction	✓ Motivation and satisfaction
✓ Own reflection	✓ Employability	✓ Organizational change
	✓ Psychological support	✓ Retention
	✓ Creativity	✓ Recruitment
	✓ Networking opportunities	✓ High-flyers
	✓ Organizational change	✓ Organizational learning
	✓ Personal change	✓ Cost-effectiveness
	✓ Time-effectiveness	✓ Organizational culture
		✓ National and cultural diversity
		✓ Development
		✓ Time efficiency
		✓ Internal and external communication
		✓ Strategic succession planning

Disadvantages for mentors and mentees

It was very difficult to write a section on the disadvantages of mentoring, not least because there are so few critical studies on the topic. Furthermore, most negative issues that occur in mentoring relationships are problems that need to be dealt with; they are not really disadvantages *per se*. Common problems of mentoring relationships will be discussed in detail in Chapter 11, which will also suggest potential solutions to these.

Let us then try to look at the few disadvantages mentoring can hold. These have been grouped together for mentors and mentees, since their problems are often the same and/or causally linked.

- *Breaches of confidentiality.* 'This is undoubtedly one of the biggest potential disadvantages of mentoring. Fortunately, however, breaches of confidentiality tend to occur very rarely – at least breaches of mentors' or mentees' confidentiality. Interestingly, mentors and mentees tend to breach the confidentiality of third parties much more frequently.
- *Other's negative emotions.* In cases where a third party feels compromised by any one mentoring relationship, mentor and/or mentee can be put at a disadvantage. For example, if the mentee becomes the subject of someone's envy (most likely an individual who was unable to enter a mentoring relationship), the scene could be set for some unpleasant events. These may include active attempts by this third party to harm the mentee's reputation and obstruct his or her progress.

Similarly, the mentee's line manager might begin to resent the mentoring; this would be a classic case of struggling to protect one's turf. The manager might feel that the mentor begins to influence his or her work remit by way of the mentee. To avoid such anxieties, managers should be actively briefed about the mentoring program and encouraged to support their direct reports in taking part.

- *Dependence or counter-dependence.* Mentees may become too dependent on their mentor and cease thinking for themselves. This is not productive for either party, and may encourage the mentor to back away from the relationship. First and foremost, it simply defeats the objective of a mentoring relationship. Equally unproductive is the situation in which the mentee begins to rebel against the mentor, disagreeing with anything the mentor says and never sticking to action plans.

Risks for the organization

As for mentors and mentees, there are very few *real* risks for the organization as a result of running a mentoring scheme. Most, if not all, of them can be avoided by planning, implementing and monitoring the program carefully.

- *Legal proceedings.* Legal cases could ensue from a few unfortunate circumstances. The most common ones relate to grossly unethical behaviour on the part of either mentor or mentee (e.g. sexual or racial discrimination and/or harassment; see Chapter 7). Organizational members who might have been 'excluded' from the mentoring scheme could feel that they have been discriminated against.

- *Ill-prepared schemes*. The importance of carefully planning and implementing a mentoring program cannot be overemphasized. For example, introducing an ill-prepared scheme, even if only initially as a so-called 'pilot', may have long-term negative repercussions. These may be such that the initial scheme has caused so much frustration that an irreversible anti-mentoring climate has spread throughout the organization. This climate may prevent the introduction of any follow-up scheme. So, if you decide to implement a mentoring scheme in your organization, be sure to be prudent about it and invest the time and effort this requires.

- *Underutilization of the scheme*. One of the most important steps in designing a mentoring scheme is to assess employees' expectations and needs. They are, after all, the recipients of the mentoring services, and the program should therefore be congruent with their interests. If the needs of the potential mentee groups have been carefully assessed, if it is clear how to access the scheme, and if the program has been marketed well, underutilization should not really be an issue. In fact, excess demand and finding enough quality mentors to match this is more likely to be the problem.

- *No positive performance changes*. Again, in a carefully designed and implemented scheme this should not be a regular feature. However, there will always be some individuals whose performance does not improve as dramatically as that of others. Furthermore, when running a mentoring scheme you should not expect to see any substantive behaviour changes in less than 1 year (Murray and Owen, 1991).

Summary

The potential challenges for mentees, mentors and the organization are summarized in Table 2.2.

Myths of mentoring

There are many stories about mentoring, most of which have little or no basis and in fact do damage to the reputation of mentoring as an ethical and effective work function. Some are misconceptions about what the relationship entails and what the

Table 2.2 Summary of the potential challenges for mentors, mentees and the organization

Mentors/mentees	Organization
✓ Relationship breakdown	✓ Legal proceedings
✓ Breaches of confidentiality	✓ Ill-prepared schemes
✓ Other's negative emotions	✓ Underutilization of scheme
✓ Independence	✓ No positive performance changes
✓ Unmet expectations	✓ Undesirable performance changes

relevant parties can gain from it. This section is intended to unravel some of the myths surrounding mentoring, suggested by Warner (1994). These myths are as follows:

'Managers make good mentors'

Managers have often carried out the role of a mentor to one of their direct employees. This frequently happened (and still does happen) without either party even realizing it. That is, it happens 'informally', where mentees receive mentoring only occasionally and in an unplanned manner. Most importantly, this type of mentoring will be in relation to needs, which they feel comfortable discussing with their line manager. In such situations, being mentored by your line manager can certainly be advantageous. However, in terms of *formal* relationships, line managers are certainly not ideal candidates for mentoring. This is even the case if a manager possesses the characteristics of a good mentor and would therefore, theoretically, qualify for the role. The incompatibility between manager as mentor and direct report as mentee can be explained in various ways. For example, managers are primarily results oriented and may bend employees' development needs towards short-term goals. Managers are also able to influence employees' status and pay. It is understandable that mentees will not want to be as open under these circumstances, which may compromise the quality of the relationship.

'A mentor has to be older than the mentee'

> Although it is true to say that someone older will frequently have a wider range of experience, it is not true to say that a younger mentor will have nothing of value to impart. Younger mentors may not possess the same *scope* of experience as an older person at the same hierarchical level, but they might be extremely competent overall or very ingenious in a particular area. New technology is one obvious example where younger people often display significantly greater skills. Additionally, they are often more comfortable with new developments in general and may be able to pass on some of this openness to older mentees.

'Mentors are teachers'

> Although a mentor may be inclined to 'teach' (as in the act of instructing a person in a directive manner with the expectation of passive reception of the material by the person), he or she ought to refrain from it. The reasons have been laid out in the previous chapter and relate to the fact that teaching is of little long-term benefit, which is contrary to the aim of mentoring. As aforementioned, the purpose of mentoring is to facilitate learning in such a way that mentees will 'learn how to learn'. Moreover, mentoring also aims to encourage people to make 'learning to learn' a long-term objective, which they are motivated to obtain even without the mentor's support. It is the responsibility of the mentor to allow mentees to find their own way without fear of reprisal or judgment. None of these are elements of teaching. That is not to say that mentors can never provide any feedback or state an opinion! It simply means that mentors must allow mentees to have their own, and to act on their own instincts.

'A mentor should be chosen for you'

> Mentoring relationships are unlikely to work unless they are voluntary associations. This implies that the mentee will want to be mentored in the first place, regardless of who the mentor is. It also implies that the mentor–mentee match has to be a 'good' one, i.e. one that is desirable to both parties. A mentoring relationship is perceived as desirable if, for example, it fulfils the mentor's and mentee's expectations. A relationship is also desirable if rapport is built quickly.
>
> In the case where an employee does not perceive mentoring as an appropriate learning method for him or herself, choosing a

mentor for that individual is not an option. A relationship started on that basis is doomed to failure. If, on the other hand, an employee is motivated to enter into a relationship, a decision regarding how much to influence the matching process has to be made – and this is not an easy one! Both allowing employees to choose for themselves and choosing for them have advantages and disadvantages. Mentees who select a particular mentor usually do so because they respect that person, feel they can learn from him or her, and like the mentor because they are similar types of people. The advantages include the fact that rapport is likely to be built more easily, the relationship will develop faster, and the motivation to learn and impress is high (at least on the part of the mentee!). The downside is that the mentor and mentee may be too similar and that the scope for potential learning may therefore be limited. Additionally, they might like each other so much that they end up merely enjoying each other's company instead of setting challenging learning objectives.

The advantages of choosing a mentor for an employee include the potential to avoid the mistakes mentioned above. If the organization chooses a mentor for an individual, it might be able to ensure that the mentee gets stretched in a way that is in line with succession planning. Why did we write '*might* be able to ensure'? The answer to this is simultaneously one of the disadvantages of choosing a mentor for someone: the person responsible for this task might assign a mentor to an employee who cannot establish any rapport with the mentee, who does not really meet the mentee's needs, and/or who is too challenging. So, the ideal method of matching mentors and mentees probably lies somewhere between the two. It might involve getting some information on both of them beforehand, choosing a pool of candidates that could be suitable, and allowing mentors and mentees to select one another from this pool.

'Having a mentor will increase your promotional potential'

Having a mentor is highly likely to increase your performance. It is also highly likely to increase your ability to network. Yet, there are no guarantees that a mentee will glide up the corporate ladder with little or no effort besides engaging in a mentoring relationship. A mentor will often have many useful contacts and knowledge of job opportunities, and may also be in a position to speak highly of a mentee to the appropriate people. However, eventually it is still the responsibility of the mentee, not the mentor, to manage his or her own professional future.

'A mentor has to be of the same gender and race as the mentee'

This is a limiting belief, and should not be adhered to. If we only seek out mentors of the same race and gender, we limit ourselves to a narrow perspective. The basis of a mentoring relationship is to learn, and mentees cannot fully appreciate the diversity of life and work if they solely seek out opinions similar to their own. A mentor should aim to challenge and stimulate the mind of mentees, and mentees should be hungry for new ideas and creative solutions.

'You only need one mentor'

Something we feel very strongly about is that we can have multiple mentors in our lives. Different mentors can provide different gifts. For example, you might have a mentor to help you in your profession, another who stimulates your creativity, another who can teach you to be a better listener, and another who shows you how to be a better volunteer. Mentors can tap different facets of our lives, fostering holistic growth.

'Mentor–mentee expectations are the same for everyone'

Individuals, regardless of gender, race, sexual orientation or socio-economic level, seek mentors for many of the same reasons. This may be for resources, visibility, enhanced skill, and counsel. However, each individual or mentee brings different expectations. Successful mentors assess where a mentee is, not where the mentee should be. The mentor provides ample opportunity for 'expectation discussions' to take place, which in turn will guide and enrich the experience.

'Once your mentor, always your mentor'

Before you begin a relationship with a mentor or mentee, decide how much time you are willing to invest. As the skills, attitudes, confidence and situation of mentees change, so their needs may change. The mentor should pull back and let mentees go their own way if this is the mentees' choice. The goal in a mentor–mentee relationship is to move beyond the restricting confines of dependency to the higher state of interdependency. Although a mentor and mentee may maintain contact for a long time, the relationship can have time parameters.

'Mentoring is a complicated business'

> The most complicated thing about a mentor–mentee relationship is how to get out of a bad one. If the relationship is not productive, find a tactful way to disengage. As with all relationships, do not stay in a bad one. Remember, though, only terminate the relationship after attempts have been made to establish its limitations and improve it.

> The key to successful mentorhood is the commitment to the growth and development of another individual.
>
> (Warner, 1994)

Summary

In this chapter, we have considered the dimensions on which mentoring outperforms other methods of employee training and development. These include being an integrated approach, fostering motivated continuous learners, and effecting very rapid as well as customized development.

Although these are clear advantages of mentoring over alternative forms of learning, the issue has to be put into perspective – thus, it really depends on your organization's and your employees' needs, as well as your company culture, as to which learning method is most appropriate. This means that mentoring should only be chosen if it seems to be the approach that is best suited to your particular situation. As you will remember, Chapter 1 described the circumstances under which mentoring should be selected as an employee development method over and above other alternatives (see Table 1.2).

This chapter also devoted a large part to elucidating the benefits and challenges of mentoring for mentees, mentors and the organization. In a nutshell, there are many benefits and few real risks associated with mentoring. Furthermore, benefits can be maximized and challenges minimized through carefully planning and implementing your scheme – something that this book endeavours to help you with.

A hugely important part of implementing a successful program involves making very clear to everyone in the organization what mentoring actually is and what it aims to do. This will go a long way toward demystifying mentoring and preventing problems that may ensue as a result of wrongly conceptualizing it.

References

Gregg, C. (1999). Someone to look up to. *J. Accountancy*, **188**, 89–93.

Herzberg, F. (1987). One more time: how do you motivate employees? *Harvard Bus. Rev.*, **Sep–Oct**, 5–13.

Higgins, M. C. (2000). The more, the merrier? Multiple developmental relationships and work satisfaction. *J. Man. Dev.*, **19**(4), 277–96.

Murray, M. and Owen, M. A. (1991). *Beyond the Myths and Magic of Mentoring – How to Facilitate an Effective Mentoring Program*. Jossey-Bass.

Oxtoby, B. (1999). United by learning. At:
http:/www.learningbuzz.com

Tyler, K. (1998). Mentoring programs link employees and experienced execs. *HR Magazine*, **April**, 99–103.

Warner, M. J. (1994). Mentor myths. *Exec. Excellence*, **11**, 20.

Objectives of mentoring programs

At a societal level, mentoring has been found to be an effective method of helping individuals cope with or adjust to significant changes in their circumstances. For example, mentoring is useful for students working through higher education, offenders adjusting to life outside prison, and older people coping with retirement. Similarly, in a business context, mentoring schemes can also be used to address a whole range of organizational and individual needs. The following sections will consider the many different objectives that mentoring programs can focus on. Each of these meets different employee requirements, and therefore also involves different mentee groups. The scheme objectives that will be considered are as follows:

- Change management.
- Diversity.
- Graduate recruitment and induction.
- Executive/partner/director.

- International management (including 'international assignments').
- Cross-cultural management.
- High flyers/succession planning.
- Professional development (BAA – Ian Skerrit/EMC conference).
- Retaining talent.
- Returners.

Each section will detail the *specific objectives* that a scheme involves, what particular *characteristics* (if any) its mentors ought to display, and what benefits any particular program brings to the organization. Some of the schemes will be explored in greater detail than others. This might be the case because the scheme in question is more popular and therefore more likely to be of greater application. Alternatively, it might be more complex or perhaps more controversial than others and therefore warrant closer examination. Either way, some of the schemes require more in-depth coverage than others.

While reading through the following sections, you will see how the focus of a mentoring scheme influences the relationship dynamics. It does so by way of determining the nature and range of mentee needs and the type of mentor and mentee to be recruited into the program. You might also want to think about which objective the scheme that you are currently running or intending to run maps onto. Bear in mind, however, that it might not categorically match any one of the schemes that will be discussed in this chapter. Perhaps your scheme is a mix of several types?

Change management

Mentoring and change are inextricably linked. Think about it: receiving mentoring means that people will learn and develop, and this in turn means that they will change. Regardless of the orientation of a scheme, triggering change is the main task of mentoring, and making mentoring a substantial component of your change process will help you to accelerate and optimize it: mentoring enables stress management, the minimization of resistance, and the achievement of individual and organizational change objectives. Mentoring can be used in isolation or, where appropriate, in conjunction with other training and development methods to maximize its effect. Either way, the benefits of supplementing change programs with mentoring are substantial – a fact that is demonstrated time and again in both case studies and academic literature (Conway, 1998; Clutterbuck and Megginson, 1999; Whittaker and Cartwright, 2000).

Figures 3.1 and 3.2 provide you with a visual model of how processes and outcomes differ between supported and unsupported change. When a company's leadership supports employees during transformations through, e.g. offering mentoring, employee reactions to change are more productive and acceptance occurs sooner and will also be more profound.

Mentoring schemes can be incorporated into any kind of business transformation, including:

- Mergers, acquisitions, flotation or the (partial) sale of a business.
- Expansion into new markets and/or the development of new types of business relationships (e.g. customer or supplier) across national boundaries.
- Structural, cultural, strategic or operational changes as a result of the above.

Whether change is planned or unplanned, and whichever focus it adopts, mentoring can easily be incorporated into the process. However, the type of scheme to be introduced will vary depending on the type of change an organization is facing. For example, if you *respond* to changes in the business environment (e.g. legal amendments such as market deregulation), you are likely to focus your mentoring scheme on the people involved in strategic decision-making. During a *planned* change process, on the other hand, you might also want to involve other levels of employees for maximum effectiveness.

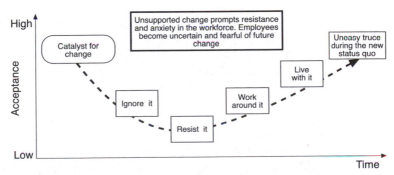

Figure 3.1 Employee reactions during unsupported change.

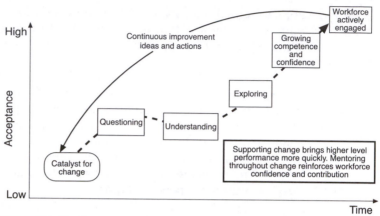

Figure 3.2 Employee reactions during supported change.

In what ways does mentoring benefit change?

By now, you are probably wondering how exactly mentoring benefits business transformations. To answer this question, we first have to take a step back and consider what organizational change is and what it means for an individual. In virtually every case, and naturally so, business transformations are driven from the top down. They are the result of management/board decision-making in response to a given set of circumstances. These decisions eventually cascade through the organization with consequences for employee feedback and participation.

Unfortunately, change is not a concept readily embraced by most human beings. To the contrary, most individuals fear change, and fear often engenders resistance. The manifestations of resistance are multifarious: some individuals will sabotage the change by obstructing its implementation, others will lie low and hope to escape the changes, and others will throw in the towel and leave. The single most common consequence of change, however, is stress, which in turn can lead to bouts of physical and/or psychological illness (Karasek, 1990; Begley and Czajka, 1993; Callan, 1993).

Psychologists, managers and other people with interest in (employee) behaviour have long tried to explain why change is associated with this range of negative outcomes. Some have asserted that resistance to business transformations is the consequence of change creating a state of disequilibrium within individuals, and that the consequent struggle to restore equilibrium renders the organism vulnerable (Pearlin et al., 1981). Others have suggested that human beings are essentially 'creatures of habit', and are very sensitive to changes in their usual circumstances. Either way, employees are at different stages likely to feel stressed, fearful, angry and/or resigned to the changes.

What can managers do to foster employee acceptance of change, and to support the change process? *'Information'* is one obvious solution. That is, providing employees with as much information as possible regarding the planned transition can help to minimize fear by giving people a chance to be prepared. However, although hugely important, in reality there is often a limit as to how much information can be revealed whilst the change strategy is still being worked out. Furthermore, even if a lot of information is being provided, some employees may still feel dissatisfied since 'feeling ill-informed' did not constitute their true anxiety.

'Employee involvement' is another viable solution. Encouraging employees to participate in the change-planning process and allowing them to contribute to setting targets is a very powerful way of reducing resistance. However, the degree to which involvement is feasible will vary greatly depending on a company's circumstances. Sometimes decisions and plans have to be created fast and consultation is not an option. Even if you have managed successfully to integrate your employees, you will still find a substantial proportion of unhappy staff amongst them.

This is where mentoring comes in. Its powerful methodology picks up where the other solutions fail. Its dialogues will support your employees both by providing a cathartic element and by helping mentees to define their (change) problems and to develop solution strategies.

In sum, mentoring during business transformations is likely to have a positive impact by:

- Helping individuals to manage stress.
- Improving communication and, therefore, the distilling of information regarding the change process (e.g. about its purpose, goals and the role any one individual is supposed to play); this orchestrates and focuses the transformation.
- Altering individuals' perception of the business transformation by, for example, helping them to see it as a (learning) opportunity.
- Making employees feel valued, reducing resentment and enhancing commitment.
- Encouraging collaboration between employees and minimizing competition.
- Exploring and resolving mentees' concerns regarding the change program, reducing resistance.

- Moving employees away from feeling victimized by supporting them to exercise influence.
- Providing employees with direction by encouraging them to define their new role in the changing organization, and, last but not least,
- Accelerating the change process and driving it towards desired outcomes.

The three case studies that follow demonstrate how mentoring can be used in organizations to support and enable organizational change.

CASE STUDY 3.1

by David Megginson and Paul Stokes of Sheffield Hallam University

David Megginson and Paul Stokes initially received funding for the scheme from 'Yorkshire Forward', a government funding body for regional development, to research the potential of a mentoring program designed for companies in the South Yorkshire area that wanted to expand into the export business. Later on, the scheme included match funding from other bodies, including Rotherham Business Links. In the autumn of 2000, funding was granted to proceed with setting up the actual scheme. The scheme's objective can be described as 'increasing mentees' knowledge of the export business and helping them to make the transition using mentoring relationships'. In this case, the mentees are company directors or executives who have so far mostly only traded nationally, and the mentors are directors or executives with experience in the export business.

Intermediaries were used as far as marketing and mentor and mentee recruitment were concerned. These intermediaries included the Business Links community, Change Management alumni from Sheffield Hallam University, other private contacts, and newspaper advertisements. However, as it turned out, most mentors and mentees were eventually obtained via the Business Links community. Furthermore, some mentors used their own networks to win other mentors for the scheme.

Written support packs and workshops were utilized to prepare mentors and mentees for the scheme. The support packs covered topics such as the skills needed for mentoring, the ethos of mentoring and information on its benefits, whilst the workshops were more practical in nature, addressing the following aspects:

- *Using a framework of mentoring developed by David Megginson and David Clutterbuck (Megginson and Clutterbuck, 1999), participants were asked to rank how they viewed the role of the mentor. This was followed up by a discussion regarding the outcomes.*

- *Participants were encouraged to think about the potential contents of the meetings. For example, they were asked to consider the question of their impact on the other person and to think about how much of the talking they were meant to do.*
- *Participants were encouraged to think about the processes of getting to know each other and terminating the relationship.*
- *Mutual expectations were brought to the surface and discussed. Furthermore, the expectations of the program co-ordinators were also explained, which included topics such as the frequency and duration of meetings. In this respect, 2-hour sessions once a month were deemed appropriate.*

For the mentors, skills training was deliberately omitted, since all of them were seasoned MDs who had mentored all their lives and who valued discussing their practice once they were immersed in it but did not seek disembodied training beforehand. There was also no skills training for mentees, but discussions were held before and during the scheme about their experiences and support was given where needed about how to get the best from their mentors.

Initially there were different workshops for mentors and mentees, but they were soon asked to attend joint ones, although certain aspects were still discussed separately. Running joint workshops proved much more successful and popular with participants, because they felt that they better understood how the scheme actually worked. Furthermore, once mentors and mentees started to attend the same workshops, it was possible to commence with the first step of matching during these sessions. This involved providing mentees with a pen picture of each mentor as well as a preferences form, and asking them, at the end of the workshop, to indicate both their top three favourites and those mentors they would not perceive as suitable at all.

After these workshops, the matching then remained the responsibility of Paul and David. The criteria they applied included paying attention to mentees' preferences as well as making pragmatic decisions regarding questions such as compatibility between mentors and mentees. Once they had decided which mentor to assign to which mentee, they contacted the mentees first in order to make them a particular offer. If the mentee accepted, the mentor was informed and both mentor and mentee received each other's contact details by e-mail. In line with what had been discussed during the workshops, it was then the mentee's responsibility to take charge of the relationship and to, for example, arrange the first meeting. Interestingly, it was found that the mentees lagged behind in the recruitment of their mentors because although there were many more mentors than mentees, the latter group was found to be much more selective in terms of choosing a mentor.

One and four months into the mentoring program, David and Paul held two additional workshops for mentors and mentees, which were part of the support provided to scheme participants. These workshops could be described as review meetings during which mentors and mentees were given the opportunity to talk about how the relationships were progressing, and what problems and successes they had experienced both with the relationships and/or the development of their business. These workshops were highly valued, particularly by the mentees, since they gave the mentees the opportunity to form informal networks with people in a similar situation and to exchange their newly gained knowledge on the subject of exporting. In fact, it was observed that mentees at times began to mentor one another. As far as supporting the mentor and mentee pairs was concerned, they also had the option of contacting David and Paul in order to ask questions, exchange thoughts or receive advice.

A formal evaluation of the 10 mentoring pairs has not yet taken place although some anecdotal evidence suggests that the scheme is beginning to benefit some businesses. Plans to carry out an evaluation do exist, and the methods to be employed are likely to involve both joint as well as separate interviews with mentors and mentees.

CASE STUDY 3.2

by Trish Longdon and David Rowlands of District Audit

The Audit Commission for England and Wales promotes proper stewardship of public finances and helps local authorities and the NHS to deliver economic, efficient and effective public services. The Commission also owns District Audit, which it appoints to carry out many of the audits for which the Commission is responsible. District Audit operates as an arm's-length agency.

The District Audit mentoring scheme came into existence in 1995 as a result of a major re-organization and an ensuing need for a sizeable increase in senior managers. It helps newly appointed senior managers to develop into their roles using the experience and knowledge of existing senior staff.

In the absence of any appropriate training alternatives to the needs of these new senior managers, District Audit commissioned David Clutterbuck to evaluate whether 'mentoring' could help. He suggested that the senior managers would be likely to benefit from mentoring in terms of rapidly adapting to their new roles. As a result, Trish Longdon, then People Development Director for District Audit and now in a similar role for the Audit Commission, sought the support of senior colleagues for the mentoring scheme.

The scheme is funded from the annual training and development budget and is managed by David Rowlands, who as HR Manager has also successfully implemented the Investors In People standard in the organization.

At any one time there are up to 25 mentees actively engaged in mentoring relationships. A total of 75 mentoring relationships have been embarked upon since the inception of the scheme. Mentees are nominated by their Directors, based on individual needs and circumstances. David Rowlands is then responsible for matching mentees with suitable mentors usually offering several options to the participants in the scheme. Matching is based on mentor availability, the nature of the learning needs of the mentee, and a desire to keep the mentoring relationship out of their immediate line management tree by perhaps offering mentors from another region in the country.

Training for mentors and mentees is provided by David Clutterbuck, and includes the following agenda points:

- What is mentoring?
- How does it differ from coaching, counselling and managing?
- What skills and behaviours are associated with mentoring?
- Practising skills and behaviours in role play situations.

Mentors and mentees typically meet once each month, with a focus on how the mentee is developing into the senior management role. Often the issues relate to managing and implementing change in their teams. Line managers are kept involved by the mentor and mentee so as to keep them from feeling excluded. The scheme co-ordinator may also check with the line managers to ensure that they are aware of developments in the mentoring relationship, and that they are happy with progress.

In terms of the success of the scheme, David Rowlands comments that: 'It's been excellent; our best training and development initiative of the past 6 years'. The scheme is more formally evaluated with confidential questionnaire surveys to ensure that scheme participants are gaining from their investment of time and effort. The results have shown that mentors benefited even more than the mentees! They felt they had developed as a result of being challenged and stimulated by the mentee's learning. The main difficulties encountered during the operation of the scheme have been about mentor–mentee logistics – simply getting meetings to happen as planned. As for improvements to the scheme, the main area for attention seems to be publicity – making sure that more people are aware of the mentoring program. Until now, the scheme has been promoted in a relatively low-key manner.

CASE STUDY 3.3

by Paul Burns, formerly of British Telecom (BT)

In 1995, BT's Consumer Division underwent an internal change program called '... for a better life'. One aspect of the change program involved working with four charities that already had mentoring schemes to provide opportunities for BT employees to participate as mentors in business-to-community schemes. These four schemes were:

- *Roots & Wings, a school mentoring scheme.*
- *The Leadership Consortium, a scheme for very talented people with disabilities.*
- *The Business Enterprise Long Term Support (BELTS), a scheme for prisoners about to be released, with ideas for self-employment; and*
- *The Princes Youth Business Trust (PYBT), a scheme for disadvantaged young people requiring support with setting up a business.*

At the time of 'better life', the Consumer Division was headed up by the late Stafford Taylor and, as well as improving shareholder value and customer satisfaction, he wanted the change to benefit employees and the wider community.

As Paul Burns explains:

I was part of the team responsible for designing and implementing the better life program. I began the community benefits through funding to charities in return for responses to activities related to better life by (BT) employees. Meanwhile Stafford went on a Business in the Community (BitC) 'Seeing is Believing' visit to one of the first two schools in this country to try business-to-community mentoring. As a result of this he decided better life should pilot the mentoring, called 'Roots & Wings', by both BitC and BT.

With particular support from Bob Mason, then Head of HR for Consumer Division, schools were chosen in Peckham, Stoke-on-Trent and Manchester, and I was given the job of finding and, along with Business in the Community, supporting local program co-ordinators and schemes. Stafford Taylor continued to give strong moral support, visiting schemes, meeting mentors and encouraging his Directors to do the same.

At this stage the objectives of the scheme were to contribute to the community, provide development for BT people and build local relationships (which had suffered when BT moved from regional units to national). Later we realized that the novelty of the schemes as part of a change program was helping to make better life more attractive to employees.

There were several queries from BT employees from other parts of the UK about

Roots and Wings. Setting up more school schemes was limited by budget (fees to BitC and grants to schools in support of the mentoring) and the number of people who could be released from work to support them. I persuaded better life to begin working with other mentoring schemes, which would allow a smaller number of additional BT employees around the UK to get involved. Three national schemes were made accessible to them: the Leadership Consortium, BELTS and the PYBT.

At the end of the 1995/1996 school year, the schools mentoring scheme was evaluated, partly externally, and judged to have been a success in terms of assisting students, developing BT people and PR. From three schools and 70 mentors, we expanded the next year to eight schools and 198 mentors. Again following external evaluation in 1997/1998, Roots & Wings was expanded to 13 schools, including two in Northern Ireland, and 305 mentors. That year, BT Roots & Wings won the Dragon Award for employee involvement in the community.

The other schemes have always been smaller. Typically the Leadership Consortium has had 20 mentoring pairs, and BELTS has had 8 between 1996 and 1999. PYBT probably had about a dozen BT mentors over the same period. (Because PYBT has so many regional offices, it was difficult tracking what happened to names that were forwarded and in the end we asked BT people to make contact with their local offices and keep us informed of progress).

With the changes in BT it has been difficult to support the schemes, and last year it was decided formally to withdraw from the Roots & Wings schools and the BELTS Scheme. However, the Leadership Consortium has just recruited another 20 BT people.

Day to day management of the schemes was left with me, and comprised at least half of my workload over 4 years. It has since been handed on to other people. Roots & Wings only worked because of the dedication of Local Co-ordinators who built up and maintained relationships with a school, recruited mentors and supported the pairs.

After the first year we used video-conferencing to bring all Co-ordinators together for a 2-hour review meeting at least every 2 months. Video studios in up to six centres were used. In between I had telephone contact and occasional visits. The latter were most likely when a new school was being approached, or if there were particular difficulties.

We also held an annual overnight event, partly as information sharing and partly to recognize the Local Co-ordinators. The time given by the Co-ordinators was substantial; they estimated 2 days a week on average, and many had no exemption from other duties while doing this.

Funding was provided by BT Community Partnership. This covered BitC costs, grants to schools, the video-conferencing and annual events. However, each BT unit that agreed to allow people to mentor gave paid time. This was especially generous when units allowed large numbers to mentor. Some units also funded special events. For example, Payphones paid for an end-of-year event for mentors and mentees, and some of my costs and my salary came from the better life budget.

Most costs of BELTS and The Leadership Consortium were first met by the BT Community Partnership. This included an annual £15k membership fee for the Consortium, but after 2 years this fee was paid out of HR budgets, partly in recognition of the contribution this made to the development of BT people.

For Roots & Wings, mentors were recruited through national publicity (articles in BT media and intranet) and local publicity (e.g. talks to groups, events put on by partner schools in BT buildings). Mentees were recruited following a talk to pupils about the nature of the scheme.

With BELTS, it was very much left to people to approach me if they were interested after hearing about the scheme in BT media or from colleagues involved. The mentees were already clients of Instant Muscle, a charity that works with a range of people seen as 'doubly disadvantaged'. These people, prisoners, had been visited by one of the charity's business advisors, individuals supporting hundreds of prisoners with ideas for self-employment after release. For example, prisoners had often already started work on a business plan with a business advisor before being given a BT mentor who would visit and work with them on a much more regular basis.

The Leadership Consortium worked in a different way. I was given a list of people who the Consortium wanted a BT mentor for, and then looked to find a suitable person who lived near the mentee. As the standard of mentees got higher each year, this sometimes became difficult and on occasions impossible in areas with few or no experienced BT managers. It was not appropriate to assign a manager with less experience of managing than the mentee. The mentees were people who had applied for a Leadership Consortium Development Bursary following public advertisements. While being interviewed for the bursary, they were asked whether they would be interested in a BT mentor and access to some BT training in case their application was not successful.

Mentor and mentee selection/training/matching

Mentors were all volunteers and effectively self-selected for the schemes other than the Leadership Consortium. There were 4-page descriptions of each scheme, and additional details for people considering Roots & Wings. It was made clear that we did not want those interested to decide about the scheme until they had been to a training day and fully understood what was involved. I can't remember anyone not continuing after the induction day.

For the Leadership Consortium, I used my networks within BT to identify a likely mentor in a given area. If this didn't work, I would use the database of BT people and contact details and make an initial approach by e-mail followed up with a telephone call. The e-mail contained a description of the mentee without giving away the identity, and what the mentee hoped to achieve from the mentoring. An attachment gave the background to the scheme and what was expected. Sometimes I asked people to mentor, at other times to find a mentor, and sometimes both options. This approach eventually led to a mentor about eight times out of ten. For the secondary school mentors, a police check was carried out. We were upfront about this, and I hope it deterred unsuitable people.

In Roots & Wings, matching was carried out by the BT Local Organizer and a teacher from the school designated to lead on the mentoring. Both mentees and mentors completed forms to help with the matching. This asked about personal characteristics (age, gender, ethnicity), preferences (for male or female mentoring partner) and interests.

All of the schemes were open to non-managers. Management or business experience was needed for the adult schemes, but it was made clear this did not have to be within BT or a large business. Non-managers made up 60 per cent of the mentors, but nearly all of these were in Roots & Wings.

The training or induction was usually a day. It included the background to the partnering organization and to the schemes in BT, information on what mentoring is, what was expected of mentors, and where to get support. Mentors and mentees were also encouraged to talk about prior experiences with mentoring. For the Leadership Consortium, we twice ran a combined induction for mentors and mentees. For some of the senior managers on the Leadership Consortium, one-to-one briefings were held if they could not make the training day. Roots & Wings used case studies to think through some of the issues that might arise, and a presentation by a member of the school staff on the school, its community and on how they viewed the mentoring. Apart from the training for the Leadership Consortium, mentors and mentees were prepared separately. However, there would often be input from a mentee who had already benefited in a previous mentoring relationship.

The mentoring relationships

The ideal for all of the schemes was for mentoring meetings to take place at least once a month. The target for schools was 10 mentoring sessions between October and June. The commitment was only for 1 year, but about a third of pairs continued into another year. For the adult schemes, mentors were asked to meet at least 10 times over 12 months. Many exceeded this.

For BELTS and PYBT, the mentoring focused on setting up a business or expanding one. For Leadership Consortium, the focus was on helping talented people to use more of their potential – identifying career options, selecting goals and taking steps towards those goals. It also included helping people select and be invited to BT training courses.

For Roots & Wings, the nature of mentoring was more varied. Some schools chose 'hard cases' for mentoring, some chose high flyers, some chose quiet kids who tended to be overlooked in class, and others chose those they felt would respond most to mentoring. It was not generally about helping with school work, but more typically about helping to build confidence, improving attitudes, making aware of career opportunities, investigating possible careers and developing life skills.

All BT employees expressing interest in mentoring were asked to seek the agreement of their line managers, and materials were produced to help line managers understand the nature of the commitment, the benefits, and how a line manager could support the mentoring. Management support was seen as key for mentoring to succeed, and the best development of BT people would come when managers were informed and involved.

Evaluation

Evaluations were carried out for BELTS (once), Leadership Consortium (four times) and Roots & Wings (four times, the first two times involved the North West Consortium for the Study of Effectiveness in Urban Education – an alliance of education academics and school inspectors based in Manchester). Broadly speaking, the schemes were judged as very worthwhile by mentees, mentors and line managers, and were seen as contributing to the success of better life. Another benefit was the way these community schemes encouraged in-company mentoring and coaching. The vast majority of community mentors had not been a mentor or mentee before. On a number of occasions people told me that, having seen how their mentoring was helping someone else, they had sought out their own mentor. Or, if they were more senior managers, they had begun to promote mentoring in their area of work. Before these schemes were introduced, mentoring had been an elite activity in BT.

The greatest difficulties came from the time needed to organize the mentoring and the fact that not enough time was given for this. I had a job and a half, and so did the Roots & Wings Co-ordinators. Everything depended on good communications, and without this, mentoring relationships could begin to unravel or we lost mentors for the next year because they were not getting enough satisfaction from the schemes.

Having said that, BT was in other ways extremely generous in supporting the scheme and providing recognition for mentors. For example, each year mentors were presented with a memento as a way of thanking them for their contribution. And when I received an MBE for my work in setting up the schemes, BT provided a limousine to take me and my guests to Buckingham Palace.

Mentoring for diversity

Mentoring is one of several methods used to manage organizational diversity. Although diversity management has been around for a long time, only recently has it become a priority for the Board. This is the result of many factors, including changes in equal opportunities legislation, that have put increasing demands on organizations to attend to diversity. Furthermore, the recent and dramatic increase in globalization has caused an equally steep increase in the extent of organizational diversity. There is now a much broader range of nationalities, ethnic groups, and age groups in many organizations than, say, 10 years ago.

What does the term 'diversity management' actually mean? As

with mentoring, the term has recently been stretched to include many things, setting the scene for bewilderment at the very least. Most commonly, it refers to the efforts of companies to attract, recruit and retain so-called minority groups (e.g. women, racial minorities, ethnic minorities, gay men and women, and the disabled), and to represent them proportionately in upper management and on the Board. In other words, diversity management is typically intended to prevent discrimination and ensure equality and satisfaction for all employees. For example, Aer Rianta in Ireland established a diversity mentoring program that was aimed at redressing the balance of women to men in middle and senior management. In this scheme, mentors supported their mentees in identifying what positions they would like to reach and when by. They then devised a development and career plan intended to guide the relationship throughout the time it will take to reach the mentee's career goal. Similarly, Proctor and Gamble ran a diversity mentoring program aimed at retaining and advanc-ing female managers in the company. The case study that we will consider here as an example of mentoring in this situation is one currently run by AN Post.

CASE STUDY 3.4

Mentoring for diversity at An Post

An Post is Ireland's national postal service provider. As the parent company operating Ireland's largest communications, distribution, logistics, and financial-related service networks, An Post provides a wide range of services to both business and personal customers.

In 1999, An Post launched a project in collaboration with the European Social Fund (ESF). This project, called MIDAS, was a Development Program for senior managers of An Post and other organizations, and was funded by both the ESF and An Post. It aimed at fostering senior managers and leaders who would be able to reinforce and value an organizational culture in which diversity and individuality were appreciated and utilized. Since initial research for the MIDAS project revealed that mentoring is a very effective development method for senior managers, a mentoring scheme was implemented to support this overall Development Program. The project received its name from the Greek King of Mygdonia, Midas, whose wish that everything he touched should turn to gold was granted by Silenus, to whom he gave shelter. Similarly, the outcome of the MIDAS project is to reap superior organized performance and contribute to competitive advantage through a strategy of diversity management.

The scheme was implemented and co-ordinated by a MIDAS project team, which consisted of three women: Sheila Flannery, the Project Manager, Keara Dunne, the Project Executive, and Adrienne Buchanan-Murphy, the Project Officer. Having formerly implemented a mentoring scheme at a division of Aer Rianta, Sheila Flannery possessed substantial experience with running such programs.

In order to design the entire Development Program, the MIDAS team carried out initial research, part of which involved conducting semi-structured interviews with general managers, directors, and chief executives to ascertain what competencies were crucial for, for example:

- *Managing diversity.*
- *Dealing with crises in work situations.*
- *Certain leadership styles, and*
- *Establishing and addressing one's own and other's learning needs.*

These interviews served as a feeder pool for mentors because they enabled the MIDAS team to identify general managers in An Post who were adept at mentoring. Through this method, four mentors were recruited who the team later matched to mentees. Mentees were recruited through the selection process associated with the overall management Development Program. In total, 12 mentees were selected, six of which were internal and the remaining six external to An Post.

Notable in this program is that it employed a form of group mentoring in which a total of 12 mentees was split into four groups of three, each of which was then assigned one of the four mentors. The program ran from the middle of 1999 until the end of 2000, and during this time mentoring sessions took place within these groups – a minimum of three meetings per group was required, and arranging any sessions beyond that was left to the discretion of the groups.

The developmental focus of the mentoring was on the specific project that each group was obliged to undertake as part of their participation in the Development Program. Although there were variations between groups, all of the projects were concerned with implementing change in the organization in relation to diversity.

Prior to commencing the mentoring sessions, both mentors and mentees received training. For both groups, this included an introduction by David to mentoring in general. In addition, the mentor's half-day workshop covered:

- *Basic concepts in mentoring.*
- *What it takes to be a good mentor.*

- *The management of relationships.*

Mentors were also given the chance to practice, and the whole training workshop was supplemented by question and answer sessions. For mentees, the MIDAS project team decided to run a 1-day workshop, which addressed issues such as:

- *Mentoring – theory and practice.*
- *Diversity issues.*
- *Group mentoring.*
- *Individual mentoring.*
- *The development of the relationship.*
- *Key skills and pitfalls.*

To date a formal evaluation of the mentoring scheme has not been conducted, but it is believed to have been successful. According to Adrienne Buchanan-Murphy: '... each group commented that they found having a mentor during the project beneficial in seeing through the change'. In terms of challenges that had been experienced in relation to the program, Adrienne named 'organizing dates for mentors and mentees to get together for the initial meeting'. When asked what components of the scheme she would like to improve, she replied that '... more training at the initial stage on the role of the mentor and mentee would be good. Also, a training workshop, which both the mentor and mentee could attend to discuss the concept of mentoring, should become part of the preparation process'.

Mentoring for diversity – issues of definition

Case study 3.4 aimed to illustrate how mentoring can success-fully be used for diversity management. We previously noted that the most common interpretation of this term relates to the recruitment and retention of more people from traditionally under-represented 'identity groups' (Thomas and Ely, 1996), and to the proportional representation of these groups in the upper echelons of management. However, this is no longer the only definition of diversity. David Thomas and Robin Ely of the Harvard Business School suggest that diversity management should also be taken to refer to the 'management of the varied perspectives and approaches to work that members of different identity groups bring'. Another interpretation of the term considers it to be the 'integration and use of the diverse talents of all employees'. Without wanting to impose a solution to the problem, we would like to propose that the latter two interpretations should not be considered here as an issue for diversity mentoring. Instead, we would like to suggest that they should be addressed in 'cross-cultural mentoring' schemes, which will be discussed later in this chapter.

Given that neither 'mentoring' nor 'diversity' hold a universally accepted definition, attempting to use 'diversity mentoring' to manage differences sets the scene for even greater bewilderment. For example, how wide should we extend the notion of diversity mentoring? If a particular scheme is aimed at enforcing equality, should it include mental illness and obesity as sources of disadvantage? Does diversity mentoring mean supporting the maximization or the minimization of differences between employees? If it means helping to maximize differences, would it not become even harder to penetrate the glass ceiling, given that the upper echelons are typically very conformist?

The main problem with lacking a shared interpretation of 'diversity', 'mentoring' and 'diversity mentoring' is that it hinders the development of best practice in managing mentoring relationships and designing mentoring schemes in this area (Clutterbuck and Ragins, 2001). Best practice arises from discussions and observations in which everyone has the same concept of the subject matter. Furthermore, best practice guidelines are supposed to be transferable to the design and implementation of virtually all schemes with a particular orientation (e.g. diversity mentoring). However, if an orientation means different things to different people, best practice guidelines can no longer be relied upon. Lastly, not having a shared understanding of the meaning of diversity mentoring also makes it difficult for organizations to define the purpose of their scheme. This, in turn, seems to have an immense impact on the mentoring relationships within the scheme: clarity of purpose in the program appears to create a clear focus in the relationships. Too vague or too grand an objective often proves unattainable. In addition, participants may find it hard to relate the objective to their personal needs.

Until an official, universally accepted definition of diversity mentoring exists, precisely defining the program's purpose is of even greater significance in these types of schemes than in others. You should also consult widely in this process, taking into account the views of everyone affected by the program. This should prevent the unpleasant consequences of unmet expectations.

Graduate recruitment and induction mentoring

Commencing a new job is both an opportunity and a challenge. Most of us will recall the feelings of excitement as well as trepidation and inadequacy that can accompany the first couple of weeks in a new job. This emotion is likely to be pronounced if a job is your first full-time one after the completion of formal education. Under these circumstances, individuals are often extremely uncertain of what to do and when as they have no previous experience against which to benchmark their behaviour as a full-time employee. For these people, most commonly recent graduates, guidance and support is urgently needed. Even if a particular job is not your first one, there will always be times when you would really appreciate having someone to turn to, someone to 'show you the ropes', someone to help you acclimatize to a new organizational culture. Companies utilizing graduate schemes are numerous, and include British Aerospace, PricewaterhouseCoopers, Accenture, and Kingfisher.

Reasons for introducing graduate schemes

Currently the most frequent type of mentoring program, graduate and other new recruit schemes are implemented for several reasons, including:

- Attraction of individuals with employment potential.
- The accelerated induction of individuals.
- Retention of new recruits.
- The timely and high-quality development of the job performance of new recruits.
- Providing a safety-valve and sounding board for the concerns of new recruits.
- Diffusing feelings of self-consciousness and uncertainty.
- Helping graduates to find their place in the organization/ define their role.
- Supporting career development; helping graduates to establish career goals and identify appropriate actions.
- Ensuring greater organizational understanding (e.g. of culture goals and strategy).
- (In some cases) the mentor acting as a role model.
- Facilitating the relationship between the graduate and his/her (new) line manager/team leader. (NB: Although the involvement of third parties in mentoring relationships will be discussed in more detail later in the book, it is worth noting at this stage that line managers should be encouraged to support the relationship. There are a variety of reasons for this, such as avoiding line managers feeling resentful of the mentoring association because they might fear that another

person (the mentor) is influencing their work remit through the mentee).

Graduate schemes and succession planning

An additional, albeit more implicit, aim of graduate programs is that they can be used to support management succession planning by identifying high flyers and grooming them for higher-level positions. However, it is best for this identification process to happen without too much involvement of the mentor. Mentors can function as mediators, i.e. by informing management of the existence of a high-potential employee if they happen to meet one; however, mentors should never become assessors of employee's performance with regard to management potential. That is, they should not play a part in assessment or development centres or annual performance appraisals. Equipping mentors with an assessor role would seriously weaken the trust a mentee could place in a mentor, or cause them to 'look up' to the mentor.

Specific benefits of graduate schemes

Based on their long-standing experience with mentoring schemes, Clutterbuck Associates report that their clients consistently point to the following as benefits of implementing graduate schemes:

- Reduction of staff turnover and recruitment costs; this is achieved because graduate schemes increase motivation and instil a sense of belongingness.
- Improvement of internal communications including the fundamentals of the corporate vision, values and mission.
- Encouragement of employees to take on responsibility more quickly for their own career development.

Characteristics of graduate mentors

What are the characteristics of graduate mentors? These will depend very much on the focus of the scheme. In terms of organizational level, for example, a more experienced peer-mentor would probably suffice if the purpose of the scheme is induction only. If, however, the purpose of the scheme is to identify and stimulate high-potential employees, the mentor might have to be one or two ranks more senior than the graduate. This would allow for more qualified decisions to take place regarding the mentee's progress. Another reason for using more senior mentors might be the extent to which you want to make graduates feel valued: the more senior the mentor, the more valued individuals tend to feel.

Additional characteristics include:

- Impartiality – although always required of a mentor, graduates often emphasize this particular mentor quality.
- The ability to understand and empathize with the situation of the graduate – mentors must be aware of the numerous challenges faced by newly recruited graduates, such as managing organizational politics and adapting to the corporate culture.
- Availability – the mentor must be able to commit fully to the relationship and make sufficient time available.

CASE STUDY 3.5

by Bushra Ashraff and Belinda McGann of British American Tobacco

Established in 1902, British American Tobacco (BAT) is the world's most international tobacco group, with an active business presence in 180 countries. BAT employs almost 90,000 people worldwide. Its global market share totals 15 per cent, it is market leader in more than 50 countries, and it has a strong portfolio of over 300 brands.

BAT's mentoring scheme is part of an overall project aimed at creating a global graduate recruitment and development program. This program is called 'The Challenge Initiative', and has been running for the past 5 years. The main objective of the mentoring element is to support graduate management trainees in learning about the business and the industry. In addition, the scheme provides trainees with an opportunity to discuss their progress in their new roles and to talk about the challenges they are facing.

The entire graduate project, including the mentoring scheme, was championed by the then Human Resources Director, David Stevens. A project team worked with him to define the various elements of the program and to implement it. This central team established a global framework for the program with local HR personnel, who are ultimately responsible for managing the mentoring in their local market. Thus, it is up to them to find and recruit mentors and to match them with mentees for maximum efficiency. Management trainees join the mentoring scheme as part of their overall development program and the company provides the appropriate support. At any one time there are approximately 140 mentees taking part in the scheme.

Specific criteria are applied in selecting the mentors for the program. Mentors should:

- *Be middle to senior line managers.*
- *Have depth and breadth of experience.*
- *Ideally be able to fulfil the role for the complete 2-year period.*
- *Have a consistent track record of developing others.*
- *Be of high integrity.*
- *Be good communicators and listeners.*
- *Be respected by their peers.*
- *Be committed to their own development and that of others.*

The mentoring training is integrated with a larger training program aimed at supporting the management trainees in getting the most out of the development opportunities offered to them. This training program is called 'Aiming for Excellence'. The training for mentors, which was designed in collaboration with David, is called 'Mentoring for Excellence', and the agenda includes the following components:

- *Explaining the background and history of mentoring.*
- *Demonstrating the differences between mentoring and other learning routes.*
- *Showing the importance of mentoring in career development in organizations today.*
- *Identifying the skills and competencies a good mentor needs.*
- *Understanding the phases of development in a mentoring relationship.*
- *Giving mentors the opportunity to practise mentoring meetings.*

In addition to this initial training session, mentors also receive ongoing support from BAT across areas such as:

- *Identifying how to develop successful mentoring relationships.*
- *Obtaining feedback on the mentoring program's 6-monthly review.*
- *Clarifying the role of the mentor.*
- *Identifying what can be improved and considering actions to facilitate this improvement.*

Once mentors have successfully completed their training, they are then matched to a mentee. Matching is guided by the following factors:

- *Personality type.*
- *Background and experience.*
- *Age/culture.*
- *Learning style.*

- *Communications style.*
- *Gender.*
- *A lack of line relationship between mentor and mentee.*

The mentor should also preferably be in another business function than the mentee.

In terms of matching mentors with mentees, BAT takes the view that there should be balance between the similar and dissimilar personalities or backgrounds of the two parties. Compatibility depends on the individuals' personality type, learning, and communication style.

Although the frequency of mentoring meetings is not prescribed, pairs are encouraged to meet on a monthly basis. The emphasis of mentoring at BAT is strongly on developmental mentoring, and as such mentees are expected to take over the responsibility for managing their own learning. They determine the direction and pace of learning, and are required to be proactive in allocating time and discussion topics with their mentor. Mentors enable mentees to do this through, for example, prompting them to reflect creatively and intelligently. Mentors also share their experiences with mentees and focus on the long-term development of their capabilities.

The mentoring program is evaluated annually as part of the Global Management Trainee Survey. With regard to mentoring, the survey seeks to establish how many trainees enter the mentoring program and how much value it adds to their development. Mentors find the relationship to be highly rewarding, and over two-thirds of the mentees as well as the organization itself gain substantial benefits from the scheme (see Table 3.1).

In terms of organizational *benefits, BAT believes that mentoring increases organizational awareness. For example, through networking with higher management levels, mentees gain insight into the mentality and rationale of this group – they learn to 'speak their language'. In addition, the mentoring scheme also supports and is supported by four organizational principles, known as the Guiding Principles. These are:*

1. Strength from diversity – *actively utilizing diversity – of people, cultures, viewpoints, brands, markets and ideas – to create opportunities and strengthen performance.*
2. Open mindedness – *being an active listener, genuinely considering others' viewpoints and not pre-judging.*
3. Freedom through responsibility – *the freedom to take decisions and act on them obliges us to accept personal responsibility for the way they affect our stakeholders.*
4. Enterprising spirit – *the confidence to seek out opportunities for success, to strive for innovation, and to accept the considered risk-taking that comes with it.*

The aspects of the scheme that present the greatest challenge include matching mentors and mentees for maximum effect, gaining the commitment of managers to invest time in mentoring, and clarifying the difference between the role of a line manager and that of a mentor. Finally, areas for improvement that were suggested by mentees included:

- *Setting up meetings with the other trainees to exchange information about how to get the best out of their mentoring relationship.*
- *Finding additional ways of supporting trainees to stay focused on developing themselves, as this can often be pushed to the background given the daily duties of their jobs.*
- *Mentoring support could also include more on the development of managerial competence; and providing mentors with additional training and support in developing these skills.*

BAT is constantly striving to improve its mentoring program and process, and therefore feedback from our mentees is invaluable in this process.

Table 3.1 Benefits of BAT's mentoring scheme for mentors and mentees

Mentors	Mentees
✓ Improvements in communication skills	✓ Mentors add considerable value to mentee's personal development
✓ Better insight into the motivators for people's career choices	✓ Substantial improvements in managerial skills
✓ Extended networks	✓ Insights into development priorities, i.e. seeing clearly which skills and which personality characteristics really need to be developed and how
✓ Improved work relationships	✓ Excellent support
✓ Increased personal motivation	✓ Changed views and perspectives regarding one's function

Executive/director/partner mentoring

Becoming and then being a company executive, director or partner is a hugely challenging task involving many potential crises. It is also a lonely task, and coping with isolation can be tough. An excellent case for the importance of mentoring for aspiring executives, or rather aspiring 'partners' in professional service firms, was made by Herminia Ibarra (Ibarra, 2000). According to Ibarra (p. 148), '... there are few professional transformations quite as psychologically complex as the transformation to partner'. Even before having been made a partner, these individuals are expected to behave like one. Given that becoming a partner essentially involves forging a new identity that conveys credibility and competence, this is quite a challenge. For this and other reasons, Ibarra stresses throughout her article that making partner requires a phenomenal amount of skilled mentoring support from a person who is already a partner at the same company.

Based on her analyses of the process of becoming partner, she concluded that this involves three main tasks:

- Choosing and observing role models.
- Experimenting with possible selves.
- Evaluating the outcomes thereof.

The mentor's role in a mentee's transition to partner status

Within the transition to partner status, Ibarra sees the mentor's role as encompassing the following elements:

- Helping the mentee to reflect and to learn from these reflections.
- Providing high-quality feedback.

With the mentor's help, the aspiring partner is more likely to make – as well as emotionally survive – the process of forging a new identity. With the support of a mentor, this process is likely to be accelerated. Lastly, mentoring should not end upon being made a partner; it should continue, but perhaps with a different person and in a different form, such as peer mentoring.

Like partners, (aspiring) executives and directors will find the help of a highly competent and trustworthy mentor invaluable when faced with a whole array of personal and professional challenges. (Please note that the term 'executives' will from herein be used to symbolize all variations, including aspiring executives and/or directors as well as those currently occupying either of these positions).

Mentoring for executives

As is the case with mentoring for partners, the executive mentor's task consists of supporting the executive in making significant transitions. Transitions can be effected in areas such as the executive's thought processes, their perspectives and their self-knowledge.

Clutterbuck and Megginson (1999) devoted an entire book to the challenges and practices of executive and director mentoring. In their book they emphasize that, although there are both national and individual differences, the specific needs executive mentees typically want to address show recurrent patterns, and these are shown in Table 3.2.

Table 3.2 Needs of executive mentees

Aspiring Executives and/or Directors	Executives	Executive–Directors
✓ Issues of visibility	✓ Achievement through influence versus command	✓ Working with colleagues in collaborative independence
✓ Understanding senior levels	✓ Coping with stress caused by responsibility	✓ Ensuring accurate awareness of organizational issues
✓ Managing business politics	✓ Issues of credibility	✓ Being a good role model for values of top team
✓ Gaining relevant experience	✓ Enhancing own performance management	✓ Developing skills for becoming a Chief Executive or a non-executive director
✓ Creating valuable influence and information networks	✓ Developing others	✓ Life/career planning

Characteristics of executive mentors

Although the specific competencies required of mentors will always vary between schemes, executive mentors seem to be the most distinct (Clutterbuck and Megginson, 1999). This is perhaps not surprising, given the types of needs they are required to meet.

One of the paramount skills for executive mentoring is the mentor's ability to help the executive to create and use personal reflective space (PRS). PRS can be defined as 'the seized opportunity to develop personal insight through uninterrupted and purposeful reflective activity' (Clutterbuck and Megginson, 1999). Although PRS is of paramount importance to the executive's personal and professional development, research has previously suggested that executives find it hard to reflect. This can at least in part be attributed to their busy work schedules, which make it difficult to set aside time for reflection. In the context of mentor training (Chapter 10), we will explore the executive mentor's characteristics in more detail.

Apart from the differences in competencies that exist between executive mentors and other mentors, they can also be distinguished on account of another feature: executive mentors are true professionals! They are typically highly experienced and successful (retired) business men or women with a wealth of first-hand experience at executive level. This professionalism is also frequently reflected in their fees. There are exceptions, however, where fees are kept low because executive mentors view the mentoring relationship as an opportunity for personal growth and as a chance to 'give something back'. One example of this is Business Mentoring Scotland, a company providing mentoring support to directors of selected growth companies. Although the mentors are required to be seasoned and highly professional business men or women, they are asked to support the directors free of charge.

Case study 3.6 demonstrates how mentoring can be used in organizations to enable top management development.

Case study 3.6

Executive mentoring at Lex Service PLC

Lex Service PLC provides motoring and related business solutions to individual and corporate customers in the UK and Europe. Their services include the provision of BSM driving schools, nationwide repairs centres, outsourcing services for corporate customers, and vehicle importing and retailing.

From 1994 until recently, Lex has looked to mentoring as a means of top team development. The scheme is currently put on hold due to a pending major restructuring initiative. Unusually, they did not have a 'Lex mentoring program'; instead, the board started with a number of business issues, and used mentoring as one of the appropriate solutions.

In one instance, mentoring had been specifically introduced to help the business with management retention. Mentees were identified when an analysis of the succession process revealed a number of people at executive level who were critical for the future.

Each mentee was allocated to a mentor drawn from the executive team (including the Chief Executive and Chairman). Pairings were based on the mentee's development needs, the strengths and style of the mentor, an avoidance of direct line relationship, and geographical feasibility.

The mentors were tasked with ensuring that mentees had:

- *A clear view of their value to Lex.*
- *A job that was stretching.*
- *A development plan that was actively supported.*
- *An ongoing dialogue about their career needs that took into account both the company's and their own needs.*
- *Appropriate reward and recognition.*
- *Access to the Chief Executive.*

The mentoring pairs met up roughly every other month; and the lifespan of the relationship was determined by the participant's feelings about the value that they were gaining from it. The mentor's performance was regularly reviewed by the executive team, and mentees were regularly surveyed to understand the impact of the program on their needs.

Mentoring for retention has been a huge success in Lex. Whilst turnover in the general management population has remained steady, in the mentee group it has halved. This may not all be attributable to mentoring, but the indications are there that mentoring has made the difference.

Mentoring was also used to support the practical application of off-the-job training, and to help senior managers enhance their ability to tackle new challenges. Whether the mentee was matched with a mentor from within Lex, from a non-competitor organization or from a professional external practice, the control of the relationship stayed with the mentee. The central management development function was there to act as a matchmaker, but after that it was up to the participants to make the relationship work.

Mentoring in Lex has been successful because the approach has been carefully crafted to suit the needs and culture of the business, rather than being imposed as an HR agenda. The HR team had a role to play in publicizing the availability and benefits of mentoring, and in providing a framework for its implementation. However, the most important facilitator of mentoring in Lex has been the strong commitment of top management. The top team value mentoring as a means of growing the strategic competence of the business, and all have been actively involved as mentors. They were the first people to use the process, they have seen the benefits, and are now able to give credibility to mentoring and act as role models for this form of management development.

International management

Within many corporations a sea change in relation to management education is taking place: where they traditionally received *ad hoc* training, top managers with international or global responsibility are now being developed in a more systematic fashion. Amongst other interventions such as training and formal study, mentoring is an important component of this endeavour to foster internationally competent managers. This trend is not only observable in big multinational companies, but also in those of small or medium size.

International management mentoring schemes (IMMS) are strategic and long-term interventions. An important element of these involves sending managers on overseas assignments, for which they continue to receive mentoring (see 'International assignments' below). This type of intervention is extremely powerful in creating internationally competent managers.

In general, IMMS focus on supporting top management with handling the challenges and opportunities associated with international enterprise. These individuals need to think and manage globally; they need to be able to manage across cultures as well as across countries. They also need to be able to capitalize on the international status of their company, understand what it means to compete internationally, and manage risks. In short, managers need to develop a 'global brain' that allows them to understand an international company and its business environment in its entirety, so that ultimately the organization competes successfully in global markets.

Competencies to be developed by IMMS mentees

To fulfil the above objectives, strategic mentoring is required – i.e. it becomes an integral part of business strategy. It focuses on the development of those competencies that will enable managers to meet business needs.

The competencies to be developed include both behavioural and attitudinal elements. When examining these, you will understand why the development of international managers is a long-term process. It is long-term because it requires the mentee to dispense with traditional management models and adopt a new approach. This type of change is demanding, and requires time, patience and commitment – not only on the part of the mentee, but also on the part of the mentor(s) and the organization. However, given that it will ultimately develop managers who sustain (or even create) the success of an international enterprise, the investment of resources is worthwhile. The competencies that need to be developed and role-modelled by international managers can be grouped into the following sections (Conway 1998):

1. *Understanding, implementing and modelling international strategy.* This relates to all types of strategy including overall business, finance, marketing and HR. Since strategies do not exist without corporate visions, the manager also needs to acquire the ability to formulate a vision that supports international enterprise (or fully understand and buy into an existing one). In this respect, it is important for the manager to learn to ask questions such as 'what is important for international vision and strategy formulation?', 'why is it important?' and 'how do they differ from national ones?'.

2. *Cross-border coaching and co-ordination.* This competency involves learning how to think about and co-ordinate the business processes of an international business – for example, should decision-making be centralized? How can the exchange of resources (human and other) between branches be organized for maximum efficiency? How can cross-functional/ international teamwork be arranged? How do you overcome the problems of cultural diversity and geographic dispersion? Mentees aim to develop a wide range of abilities:

   • They need superb individual and team coaching skills to create a world-class team.
   • They must act as intercultural mediators, which requires outstanding facilitation skills and interpersonal sensitivity.
   • They must encourage international and intercultural collaboration and communication.
   • In order to act as intercultural mediators, it is vital that managers examine their own cultural values and beliefs.

- They have to develop the capacity to discard stereotypes, and to accept differences.
- They have to learn to understand what is happening in the different company locations – what is really going on in cases of intercultural conflict.
- Most importantly of all, managers should try to foster their own positive attitude toward cultural diversity amongst other employees.

3. *Change agent*. Although the necessity to change is a constant feature of any business, it is somewhat more pronounced in internationally operating enterprises. This includes large-scale organizational as well as smaller-scale individual changes. International managers epitomize this need for change: first, they need to go through a vast amount of personal change. Secondly, they need genuinely to embrace and champion organization-wide transformations and not be seen as hindering changes. This takes various forms such as engaging in continuous learning and being able to switch frames of reference.

4. *Management of personal effectiveness*. Managing an international business implies the investment of more than usual time, including time away from home due to international travel. To succeed in this highly demanding role, both privately and professionally, international managers must learn how to manage personal effectiveness. This entails coping with stress and establishing a healthy work–life balance.

5. *Openness to continuous learning and development*. This in itself is a competency, the importance of which cannot be overstated! The reasons for its significance have been provided throughout this section. That is, acquiring international management competency as described in the preceding points demands a sound capacity for learning as well as the willingness to do so. For example, the vehicle for personal transformation and the acquisition of adaptability and flexibility is learning and development. All of these skills are highly important, given that the internal and external business environment is constantly changing. The openness to learning and development is also important for managers' tasks of coaching and co-ordinating cross-cultural teams. In this respect, they act as role models whose positive attitude towards learning will inspire their team to emulate it. In multinational and/or culturally diverse enterprises, learning becomes crucial for everyone, since it facilitates the process of coming to terms with cultural differences.

Mentoring topics in IMMS

Having examined the types of competencies international managers need to develop, typical topics for mentoring are likely to include the following:

- Understanding and formulation of international strategy (including business, finance, and human resource strategy).
- Coping with change.
- International competitiveness and visibility.
- Managing an international career – goals, risks, opportunities, work–life balance.
- Marketing and sales in international markets.
- Organizational structure and operational management.
- Human resource management/development across national boundaries and across cultures.
- Thinking through difficult and sensitive situations.

The mentor's main tasks

The primary tasks of a mentor in IMMS include:

- Providing reflective space and encouraging the active use thereof.
- Acting as a sounding board and engaging in dialogue that can both be impartial as well as challenging.
- Role-modelling international management expertise.
- Supporting the mentee through organizational and personal change – for the mentee, this can be a difficult and even painful experience involving the discarding of many well-established mindsets and behaviours; a mentor's support is very much needed to maintain direction and motivation.

Benefits of mentoring for developing international managers

There is a whole range of organizational benefits that ensue from hosting an IMMS, including the following:

- *Increased competitiveness.* This benefit accrues in various forms. First, being able to exchange thoughts on many types of business issues with a mentor who is experienced in running a multinational company will help mentees to gain greater insight into this field, make more effective decisions and avoid harmful mistakes. Mentees will be able to think and behave in an 'international way', develop the competencies required for it, and make decisions using their 'global brains'. All of these will greatly enhance the organization's ability to compete internationally. Secondly, the competitiveness of international enterprise is further enhanced by its ability to adapt to change. Thirdly, mentoring is a two-way learning relationship, a fact that is evidenced in virtually every evaluation of mentoring relationships. This implies that the mentor also acquires new ways of looking at and approaching business situations. The likelihood that the mentor will therefore enhance his or her own international understanding and management capability is extremely high.

Underlying all of these ways in which IMMS can enhance an organization's competitiveness is the ability of mentoring to help people embrace and manage their own learning and development.

- *Stress reduction and individual effectiveness.* If nothing else, mentoring will reduce the stress levels experienced by most managers with international responsibility. Apart from having health implications, consistently high stress levels can impede an individual's ability to make effective decisions. The process of helping mentees to arrive at effective decisions is supported by the mentor's ability to remove cognitive blockages through a combination of questioning, supporting and challenging.

Additional organizational benefits accrue directly from one of the components that is often part (sometimes even the central or only part) of an IMMS: international assignments. Before looking at the benefits of international assignments, we would first like to explain in more detail what we mean by this.

International assignments

Nowadays, many multinationals (or companies with international joint ventures) send employees, particularly managers and executives, on international assignments. These require them to work for what is often a substantial amount of time in a company branch located in a foreign country. One of the reasons behind international assignments is that a company is responding to an immediate problem that has arisen in a company's foreign subsidiary and requires a highly skilled person to take over. Another reason for executives and managers to be sent on international assignments is to educate and develop them. The assignment is intended to prepare them for their successful leadership within a global organization. The underlying assumption is that having executives with international experience enhances international competitiveness. It is thought that sending them to work in a foreign country will provide them with a range of skills and insights that they would not otherwise acquire. This includes helping executives/managers to gain:

- A better understanding of what it means to lead an international corporation – for instance, executives will gain a greater appreciation of the differences in challenges and opportunities between company branches.
- The ability to take a broader focus when making company decisions, i.e. truly realizing that one's organization is international and taking that into account.
- Better people management skills.
- Greater flexibility and openness to change.

The role of preparation and support in international assignments

Taking up an international assignment is not a straightforward task. In fact, many of them turn into failed experiences, with expatriates terminating the assignment prematurely or simply resenting it (Black *et al.*, 1992). The main reason for this is the lack of personal and professional preparation and support assigned to expatriates. Even if an individual has extensive experience as a manager or executive, taking up this role in another country will be a very different task, not least due to the different national and cultural background of the new colleagues!

Executives/managers will need support prior to, during and after their stay in a foreign country (Kram, 1983). Prior to the assignment, mentors could enable the expatriate to prepare emotionally and professionally for the assignment. Issues such as challenges, opportunities and concerns should be explored. Mentoring during the assignment focuses on helping the mentee to settle and get started. Since this is usually a rather awkward process, the mentor should be available to the mentee quite frequently and at short notice. The mentoring sessions should, at least initially, also take place quite often, such as once per week.

The mentoring that is to take place after the assignment is crucial as well; it is important to individuals to conduct a retrospective analysis of the experience on the basis of which they can draw out the main learning points. Mentees may want the opportunity to work out how they can leverage the experience gained abroad, and they need support in re-adjusting to their old (work) environment. Indeed, this endeavour is so important to individuals that some, once repatriated, have been reported to have left their companies because they did not receive this type of guidance (Black *et al.*, 1992). This is regrettable – particularly if the person who resigned is of crucial importance to the business!

Although mentoring schemes aimed at supporting expatriates seem an ideal way to address many of their problems, they are still fairly rare (Siegel *et al.*, 1999). In our collection of case studies, Allianz was the exception in providing mentoring support throughout the process of expatriation. Consequently, little evidence has been accumulated as to the outcomes of these schemes. However, the evidence that does exist shows mentoring to exert a positive influence on expatriates (Feldman and Thomas, 1992).

Objectives in expatriate mentoring

Where established, the mentoring relationships were intended to address some or all of the following objectives:

- To support executives' or managers' professional adaptation. This involves, for example, facilitating their adjustment to the national and corporate culture by helping them to develop national, cultural and interpersonal sensitivity. Mentors are meant to promote individual's abilities to understand and manage differences in beliefs, values and behaviours. Supporting the mentees professional adaptation further involves promoting the accelerated acquisition of technical and professional knowledge and skills.
- To enable them to anticipate and/or learn from common failures of international assignments, which are often caused by a lack of professional preparation.
- To support executives' or managers' personal adaptation, involving helping them to understand and prosper in a new cultural and social environment.
- To improve their personal flexibility, self-monitoring and reflective skills; although the latter two elements are always integral parts of any mentoring relationship, their importance is emphasized in expatriate mentoring: self-monitoring and reflective skills are essential for developing the cultural and interpersonal sensitivity mentioned above.
- To be a sounding board for any general questions and issues that may arise from being an expatriate.
- To facilitate expatriates' ability to learn from the assignment and to become more effective for it.

- To alleviate stress and emotional turmoil.

The mentor helps expatriates turn an international assignment into a successful experience by:

- Helping mentees to perform well during the assignment, ensuring that they do not compromise, but improve the business.
- Fostering learning in the assignment, which enhances the mentees' leadership and professional skills as a result.
- Ensuring that the expatriates find the experience to be enjoyable and enriching; this is important because failed expatriate years (i.e. those that have turned into an unpleasant, unsuccessful experience and/or were terminated prematurely) can have long-standing repercussions for an individual's ability to lead an international corporation.

The costs incurred by a business as a result of a failed expatriation can be substantial (for example, costs for downtime, early repatriation and other direct and indirect outgoings). Although mentoring can exert a positive influence here it is not a panacea and will not solve all the problems associated with international assignments. Mentoring should be seen as complementing formal training programs geared towards preparing individuals for expatriation and repatriation.

Characteristics of IMMS mentors

We have now considered mentoring schemes for international managers on a generic level as well as examining one of their elements, international assignments, in more detail. Looking back over the information provided, the question of 'the right kind of mentor' arises. In keeping with the structure embraced so far, we will first have a closer look at the characteristics of the mentors involved in IMMS in general before turning to the characteristics of an expatriation mentor.

So, what do the mentors of IMMS look like? The mentors are either from the same or a more senior organizational rank, and are likely to be from within the organization but could on some occasions also be recruited from outside. This decision entirely depends on the size of the organization as well as on the availability of suitable mentors. Either way, an important selection criterion for mentors is that they possess a lot of experience with multinational enterprise. Although it should go without saying, it is also crucial to select individuals who are indeed capable mentors! This statement relates in particular to their motivation, which needs to be carefully investigated when selecting individuals for mentors. This is in the interest of the organization, not only because the mentees' development is so important but also because it is likely to be a very long-term and close relationship. Having said this, any mentoring relationship is at some point likely to reach a plateau, and a new mentor might be needed to advance mentees' development.

Although expatriate mentors have to possess many of the characteristics required by all mentors (see Chapter 5), they will need to display certain additional qualities. For example, expatriation mentors should ideally:

- Themselves have experienced international assignments.
- Be familiar with the culture/nationality to which the mentee is to be assigned (that means they should either be from that culture or have spent considerable time within it).
- Be culturally, nationally and interpersonally sensitive.
- Be highly motivated to see the mentee through the phase of the assignment for which the mentor has been allocated (i.e. either prior to, during or after the assignment).
- Be a person the expatriate will trust.

Whilst the same mentor could be used for the 'before' and 'after' phases, a different person is likely to mentor the expatriate during the assignment. Thus, the person mentoring the expatriate during the assignment should ideally be local and familiar with the culture, politics and processes of the business site the mentee is allocated to.

Where possible, it might also be a good idea to assign two mentors – a peer and a more senior one – to the expatriate during all three phases of the assignment. The reason for this suggestion is that different learning points will ensue from both sources. For example, since the peer relationship is likely to be more informal than the senior–junior one, the mentee is more likely to be open regarding social and emotional adjustment problems. The senior mentor, on the other hand, might be better suited to helping the mentee to develop a career strategy.

Case studies in this book that describe mentoring schemes for fostering international management capability are Allianz Insurance (Case study 3.8) and Ericsson (Case study 8.1). Furthermore, the Fisher College of Business, whose mentoring activities are briefly discussed in Chapter 4, also runs a mentoring program to help managers improve their global management capability.

Cross-cultural mentoring

Before describing this type of mentoring scheme, we would like to explore what we mean by cultural diversity and evaluate its advantages and disadvantages.

Over the past decade, the face of the workforce has changed in many ways. There are more women in employment than ever before; so-called minority groups are advancing into higher positions; and highly responsible roles are frequently filled by very young people. Another noticeable trend, particularly in multinational corporations, is the diversification of the work-force in terms of national culture. Many managers and leaders perceive cultural diversity as generally positive, and maintain that it benefits organizational effectiveness and competitive-ness – a view that is frequently supported by anecdotal and academic evidence (Thomas and Ely, 1996).

How does cultural diversity enhance organizational performance?

If an organization is open to diversity of national culture, it can enhance its performance by recruiting the best people for any given job, irrespective of nationality. In addition, the diversity of perspectives, knowledge and opinions enhances overall creativ-ity as well as insights into foreign markets.

The downside of cultural diversity is that its benefits do not accrue automatically: the line between the advantages and dis-advantages of diversity is very fine, and diversity must be managed carefully to reap the benefits and avoid the traps! Let us now take a look at the two main challenges that are faced by organizations with large proportions of cultural diversity. Bear in mind, however, that these *challenges* only transcend into *dangers* if left unmanaged. Furthermore, the danger will be greater the more diverse an organization is.

Cultural diversity – the challenges

The first main challenge is to prevent persistent and harmful employee conflicts – that is, the balance between diversity and similarity (or 'organizational norms') can in some cases lean too far toward diversity. This implies that the differences in perspec-tives, behaviours and work concepts become dysfunctional and lead to culture 'clashes' (Loden and Rosener, 1991). The mani-festation of these involves misunderstandings, feelings of threat and conflicts, which can seriously compromise important work behaviours such as communication and collaboration.

The second challenge lies in preventing the diversity of national cultures from undermining (or obstructing the development of) a unified corporate culture. To illustrate this point, let us first consider what organizational culture is and what influences its development. Schein (1992) defines organizational culture as the system of beliefs, attitudes, values and behaviours that is shared by all organizational members and that integrates its processes. Organizational culture is also often described as 'the way we do things around here'. Top management typically model a certain type of culture, and seek to reinforce it amongst the other organizational members.

Organizational cultures are influenced by many factors, such as the vision of the founder, the economic and market environment, technology and organizational structure (Handy, 1993). Another factor that impacts on organizational culture is national culture (Schneider and Barsoux, 1997). Leaving aside for a moment individual differences, every nation is thought to hold a set of beliefs, values and behaviours that are considered unique to them. These determine how people do things both at work and in their personal lives.

Within organizations that have a high proportion of cultural diversity, there will be a more than usual accumulation of diverging belief and value systems. The danger is that these differences might interfere with the creation or maintenance of a unified corporate culture.

This is where cross-cultural mentoring schemes come into the picture: the powerful one-to-one dialogues of mentoring can be used to help employees from widely varying national and ethnic backgrounds to work together as effectively as possible (Kogler-Hill and Bahniuk, 1998). In fact, many North American companies now consider coaching and mentoring to be a key strategy for integrating diverse employees (Thomas and Ely, 1996; Ragins, 1997).

Advantages and aims of cross-cultural mentoring schemes

Cross-cultural mentoring schemes can:

- Create a balance between national and organizational cultures.
- Replace expatriates with indigenous people in (Western) companies located in other, particularly Third World, countries; mentoring can help to manage cultural issues.

- Familiarize employees with the corporate culture and corporate objectives, and ensure that they work in line with these.
- Support employees in avoiding misunderstandings.
- Help individuals to recognize the added value of cultural diversity.
- Help managers to integrate and capitalize on the different talents of a culturally diverse workforce.
- Create a learning organization that inspires employees' to learn from one another's differences with a view to maximizing competence.
- Create mutual understanding and, therefore, enhanced communication.

The ultimate aim of these objectives is to create a shared culture, one that improves the overall performance of a culturally diverse workforce.

Mentor characteristics

When considering the different aims of a cross-cultural mentoring scheme, it becomes clear that the mentors ought to be people who:

- Have had diversity training and/or experience with cross-cultural management/training.
- Possess extremely sophisticated interpersonal and facilitation skills.
- Are sensitive towards and appreciative of cultural differences.
- Whole-heartedly espouse company values.

Case study 3.7 illustrates a cross-cultural pilot mentoring scheme set in a Western company located in Borneo. It is interesting to note that this type of mentoring may be both more difficult as well as different to other programs. For instance, due to cultural variations, Malay mentees were not so comfortable with the focus on self-managed learning within developmental mentoring – mentors were expected to be much more proactive than in a European environment.

Case study 3.7

Mentoring in a multicultural environment

In 1995, David helped a well-known blue-chip oil company to develop a pilot mentoring program in a Pacific subsidiary. The program encompassed four cultures: Malay, Chinese, British and Dutch. It was the aim of this pilot to find an effective way of replacing expatriate staff (British and Dutch) with talented indigenous employees. This process, however, is not very straightforward, particularly in Asian countries, where there are multicultural issues to take into account. These include reluctance on the part of the Malay to network with people who occupy hierarchically higher positions, and a disinclination to show open disagreement. It was thought that mentoring might be an effective method to both facilitate these cultural issues and enable the indigenization process. The decision to use mentoring for this purpose arose partly from observation of its use elsewhere in the group and partly from the recognition that the methods used to date (coaching and traditional training courses) were not achieving sufficient results with regards to indigenizing Malays.

The mentee group consisted of seven Malay and Chinese high flyers (male and female) who had been with the company for some time but had yet to achieve a managerial role. The seven mentors were drawn from all four cultures. Prior to training, the individuals were interviewed and asked to indicate what concerns, hopes and expectations they held for the mentoring relationships. Using the European Mentoring Centre's 'Dimensions and goals of mentoring' model, prospective mentors and mentees were also asked to draw the shape of the relationship at the beginning and after 2 years. This exercise revealed big differences between the mentor and mentee groups. These formed the basis of an insightful discussion during the training workshops for both mentors and mentees. The discussion allowed mentors to think through how much they were prepared to accommodate the mentees' expectations, and how much they were going to try to change them.

Training the mentors and mentees for the pilot

The seven mentors attended a 2-day intensive workshop that looked at the nature of mentoring, the skills required, and how to manage the relationship. The mentees had a 1-day workshop, with the mentors joining them towards the end of the day. The second day of the mentors' workshop involved a variety of role-plays designed by the participants themselves to reflect the kind of issues they had already encountered between the cultures.

Evaluation

The evaluation involved detailed interviews with all but one of the mentees, and all the mentors, plus the mentees' line managers. Inevitably, there was a significant variation in what had been achieved. Some of the relationships had moved firmly into the experimentation and progress-making stage. They had begun to set goals for the relationship and were working towards achieving them (for example, developing more effective skills of communication and presentation). Some other relationships had more difficulty getting through the rapport stage, and mentor and mentee had not developed a relaxed and trusting atmosphere. These less successful relationships were both cross-cultural and between people from the same culture; personality and mentoring style were the critical factors.

Only one of the relationships had involved the mentor and mentee working together on a major project. Both mentor and mentee had felt it to be useful, but the mentee was unable to see a substantial purpose for continuing the relationship – the learning had been confined to the technical aspects of project management. Counselling was provided to the mentor and mentee to help them refocus the relationship around some clear behavioural objectives. Counselling was also provided to the only mentoring pair in which it was clear that a mismatch of personality had occurred. This was an extremely difficult task in which the need to avoid any suggestion of blame or personal failure was crucial. The focus of the discussions had to be on what sort of mentor would best suit the mentee in future.

Overall, at least five of the mentees in the seven pilot pairs had made significant progress and learning. Some quantitative feedback was obtained using questionnaires from the 'Mentoring Diagnostic' and this provided a generally positive picture of the range of developmental behaviours used by the mentors.

Other conclusions from the evaluation were:

- *While there was little observable behavioural change among mentees (it was far too soon in most cases), most were actively working on specific goals.*
- *Some mentees were still reluctant to establish their own development goals, and wanted the mentor to tell them what to work on.*
- *Some mentees were much more comfortable discussing technical issues, but a lack of deep rapport made it difficult for them to open up on behavioural topics.*
- *Mentees' supervisors sometimes felt left out – they wanted to be brought into the picture, though not in a way that would undermine the confidentiality of the mentoring relationship; in particular, supervisors were interested in knowing the learning objectives of the relationship, so that they could help in turn.*
- *The number of meetings varied significantly between one to five over a 6-month period. Time pressure was a significant factor here, along with a reluctance by some mentees to interrupt the busy schedule of their mentor.*
- *Mentors learnt as well – dealing with their own direct reports, and adapting their behaviour (especially listening).*

Out of the evaluation came a number of recommendations, including:

- *Establishment of support groups for both mentors and mentees.*
- *Greater emphasis on rapport-building skills for both mentors and mentees.*
- *Recognition that mentors may have to be more proactive in setting meetings than European cultural norms would recommend.*
- *Creation of a bigger pool of mentors from which people can choose suitable partners.*
- *An obligatory self-management course for anyone wishing to become a mentee.*

High flyers/succession planning

Mentoring schemes can be used both to identify and to develop high-potential employees. Programs established for developing high flyers involve a strictly limited mentee target group: they are only open to those who others (e.g. their managers) have identified as possessing a lot of potential. 'Potential' is, in this context, defined as an individual's ability to grow and develop, to make a significant future contribution to the business, and/or to fulfil the responsibilities of an executive position.

Once a high-potential employee has been identified through, for example, a development centre or simple observation by his or her manager, a targeted development program can be established. Mentoring might be the central element of this, or simply one of many components including training, university courses, secondments or self-study.

The objectives of mentoring schemes set up to develop high flyers are likely to involve one or more of the following:

- Coping with the stresses of the role – to many people it might be both physically and emotionally demanding to be identified as a high flyer, to live up to the status of a high-potential employee, or to develop competence in line with others' and one's own expectations.
- Developing capability (e.g. leadership and operating styles) at an increased pace in comparison to others.
- Motivating and retaining high-potential employees.
- Assuming credibility in the eyes of subordinate employees who might be substantially older than the high flyer.
- Career management/development – mentors can support this process by helping mentees to take control of their careers and make relevant career decisions.

- Understanding what it means to occupy a senior role, for example, developing strategic insight and greater cross-functional/cross-team understanding.
- Selecting projects, assignments and roles that will promote appropriate 'stretch' and experience.

What are the characteristics associated with mentors of high flyers? They are likely to be:

- More senior than the mentee.
- From a different function to the mentee – breadth of experience is more important for the mentee.
- Substituted or complemented by other mentors after a certain period of time. This might be necessary to provide the mentee with the best opportunities to acquire all the competencies required by top company positions. Given that mentors can function as role models that mentees seek to emulate, considering a variety of models will help mentees in several ways – by observing a range of top management styles, trying them out and adapting the elements that seem most true to one's nature. This will enable the high-potential individual to develop a credible new self (Ibarra, 2000).

Taking on the role of a mentor for a high-potential employee is far from easy, though. The main difficulty faced by the mentor lies in having to juggle ethical mentoring behaviour (e.g. maintaining confidentiality and allowing the mentee to set the agenda) with supporting the organization's succession planning efforts – the latter clearly being the aspect around which the mentoring relationship revolves. Supporting organizational succession planning typically involves occasional assessment of the mentee's competence. However, to preserve confidentiality, mentors ought to refrain from taking part in this assessment process. They should never reveal any of the contents of the mentoring sessions to other decision-makers, leaving the assessment of the high flyer to them instead.

Benefits of mentoring schemes for high flyers

These include:

- Support of implementation of succession plans.
- Motivation and retention of the people intended for higher-level positions; mentors can help their mentees to resist succumbing to the challenges inherent in a fast progressing

career, and mentoring can also go a long way towards preventing people from transferring to competitor organizations – which, if they did, would be a substantial expense for the company.

- Conflict management; although this is only an indirect function of a mentor, being able to talk about conflicts with external parties during a mentoring meeting can help to calm down and facilitate conflicts.
- Enhanced competitiveness; competitiveness is harnessed through the development of high-potential individuals in two main ways. First, better people create better products and services. Managers in particular have a substantial influence on organizational performance, as they influence a number of people who carry out the tasks. Managers also exercise a direct influence on organizational strategy. Overall, this means that high flyers who are being developed for management positions will become powerful shapers of the company's ability to compete. Secondly, through pairing high-potential employees with more senior personnel in mentoring relationships, individuals are given a chance to contribute directly ideas for alterations to products and services. Some of these ideas might well contribute to the enhancement or maintenance of a competitive edge.

The negative side of high-flyer programs

As with many things in life, there is a less glorious side to high-flyer programs, too. Since their main aim is to further develop the skills of those already talented, they can promote elitism. Furthermore, they may also not be sufficiently supportive to include or retain those less willing or able to focus everything on their career (e.g. those with dependants).

Succession planning

Mentoring is often used to support succession planning. In this capacity, it is essentially identical to mentoring schemes for high flyers – that is, although succession planning should ideally be undertaken for every employee, this is rarely the case. In fact, due to time and financial constraints most organizations do not engage in succession planning at all – and if they do, it is typically focused on high-potential employees who are then singled out and groomed by various developmental techniques such as mentoring.

Case study 3.8 illustrates a scheme that was designed primarily to develop high-flying employees. However, the case is also a good illustration of a mentoring scheme intended to foster international management capability.

Case study 3.8

A high-flyer mentoring program, by Bernard Wynne of Bernard Wynne Associates, External Training and Development Consultant to Allianz Insurance

In 1997, Allianz Insurance introduced a mentoring scheme in the Asia Pacific Region. This scheme was and still is part of an international management training program aimed at developing employees in every aspect of a global business. Within this training program, the mentoring scheme was implemented in order to support the trainees in their development. The traineeship required employees to work in a number of countries in the Region, but they would eventually return to their country of origin. Both the training program and the mentoring scheme have been running since 1997, with different groups of employees starting every 2 years.

The training program was primarily designed by Bernard Wynne, an external consultant. It was implemented by him and the regional HR Development Manager, Frank Stelter, who was also then bearing the responsibility for the running of the program. Furthermore, the regional CEO, Michael Diekmann, sponsored and supported the scheme.

The training program is highly select, and only a handful of high-potential employees are allowed to enter it. In order to be accepted onto the program, candidates have to pass through a tough four-stage selection process, which is comprised of the following elements:

- *Initial interview by a local manager and local HR professional.*
- *A simple, locally organized assessment process, including assessment activities and a further interview.*
- *An interview by a senior regional manager.*
- *Attendance at an assessment and selection centre.*

According to Bernard Wynne:

this somewhat extended process was necessary because of the large number of applications. I recall once in the Philippines some 250 registered interest, 80-plus applied and three were selected for the final assessment and selection centre. Two were successful and the other one was selected to work for the business in the Philippines. This was often the case with people who attended the assessment and selection centre, but were not selected for the international training program.

During the training program, mentees have three types of mentor: an off-line senior manager in the person's home country, who is also regarded as the primary mentor; a placement mentor; and a senior manager in the regional office, who may sometimes have been the individual's line manager as well. The majority of companies located in countries in the Region recognized the importance of providing trainees with mentors, which meant that there was no problem with recruiting the home country mentor. Mentors are selected on behalf of the mentees, since the mentees are always new to the company and it is felt that better matches can be achieved if the company takes over this responsibility.

As highlighted in the example above, the training program is extremely popular and the mentoring element within it is typically regarded as a very welcome part of it. This means that it is not necessary to undertake any additional marketing in order to interest mentees.

As far as preparation for the mentoring scheme is concerned, both mentors and mentees receive training. For mentees, the training is part of their induction to the overall traineeship program. It usually lasts for about one-half to three-quarters of a day, and covers:

- *Career paths in modern organizations.*
- *The background and development of mentoring.*
- *Guidelines for mentoring.*
- *The benefits of mentoring.*
- *Barriers to mentoring.*
- *Exploring the mentoring relationship.*
- *The mentoring meeting.*
- *Reviewing the learning and applying the skills.*

For mentors, a $1\frac{1}{2}$-day training course covers the following aspects:

- *Why are we introducing mentoring?*
- *The role of mentoring in development.*
- *Building competence and confidence.*
- *The background and development of mentoring.*
- *The benefits of mentoring.*
- *Barriers to mentoring.*
- *Mentoring and coaching.*
- *Exploring the mentoring relationship.*
- *The line manager and the mentor.*
- *What do mentors do?*
- *The mentoring meeting.*
- *Reviewing the learning and applying the skills.*

For both mentors and mentees, training is active and involves a lot of discussion, role-plays and practical exercises.

The frequency of mentoring meetings varies between people, but rough guidelines concerning mentees' primary (i.e. their home country) mentors exist. Thus, mentees are encouraged to meet monthly face-to-face if possible. This is usually the case in the first 1–2 months of the traineeship, during which time they are typically located in their home countries. For most of the time, face-to-face meetings are even possible when mentees are stationed in a different country as long as this is within the Asia Pacific Region. If face-to-face meetings are not possible because, for example, mentees are on a placement in Europe, they are asked to contact their mentors each week either by telephone or e-mail.

As far as topics and learning needs typically addressed during mentoring sessions are concerned, Bernard Wynne states that: '. . . there seems to be very little that is not discussed and when meetings take place, they are clearly productive'. Some of the needs that were discussed can be gauged from the evaluation outcomes reported below.

Evaluation of mentoring relationships revealed that mentees gained considerable benefits from their mentoring experiences. These included:

- *The support and help of a senior colleague who takes an interest in the personal and professional development of the mentee.*
- *Access to a friend and advisor, in relation to a range of personal issues and decisions.*
- *Help and advice in managing career decisions.*
- *Help with preparing and pursuing a plan for personal development.*
- *Help with maintaining a clear focus on the mentee's development in relation to specific knowledge and skills, and in the broader sense of professional development.*
- *A growth in self-confidence and awareness.*
- *Support on practical issues such as relocation.*
- *Help with understanding cultural differences.*
- *Improved understanding of Allianz and one's role within the company.*
- *Enhanced commitment to Allianz.*
- *Keeping up-to-date with Allianz's developments globally, in the Region and in the home country.*

Mentors, too, felt that they had gained a lot from the mentoring experience. Thus, the majority stated that being a mentor helped them to:

- *Understand the needs and aspirations of mentees.*
- *Rethink the way they interact with other people in the business.*

- *Think about their role as a developer of people.*
- *Develop personally.*
- *Regard mentoring as a valuable way of learning.*

The evaluation survey used to identify the benefits associated with mentoring also revealed some room for improvement. The improvements have since been implemented, leading to an even better service of mentoring for trainees. In particular, the following aspects seemed to be in need of revision:

- *The importance of face-to-face contact with the mentor and a desire to ensure that opportunities for face-to-face contact is emphasized.*
- *Greater clarity regarding the objectives of mentoring and expectations we, as a company, have for it.*
- *More information and greater clarity regarding the role of the mentor and mentee in the relationship, which should also specify the responsibilities of each and clarify their joint expectations for the relationship.*
- *More involvement of the mentor in planning development assignments for the mentee.*
- *A more formalized structure with written reports currently provided for Regional HRD to be copied to the mentor.*
- *Recognition that mentoring is an important development tool; managers throughout the business, and especially those not involved, should be expected to support it.*
- *Review of the training provision for mentees and mentors to ensure that in future they benefit from the experience of those who have gone before.*

When asked which aspect of the scheme had presented the greatest difficulties, Bernard Wynne replied that:

given that mentoring had to take place across national boundaries, it was certainly difficult to make sure that mentors and mentees made regular contact with each other, face-to-face whenever possible – although it should be said that in the main this was done successfully. The overall evaluation, which took place 2 years after the introduction of the scheme, indicated that the process had been successful and delivered real benefits for both mentees and mentors.

Professional development

The scheme to be introduced here simply revolves around the need for mentees to improve their competencies in a certain area. The focus of this type of mentoring scheme is often quite narrow, relating to the enhancement of a specific skill. For example, in 1997 British Airways (BA) felt that it needed to improve the way in which its staff managed information systems projects. Although this endeavour did not solely rely on mentoring as a developmental tool, mentoring formed an important part of the scheme. Other developmental mechanisms included the establishment of a skills framework, training, and focus groups.

As with any other scheme, the duration of the program and the length of the individual mentoring relationships can be highly variable, depending on factors such as:

- The complexity of the competency to be developed.
- The ability of the mentee.
- The skill of the mentor.

However, contrary to other mentoring relationships, the cut-off point is more visible in these types of programs as it ends as soon as the mentee has acquired the competency in question. There might, of course, be some informal arrangement for the mentee to contact the mentor should any further issues arise which the mentee cannot solve alone.

Characteristics of mentors

Once again, in addition to having to possess the mentor characteristics detailed in Chapter 5, the prerequisite of the mentor in a professional development scheme is, of course, that he or she must possess in-depth knowledge about the particular type of competency that is to be developed.

In other respects, the nature of these types of relationships, and therefore the mentor characteristics, can be quite variable. For example, mentoring relationships could follow a reverse mentoring model, in which the mentor is potentially (much) younger but certainly more junior than the mentee. Many senior mentees view reverse mentoring as a unique opportunity and are fully conscious of the fact that having a younger mentor is not a humiliation but a benefit.

What are the benefits of professional development mentoring? The main and most obvious benefit is the mentees' acquisition of an important type of competency, intended to enhance business performance. Furthermore, although mentoring might not be the only developmental tool employed in this type of scheme, receiving one-to-one attention is likely to enable mentees to pick up the competency more quickly than they would otherwise have done.

Case study 3.9

A professional development mentoring program, by Tony Hardwick of the Institution of Electrical Engineers

Founded in 1871, the UK's Institution of Electrical Engineers (IEE) is the largest professional engineering society in Europe and has a worldwide membership of just under 140,000. IEE members promote the advancement of electrical, electronic and manufacturing science and engineering. The IEE's professional development activities embrace a wide range of learning needs – from students to the most distinguished and highly qualified members of the profession.

Coming under the responsibility of Tony Hardwick (Head of Professional Development Accreditation), mentoring is recommended for all Professional Engineers who are pursuing Chartered Engineer (CEng) status. Mentees in the scheme who are working towards chartership are referred to as 'candidates'. The IEE does not directly organize any of these mentoring relationships; IEE accredited companies appoint mentors to centrally registered candidates and the IEE then monitors the companies, giving guidance and advice. Both the mentors and candidates generally belong to the same company (exceptions are few, such as when an organization splits and an existing arrangement leaves the mentor in a different part or in a sold-off bit!).

Additionally, the IEE professional development function is exploring the possibility for Chartered Engineers in the regions to take on 'mentees' who lack company support. There are still some reservations about ethical issues in these relationships – for example, mentors who might work for competitors of the mentee's company. This new IEE Mentoring Network will offer candidates an opportunity to find a trained mentor who is outside their immediate work place. The network is supported by the IEE Professional Development Section – principally Tony Johns (IEE Mentoring Executive Officer). A retired Chartered Engineer with many years' experience as a 'traditional' IEE mentor, Johns' role is to:

- *Handle registration of a member's interest in being a mentor, a mentee or both.*
- *Endeavour to pair interested members, based initially on geographic location.*
- *Maintain a database of mentor/mentee pairings.*

- *Work with other IEE departments to provide training workshops, etc.*
- *Facilitate IEE branches to support the scheme locally.*

In terms of selection and/or matching of mentors and mentees, the IEE recommends that a CEng candidate should have a CEng mentor who is an IEE member if possible; however, any CEng will be acceptable, and failing that an Associate Member (AMIEE), or a professional engineer who will at least be a good role model, and so on. Mentoring by a more senior staff member of any discipline is felt to be better than no mentoring at all, but Hardwick has always recommended that it should not be the line manager of the mentee.

Whilst he and his team rarely get so involved as to be able to supervise individual pairs, they are often consulted by individuals and local scheme co-ordinators to give advice and assistance, to sort out problems and misunderstandings. Says Hardwick:

When we visit companies to accredit or re-accredit we always meet a selection of mentors (or other supporters – some companies don't quite do mentoring) and then a selection of candidates, to gauge how the Professional Development Scheme is working and advise on improvements.

The dispersed and diverse nature of mentoring in the IEE means that hard evaluation data is difficult to collate and interpret. Says Hardwick:

We probably have data all over the place but it would be a real task to make it into 'information'! Having said that, several of us here have anecdotal evidence that mentoring, properly done, is of enormous benefit, not least to the mentors themselves. I see it as a major contributor to continuing professional development for the mentors, and extremely useful to mentees/candidates. From 1979 until last year I have rarely been without a mentee of some kind, and I didn't even realize it for most of that time.

Case study 3.10

A mentoring program in the Business Innovation Services Part of IBM Global Services; an account by Lindy Cozens, mentor on the scheme

IBM, a leader in information technologies, produces computer systems, software, networking systems, storage devices and microelectronics. It employs over 300,000 people and operates in over 100 countries. Business Innovation Services (BIS) is the consulting and systems integration arm of IBM Global Services. The organization is the world's largest business and technology consultancy, and has grown in just 10 years from a $4 billion to a $33.2 billion business. BIS, which is organized into specialist practices that provide expertise on specific industries such as communications and banking and offers services such as change management, customer relationship management and e-procurement, has 50,000 consultants who billed more than $10 billion in revenue in 2000.

Due to IBM's emphasis on employee development, it is running several different mentoring schemes in parallel, all of which pursue different objectives. The Business Innovation Services mentoring program has been specially designed for the 50,000 consultants in BIS. The overall objective of the BIS mentoring program is to encourage the formation of a community within IBM that facilitates skill and personal development as well as becoming familiar with the IBM way of working. Specific subsidiary objectives of the scheme include:

- Helping mentees to clarify their career goals, and assisting in creating an environment such that they feel empowered to achieve those goals.
- Supporting career goals (e.g. by providing advice and guidance in attaining professional accreditation and advising on training needs).
- Guiding mentees in the development of key skills.
- Enabling mentors to act as a sounding board.
- Providing guidance based on the mentor's past experience.
- Being for the mutual development of mentee and mentor.
- Facilitating skills development.

Remarkable about the scheme is its unusual way of being managed or rather 'not managed'. Although originally thoroughly planned and implemented, the scheme is now essentially self-perpetuating and can be regarded as fairly informal. All employees of Business Innovation Services have an icon on their laptops that connects them straight to a LOTUS notes database that drives the program and features information about the scheme. Employees can connect to the database of mentors and mentees, which contains a list of individuals who are either presently engaged in mentoring relationships or are looking for a mentor or mentee. The database also presents some basic information about mentors and mentees, and interested individuals can browse it, pick their potential match and contact them through e-mail, telephone or face-to-face.

Once a match has been made, the pair has to negotiate an agreement of their engagement. To BIS, a key part of this agreement is that both sides understand that the program is mentee-driven. The BIS mentoring program provides guidelines for both mentors and *mentees, which help them to understand and articulate what they should be looking for in a mentoring relationship.*

Guidelines for mentees

As a mentee you are responsible for this process and managing the relationship with your mentor. In addition to achieving your personal goals, benefits include learning more about the company and about yourself, adapting to the changing markets, technologies and organizations and improving your skills.

Some steps to take as you prepare for your mentoring relationship:

1. Set yourself mentoring goals, and be realistic:
   - *Consider the barriers to success in your current position. For example, these could be lack of expertise in a business segment, lack of international experience, and thinking in terms of national borders.*
   - *Decide on your development needs. For example, these could be strengthening working relationships with other team members, seeking ways to add value and revenue from current clients, listening more than talking. Discuss your Individual Development Plan with your mentor.*
   - *Establish your mentoring goals and set a suitable timeframe in which to accomplish those goals. For example, these could be learning more about how to make contact with and develop potential clients, determining whether to pursue expertise in a specific area, learning more about completion and customers, improving people management skills, improving teamwork, and modifying behaviours that hinder relationships.*
2. Define the relationship with your mentor. *Take responsibility for self-directed growth. You and your mentor should decide on the approach and means to reach your goals. This can include telephone calls and electronic communications, as well as meetings arranged when it is mutually convenient.*
3. Manage the relationship. *Prepare for your exchanges, and communicate openly to resolve differences. Your mentor's feedback is critical to the relationship. Effective feedback is prompt/immediate, specific, constructive, objective, honest and respectful. Your mentor's style may be different from yours – learning to work with people with different styles is a valuable outcome. Record progress after each meeting or telephone discussion. Handle challenges that arise. Stay on track towards achieving your mentoring goals. Arrange a final meeting to close the mentorship period, reviewing experiences and recommending possible improvements to the program.*
4. Evaluate the relationship. *Review progress toward your goals at*

regular intervals. Determine if the goals have been met. Assess your mentoring relationship and plan for personal follow-on.

Guidelines for mentors

1. *IBM's definition of mentoring – for example, 'Mentoring is a process by which an individual (mentee) strives to achieve development goals under the guidance of another individual with special expertise (mentor)'.*
2. *Mentors are expected to:*
   - *Be committed and honest. Facilitate mentees' goal achievement by drawing on their professional experience and their knowledge of IBM.*
   - *Be willing to share mistakes as well as positive experiences.*
   - *Allow and encourage mentees to manage the relationship.*
   - *Establish and attend to mentees' development needs.*
   - *Enable mentees to explore issues and generate solutions; help them to see options and possibilities.*
   - *Monitor progress towards agreed goals regularly.*

There are no prescriptions regarding the duration of relationships, the frequency of meetings or any other process issues. Thus mentors can exercise their own styles, which may or may not include the usage of formal documentation such as development plans and progress reviews. However, as Lindy Cozens (Head of Strategy and Change for BIS Communications Sector and a mentor on the program) points out, she herself does employ these measures. Given that there is a vivid exchange between mentors in order to learn from one another, she is certain that many other pairs are using these media as well. Furthermore, within IBM the creation of personal development plans is generally very much encouraged.

Mentors on the scheme can accept up to five mentees. Lindy, for example, currently mentors four individuals who she meets physically or has contact with by telephone every 6 weeks. Although the scheme is virtually self-perpetuating, some co-ordination is still necessary – for example, the program co-ordinator, Keith Gulliver, continues to manage the mentor and mentee database. There is a representative for each sector/category within BIS, and each line of business area has a mentoring program representative. The role of the mentoring representative is to act as a focal point within the business for the BIS Resource and Development Group, to 'champion' mentoring, and to assist in the overall implementation and management of the BIS mentoring program. The mentoring representative should:

- *Communicate and promote the BIS mentoring program and, in particular, the BIS mentoring database.*

- *Provide advice and guidance on the BIS mentoring program to professionals and management within their practice.*
- *Gather new mentoring requirements for mentors and mentees.*
- *Participate in the regular BIS mentoring 'brokering' teleconference calls.*

There is also still an element of marketing associated with the scheme, involving promotions on IBM's virtual 'Communities of Practice', newsletters and posters. However, Lindy Cozens emphasizes that there is a very strong word-of-mouth element to marketing the scheme from managers, and that most participants are attracted via this route.

There is at present no formal evaluation of the mentoring, but anecdotal evidence repeatedly confirms that the scheme has been highly successful – a statement that one is prepared to accept simply by considering the sheer number of volunteer participants since its start several years ago: globally, there are hundreds of mentors and thousands of mentees. So attraction has never been a problem, and management support continues to grow. Furthermore, Lindy points out that:

The scheme has helped many people to understand IBM and its clients better. By being able to choose their mentors, who can help them develop skills, understand an industry sector better or grow personally, people maximize their performance.

The main learning point to be drawn from this exceptional scheme is that it is very well matched with IBM's culture: it is voluntary, flexible in its processes, and self-sustaining – an approach that is unlikely to work in every organization, but is perfect for IBM.

Retaining talent

Keeping turnover down and thereby retaining key talent is one of the most powerful and beneficial effects of mentoring. Its significance in this respect has been demonstrated in many studies, a very pertinent example of which is SmithKline Beecham, already described in Chapter 2.

Mentoring is thought to aid retention because:

- Individuals feel more valued and respected by the organization. In most cases, this results in increased commitment on the part of employees: individuals want to give something back to the organization for having been generous and thoughtful.
- It increases motivation: mentoring can make individuals feel more motivated if it satisfies one of their needs. For example,

the mentee who has been struggling to maintain motivation for lack of focus in his or her current job could easily regain this through having a mentor who can help with establishing goals and direction and redefining their role. Also, mentoring often leads to enhanced career prospects for mentees, since they are given the opportunity to address their development needs and improve their performance in a targeted way. Possessing greater career prospects certainly motivates many individuals.

Case study 3.11

Procter & Gamble – 'Mentoring up' with women managers

Procter & Gamble (P&G) is a global consumer goods corporation that owns and operates hundreds of 'household name' brands across the world. In order to retain and develop female managers in the marketing division, P&G devised and implemented an innovative reverse-mentoring scheme. The project was so successful that is has been subsequently expanded across six other functions besides marketing.

Whilst P&G had always tended to promote senior executives from within the firm rather than hiring in talent, women were under-represented at the higher levels of management. Voluntary turnover was also higher amongst women than men, and these were the trends that a mentoring scheme sought to address. The marketing division was chosen as the place to initiate the scheme because it is an important development ground for future general managers in P&G.

Rather than tackling the retention and development of women with a 'top down' mentoring program for individual female managers, P&G attempted to do something more fundamental. By reversing the traditional mentoring process and assigning female junior managers as mentors to male senior managers, the scheme seeks to induce culture change in management ranks by influencing organizational policies and practices as well as individual behaviour. The idea is that the mentoring will have a more profound effect on the whole firm as top managers are helped to understand, anticipate and respond to issues specific to female junior managers.

The mentees gain a special insight into the needs and concerns of female managers, feedback on the potential impact of proposed actions, and a fresh perspective on problems and work issues. In return, mentors gain special access to top managers and the experience and learning from working on high-level business issues with senior executives. The ability of mentoring pairs to use one another as sounding boards on a whole range of issues has proven to be a major benefit of the program.

Potential mentors are selected from the ranks of female junior and middle management. The mentees were initially those in upper management, but the scheme has been extended to include male managers at middle and junior management level with equally positive results. In the first instance mentoring participation was voluntary, but it is now expected that all eligible male senior level and female junior level managers will take part.

The scheme is run in conjunction with the Advancement of Women Task Force (AWTF), a group dedicated to the progress of female managers. It is co-ordinated by Kristen Nostrand, P&G Marketing Director, and a small team of mentors. As in most traditional mentoring schemes, mentors and mentees are matched on the basis of compatibility in terms of expectations, needs, personality and locations. The structure of the scheme is highly flexible so that the participants can respond to their own individual needs. A central co-ordination team ensures that the Mentor Up pairs are monitored and changed if the relationships do not prove to be successful.

Formal mentoring training and an induction to the scheme is attended jointly by the mentoring pairs. This session consists of group and paired exercises, which help them to create effective relationships. Furthermore, mentors and mentees who have already participated in the Mentor Up scheme share their experiences with the new mentoring pairs. To further ensure that the building of relationships proceeds in a positive manner, mentoring pairs are encouraged to:

- Share their previous mentoring experiences and to extract lessons for the current relationships.
- Agree on the expectations and principles that govern them.
- Define their personal roles and responsibilities.
- Form their own rules about how and when to give and receive feedback.

The decisions that are made in relation to the above topics are documented in mentoring agreements, which are reviewed after the first 6 months.

Mentor and mentees meet bi-monthly on average, away from either person's office. Mentor Up co-ordinators occasionally distribute discussion guides to facilitate productive meetings and outcomes. These guides have proven very valuable in ensuring that an open and effective exchange of ideas and issues takes place in the mentoring context.

Survey results from a pilot scheme indicated positive improvement in awareness and quality relationships, and that program participants endorsed rolling out the program to other parts of the business.

> *Whilst the feedback from participants has been encouraging, it is not easy to measure the success of a mentoring program geared towards enhancing sensitivity. However, one measure stands out: female turnover for the past 2 years has fallen by 25 per cent and is now in line with that for male managers.*
>
> *The lesson seems to be that reverse mentoring can work provided that there are clear aims for the scheme, a cultural willingness to innovate and a phased approach to implementation, with specific learning and review points along the way.*

Returners

This type of scheme could focus on the broad objective of supporting anyone rejoining an organization or restarting a career after a break. Very often, however, its main objective is to help women readjust to work after they return from sometimes long periods of maternity leave.

What are the specific objectives of returner schemes? To an extent these might be similar to those of a graduate or new recruit scheme. For example, socialization will be equally important to new recruits and returners (particularly after years of leave). Furthermore, new recruits and returners both need to develop their job competencies to a certain extent.

However, in addition to these, returners to work might also need help with changing their previously gained mindsets – that is, depending on the length of their absence from the world of work, a lot of changes might have occurred concerning the company climate, processes and operations. Their particular work role may have changed, too, rendering their job fairly unfamiliar territory. For many, particularly women returners, the creation of a work–life balance will also become a significant issue. All of this can cause great distress to freshly returned individuals, and mentoring is one way of alleviating negative emotions.

In sum, the specific objectives of returner schemes include helping these individuals to:

- Acquire or revive relevant competencies.
- Re-socialize.
- Redefine their roles in organizations and assess future prospects.
- Establish a work–life balance.
- Understand the way the organization has changed.

The main benefit of this type of scheme is that it is likely to create a less stressed and emotionally more balanced workforce. This in turn enhances a company's chances of retaining those newly returned to work. Furthermore, mentoring will also benefit the company by accelerating the time it would normally take for returners to perform their job competently once again.

Case study 3.12

Supporting women with families

Having recognized that pregnant employees need additional support on the part of their employer with regards to balancing pregnancy, maternity and work, a large insurance company began to take a variety of measures to support pregnant women and those who had recently become mothers. The measures included opening up a crèche and piloting a mentoring scheme. It was the overall aim of the program to support mothers prior to, during and after their maternity leave, the intention being to help them settle effectively back into the company upon their return. The specific objectives of the program included that it was to:

- *Help improve intra-organizational communication.*
- *Link in with other maternity provisions.*
- *Help returners to be more self-assured and ready to come back.*
- *Be informal and self-regenerating, for example in the supply of mentors who were initially approached but who later entered the program through word-of-mouth.*

The mentoring program was supplementing other existing courses for pregnant women, such as one that considered pertinent issues for individuals returning from maternity leave. The process at the heart of the program entailed the following steps. In the first instance, women were encouraged to tell their managers that they were pregnant. Following that, the manager passed on this information to HR, which in turn contacted the pregnant woman in order to identify a suitable mentor for her. The mentor roles were filled by other women working at the company who had previously been through the 'maternity experience'. HR also counselled the pregnant women and provided them with a maternity information leaflet. Following this, the mentoring relationship commenced and lasted from before pregnancy leave until the women had returned to work and settled in successfully; even whilst the mentee was on maternity leave, she and her mentor sayed in contact.

The issues discussed before the commencement of maternity leave surrounded coping with the situation, handling money matters, understanding company provisions, and, of course, the imminent birth. Whilst on leave, mentors kept mentees updated on what was happening in the organization. The pairs also discussed the question of whether or not the mentee wanted to return to work, what childcare arrangements could be made, and which obligations the employer had. After the return of the woman, mentoring concentrated on supporting the mentee with her re-adjustment to work life, helping her to cope with feelings of guilt, and establishing a work–life balance.

Before mentors were allowed to act as such they were sent on a 1-day mentoring training workshop, which involved the following objectives:

- *Explaining mentoring and how it complements the existing counselling process for pregnant women.*
- *Providing a practical model for mentoring.*
- *Understanding the skills necessary for mentoring.*
- *Providing practical exercises such as role-plays.*
- *Increasing the mentor's confidence in taking on the role.*

An evaluation of the outcomes showed that:

- *Returners were immediately more effective and up-to-date with organizational change.*
- *Mentoring was fulfilling for both parties; mentors felt that their jobs were enriched, and both mentors and mentees thought that they understood the organization better.*
- *It provided the starting point for a network.*
- *Retention of staff, in whom a lot had been invested, was enhanced.*
- *Mentoring was a cost-effective method.*
- *Both parties understood the organization better.*
- *All areas of the business demonstrated tremendous interest in the program.*

Summary and conclusions

This chapter has considered a whole range of mentoring schemes, and in this section we will try to draw out a few learning points from them. In the main, these points are meant to highlight 'best practice' in the area as well as draw your attention to program features that should be avoided. Before you read on, you must appreciate, however, that not all of the 'best practice points' would really be best for every scheme. Once again, it is highly important to understand that mentoring schemes have to be adapted both to an organization's culture and to context. For example, for some companies a very informal, self-sustaining scheme (e.g. IBM) will bring the best results, whilst a well-regulated scheme may be more appropriate for other organizations (e.g. Allianz).

Let us remind you of a statement made by Lex Services plc that illustrates the importance of a cultural fit between a scheme and an organization:

> Mentoring in Lex has been successful because the approach has been carefully crafted to suit the needs and culture of the business, rather than being imposed as an HR agenda.

That said, there are of course best practice guidelines with regard to mentoring schemes. We shall try and disseminate these here and, indeed, throughout this book. However, when choosing an approach to implementing your scheme, you should nevertheless carefully assess what would work best for your organization.

The schemes introduced here were implemented to achieve different objectives. All schemes tended to define their objectives very well, making them quite explicit, which is generally considered best practice. This helps, for example, to define the boundaries of the scheme, and it provides the initiative with focus and momentum. Setting precise objectives also implies that your mentee target group will be well defined – an aspect that featured in virtually all schemes – i.e. programs were not typically 'open to anyone'.

Furthermore, most of the case studies reported in this chapter were regarding schemes that have been implemented in one particular company. Yet there were also examples of organizations such as BT, which encourage their employees to become a mentor for the schemes run by other organizations. In addition, there were some externally managed schemes, i.e. programs that were organized by one organization but offered mentoring to a range of other companies. Examples of these types of programs include those co-ordinated by the Institution of Electrical Engineers, Sheffield Hallam University, and the Fisher College of Business.

Despite these variations between schemes, there were surprisingly many similarities. The following summary is meant to highlight these as well as draw out additional learning points:

1. *Support from the top*. The extreme importance of this is demonstrated in the majority of case studies. Many believed that

the commitment of top management was the main facilitator of the success of their scheme. In this respect, it appears to be crucial that management set an example by acting as mentors themselves. Where leadership backing was absent, this was actually noticed during the evaluation of the scheme. Thus, after having run their scheme for the first time, Allianz felt that there was an urgent need for managers throughout the business to realize that mentoring was an important development tool and that it was imperative that they support it.

2. *Co-ordination of the scheme*. Typically, there appears to be one person who was responsible for co-ordinating the overall design and implementation of the scheme. However, the larger the scheme, the more likely it is to involve project teams that support the program champion/co-ordinator. Alternatively, the co-ordinator may simply call on the assistance of other (HR) staff to carry out particular tasks such as marketing the scheme and recruiting mentors and mentees. The latter is particularly the case where a scheme has been implemented on a global level such as that of BAT. As you will remember, BAT's champion utilized local HR teams to identify potential mentors.

   The program champion/co-ordinator often seems to be associated with Human Resource Management (although this is not necessarily the case), and his or her tasks tend to include:
   - Drawing up the overall design of the scheme.
   - Marketing it.
   - Selecting and matching mentors and mentees/overseeing this process.
   - Liaising with parties who could assist him or her (e.g. managers in other company locations).
   - Organizing the training/preparation.
   Most of the time the program is organized by a person who is in full-time employment in the company in question, but external consultants can also successfully be used to implement a scheme. This is typically done in close collaboration with a specific company-internal employee (see, for example, Allianz Insurance).

3. *Training*. Although mentoring training seems to come in various guises (e.g. to varying degrees of formality and often not being called 'training'), it is always recognized as being highly important. In fact, in cases in which training was not originally provided this tended to be changed for subsequent 'rounds' of the scheme (for example, refer to Case study 8.1).

Training tends to be separate for mentors and mentees, but we consider combining them to be a good idea for certain situations. Thus, uniting mentors and mentees in order to give them the opportunity to discuss their mutual expectations can be a highly beneficial practice – if well facilitated.

In most cases, the training agenda for both mentors and mentees includes at the very least the following elements:

- Defining mentoring and distinguishing it from other training and development approaches.
- Explaining why mentoring was chosen for the organization/the purpose of the scheme.
- Highlighting the skills and behaviours associated with mentoring.
- Outlining the benefits of mentoring.
- Managing the expectations of mentors/mentees.

The striking presence of the last point, expectation management, in virtually all case studies is a very encouraging finding, given its immense importance for the success of mentoring relationships! Expectation management did not, however, always take place during training, and was sometimes encouraged as an issue to be tackled by mentors and mentees during their first meeting. We recommend a combination of both approaches. Expectation management during training has the advantages that it can be facilitated and that notice can be taken of mentors and mentees who might be good or poor matches based on their expectations. Asking participants to continue this activity during their first mentoring session is good because it helps them to express, clarify and consolidate their particular expectations of each other.

Companies that did not encourage mentors and mentees to express their mutual expectations of the relationship later tended to recognize this as a mistake. Virtually all companies designed their training in an active style, which involved discussions and sometimes also role-plays and exercises.

Naturally there are a few additional topics that should be covered in a mentoring training sessions, and we will discuss these in more detail in Chapter 9.

4. *Ongoing support of mentors and mentees.* Most of the companies featured in this chapter made it the explicit (or implicit) task of the program co-ordinator to be available for mentors and mentees should they have any questions. However, few actually reported providing active support mechanisms such as workshops/networking meetings, or the co-ordinator regularly getting in touch with mentors and mentees to see

if they needed any help. Implementing mentor and mentee support groups is a very powerful way to maximize the effectiveness of your mentoring scheme. In fact, it is interesting to see that at BAT, for example, the mentees specifically asked for this facility to be established. They felt that it would be highly beneficial to them to be able to exchange experiences with other mentees.

5. *Marketing*. In cases where a scheme was not part of a larger training and development initiative and/or where the recruitment of participants was not solely based on recommendations, the preferred ways of marketing included the company intranet, newsletters, and personal invitation letters.

6. *Mentor and mentee selection and recruitment*. Mentor and mentee groups were usually very well defined, and only two cases (IBM and BT) operated a scheme that was open to anyone (within a particular division). With regard to selecting mentees, this was often done by heeding the recommendations of managers and/or directors. Alternatively, individuals were often part of a larger training and development scheme (such as the one at BAT or Allianz) for which they had been selected and of which mentoring was a regular feature. Similarly to mentees, mentors were often suggested by (other) managers and directors, and/or approached directly by the program co-ordinator. In most cases, mentors were internal to the company.

   Because of the vast differences between schemes regarding the characteristics of the mentee group, it is impossible to generalize about mentee selection criteria. In contrast to that, there do appear to be certain criteria for recruiting mentors that apply to the majority of schemes. These are:
   - A strong people-orientation.
   - Being highly regarded within the organization.
   - Excellent communication skills.
   - Experience in and commitment to developing others.
   - Being serious about making the required time investment to be an effective mentor.

7. *Matching*. In most cases it was the program co-ordinator who bore the responsibility for matching participants. Depending on the size of the scheme, he or she would delegate the matching to assistants such as the HR personnel of a company's offices in other countries. Forms were typically used to assist the matching process. These afforded mentors and mentees the opportunity to provide details about themselves, as well as an indication of their preferences with regards to their mentoring partner. In some cases it was made explicit that mentees were given the option to choose

between several mentors. This is generally recommended when matching participants.

As with all elements of a mentoring scheme, the exact nature of mentoring criteria will vary between schemes. However, there are certain criteria that seem to feature in most programs:

- An off-line relationship between mentor and mentee.
- Compatibility between the needs of the mentee and the experience of the mentor.
- Details such as age, gender, and ethnicity as well as an indication of preferences on these dimensions with regards to the mentoring partner.
- An indication of interests.
- Personality.

8. *Meetings*. These tended to be held monthly and, if possible, face-to-face. Most mentoring pairs seem to have managed this; however, if this was not feasible alternative methods for meetings were used (e.g. telephone or e-mail).

9. *Evaluation of the program*. The main point to note with regard to this topic is that evaluation was taken very seriously across the schemes. Thus, it was carried out (or there were plans to carry it out) in virtually all cases, and if the results showed that certain aspects needed to be improved, this was typically done. This is great news, since the purpose of evaluation is, in a nutshell, just that: continuous improvement for success.

In general, the evaluation results were highly encouraging in the sense that all of the schemes have been successful. They seem to have achieved their initially set objectives and reaped benefits beyond that. Leaving aside the specific objectives of each scheme, the benefits reported most frequently by *mentors* included:

- Having developed themselves as a result of the mentoring – for example, having improved their people development skills.
- Enhanced satisfaction gained from developing others.
- An altered and better understanding of the company.
- Improved work relationships.
- An enhanced understanding of the needs, aspirations and motivators of mentees.

The benefits most frequently reported by *mentees* were:

- Emotional support.
- Improved personal and career development.
- *Focused* development – i.e. having someone who enables one to see and set priorities in the development of knowledge, skills and attitudes.
- Extended networks.

- Enhanced self-confidence.
- Better understanding of the organization and/or greater awareness of important issues.
- Generally improved performance, which came in various guises such as 'being able to do one's job better and more efficiently', 'better managerial skills', and 'more rapid re-adjustment to one's work role after a long break'.

The benefits most frequently reported by organizations included:

- Improved retention (quoted by several companies, even when this was not one of the scheme's primary objectives).
- Support of other training and development methods.
- Improved organizational communication through extended networks.
- Support of business objectives.

Between schemes, there was not much overlap regarding the areas of the program that were perceived as difficult or challenging. Every scheme tended to have its own unique set of problems, but it must be emphasized that these were only very few – one or two areas in the main. That said, most of the schemes reported finding it a challenge to get mentors and mentees to meet face-to-face – timing and geographic distance often posed an obstacle to physical meetings.

References

Begley, T. M. and Czajka, J. M. (1993). Panel analysis of the moderating effect of commitment on job satisfaction, intent to quit, and health following organisational change. *J. Appl. Psychol.*, **78**, 552–6.

Black, J. S., Gregerson, H. B. and Mendenhall, M. (1992). *Global Assignments: Successfully Expatriating and Repatriating International Managers*. Jossey-Bass.

Callan, V. J. (1993). Individual and organisational strategies for coping with organisational change. *Work and Stress*, **7**, 63–75.

Clutterbuck, D. and Megginson, D. (1999). *Mentoring for Executives and Directors*. Butterworth-Heinemann.

Clutterbuck, D. C. and Ragins, B. R. (2001). *Mentoring and Diversity*. Butterworth-Heinemann.

Conway, C. (1998). *Strategies for Mentoring*. John Wiley and Sons.

Feldman, D. C. and Thomas, D. C. (1992). Career management issues facing expatriates. *J. Int. Bus. Studies*, **Second Quarter**, 271–93.

Handy, C. (1993). *Understanding Organisations*. Penguin.

Ibarra, H. (2000). Making partner: a mentor's guide to the psychological journey. *Harvard Bus. Rev.*, **Mar–Apr**, 146–55.

Karasek, R. A. (1990). Lower health risk with increased job control among white collar workers. *J. Org. Behav.*, **11**, 171–85.

Kogler-Hill, S. and Bahniuk, M. H. (1998). Promoting career success through mentoring. *Rev. Bus.*, **19**, 4–7.

Kram, K. E. (1983). Phases of mentoring relationships. *Acad. Man. J.*, **26**, 608–25.

Loden, M. and Rosener, J. B. (1991). *Workforce America! Managing Employee Diversity as a Vital Resource*. Business One Irwin.

Pearlin, L. I., Menaghan, E. G., Lieberman, M. A. and Mullan, J. T. (1981). The stress process. *J. Health Social Behav.*, **22**, 337–56.

Ragins, B. R. (1997). Diversified mentoring relationships in organizations: a power perspective. *Acad. Man. Rev.*, **22**, 482–522.

Schein, E. (1992). *Organizational Culture and Leadership*. Jossey-Bass.

Schneider, S. C. and Barsoux, J. L. (1997). Managing Across Cultures. Financial Times/Prentice Hall.

Siegel, H., Mosca, J. B. and Karim, K. B. (1999). The role of mentoring professional accountants: a global perspective. *Managerial Finance*, **25**, 30–44.

Thomas, D. A. and Ely, R. J. (1995). Managing diversity for Organizational Effectiveness. Working Paper. Boston: Harvard Business School.

Thomas, D. A. and Ely, R. J. (1996). Making differences matter: a new perspective for managing diversity. *Harvard Bus. Rev.*, **Sep–Oct**, 79–91.

Whittaker, M. and Cartwright, A. (2000). *The Mentoring Manual*. Gower.

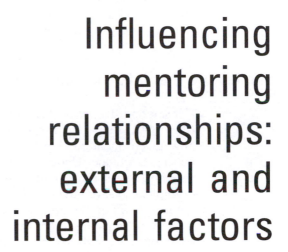

Influencing mentoring relationships: external and internal factors

So far, this book has explored the foundations of mentoring. This has included an exploration of its definition and history, its advantages and disadvantages, and the distinction between mentoring and other developmental approaches. In Chapter 3 we also took a close-up look at a variety of mentoring schemes. We identified their differing objectives, the characteristics of their mentors, and the benefits associated with each scheme for mentees and organization.

At the heart of every mentoring scheme are the mentoring *relationships* and, given the groundwork we have done so far, we are now ready to examine these on a deeper level. This chapter is the first of three that will consider the mentoring relationship in greater detail. Aspects such as the dynamics, the participants and the mentoring process will be examined over the course of these.

The purpose of the present chapter is to examine some of the factors that influence mentoring relationships. Some of these are external to the mentoring association, such as the objectives of a scheme. Others are internal to the relationship, such as personality, gender and the personal style of the mentor. Again others defy assignment to either the external or the internal category. For example, codes of ethics are a mixture of being imposed by the organization and being formed by the individual.

The factors that influence mentoring relationships

Considering the factors that impact on mentoring relationships (Figure 4.1) shows the range of permutations that is possible in any given mentoring pair. Each and every mentor–mentee pairing is unique. Understanding the dimensions of mentoring relationships is vital in the design of mentoring schemes. For example, codes of ethics or formality can play a role in hindering or enhancing the formation of rapport, affecting the degree of trust and openness present in a relationship. This in turn has an effect on the quality of the relationship, and thus the degree of learning and development that is likely to occur. Let us now take a look at each individual factor depicted in Figure 4.1.

External factors

Organizational context and purpose

The goals, mission and purpose of an organization, as well as the context in which it operates, will affect both the type of mentoring scheme that is chosen and the nature of the mentoring relationships within the scheme. For example, the nature of mentoring relationships will be very different in an organization that is downsizing as opposed to one that is expanding. In the former example, the mentoring steering committee is likely to decide that the focus of the relationships should be on 'coping with the change' and perhaps even on 'coping with redundancy and finding a new job'. In the latter example, the focus might be on 'developing employees for new roles'.

This shows how the organizational context and its purpose determine the objectives that are being set for a scheme. Since this topic has been discussed in great detail in the previous chapter, it is worth just remembering *how* the objectives you set for your program will also influence mentoring relationships. Thus, the objectives will define certain boundaries within which the relationship should be moving. That said, we would re-emphasize that the scheme's objectives must be balanced

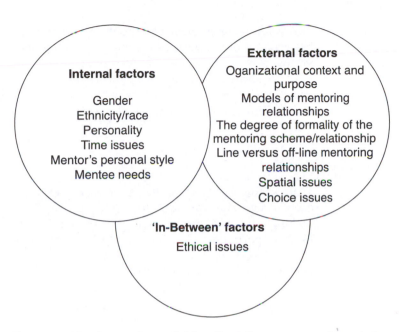

Internal factors

Gender
Ethnicity/race
Personality
Time issues
Mentor's personal style
Mentee needs

External factors

Oganizational context and
purpose
Models of mentoring
relationships
The degree of formality of the
mentoring scheme/relationship
Line versus off-line mentoring
relationships
Spatial issues
Choice issues

'In-Between' factors

Ethical issues

Figure 4.1 The interacting variables that influence mentoring relationships.

with individual's objectives. Individual mentees must be given the opportunity to meet some of their personal needs even if these happen to go beyond the limits defined by the program's objectives. If this freedom is not granted, mentees are likely to get very demotivated because they feel that the scheme is solely benefiting the organization.

A final illustration of how a company's context affects mentoring relationships involves considering its core operations. Take examples from the 'Big Five' management consultancies – Accenture and PricewaterhouseCoopers. Both of these employ a highly mobile workforce in which consultants travel frequently and are sometimes required to stay on assignments away from their home town for 6 months or longer. Any mentoring relationship that forms within this context must be very flexible in its approach; face-to-face meetings may only be possible occasionally, and e-mail or the telephone will have to be used for the remaining interaction. We will discuss the potentially differing dynamics of face-to-face and e-mentoring (i.e. using e-mail and telephone) in the next section.

Models of mentoring relationships

Most mentoring research has focused on the benefits and principles of mentoring in one-to-one and/or face-to-face situations.

Furthermore, it is most commonly assumed that mentoring is between an older, more senior person, who is the mentor, and a younger, more junior person, who is the mentee (a myth that we tried to address in Chapter 1). However, there are many more variations of mentoring models, including e-mentoring or team-to-team mentoring, and we will consider some of these variations here.

Inter-team mentoring

Teams from different shifts or sites, for example, can mentor each other. This can take the form of less experienced teams seeking the expertise of more experienced teams from the same department/unit. For example, a new sales team might be mentored by a more experienced one, which could prove very beneficial for the novices' performance.

Team mentoring

The three most common types of team mentoring, which are quite different but are all unfortunately listed under the name of 'team mentoring', can be described as follows:

- One mentor might take on a whole group of mentees. This is useful when an organization cannot provide sufficient mentors, or where a mentor's time is limited but he or she possesses expertise in an area that might interest multiple mentees.
- A group of mentors might take on one or more mentees. This model is encouraged by an increasing number of firms who believe that their employees benefit most from working with a diverse group of mentors. Some even establish formal programs in which one or more individuals are mentored by a mentor team composed of a departmental manager, a human resource professional and a senior partner (Gregg, 1999).
- Team members might mentor each other.

An example of the latter approach is the international management mentoring program run by The Ohio State University, Fisher College of Business, in Columbo. This program was the brainchild of Toshi Amino, a retired executive of Honda America. The scheme is called TARGET (To Aim and Realize Globalization Together), and brings together highly experienced executives with eight to ten less experienced executives from different companies. The aim is to support the less experienced executives in learning the ropes of international business. These executives then mentor each other with regard to various learning needs such as coping with and benefiting from international assignments.

Reverse mentoring

As briefly discussed in Chapter 3, reverse mentoring implies a mentoring relationship between a mentor and mentee in which the mentor is on a lower hierarchical level than the mentee. This type of relationship could occur whenever a (hierarchically) more junior person possesses insights and experience that will be helpful to a (hierarchically) more senior individual.

Peer mentoring

Peer mentoring is used in many British and American organizations. For example, PricewaterhouseCoopers (PwC) ensure that each new employee within the financial advisory services is matched with a peer mentor. For a few months, mentors are the new recruits' first point of contact, helping them learn the ropes (for example, mentors may assist mentees in understanding the IT systems).

Peer mentoring appears to be very advantageous for individuals. Kram and Isabella (1985) confirmed the importance of peer relationships for psychosocial and career development across all stages of an individual's career. They found that through peer relationships, individuals:

- Shared information.
- Planned career strategies.
- Provided job-related feedback.
- Engaged in emotional support and friendship, and
- Shared mutuality of needs and interests.

In particular, their research established that peer relationships provided higher quality exchanges, greater reciprocity, and greater continuity over time.

Online-mentoring/e-mentoring

Harrington (1999) proposes that technology will have a part to play in enabling mentoring relationships under otherwise difficult environmental factors, such as large geographical distances between mentor and mentee. The terms 'online' and 'e-mentoring' are still ill defined and therefore quite variable in meaning, but typically they are applied to include the use of e-mail, chat rooms and telephone.

One company that already practises online mentoring to quite a large extent and endeavours to increase its usage is the Oxford School of Coaching and Mentoring (OSCM). The School, founded and led by Eric Parsloe, offers qualifications in mentoring, as well as development programs in which coaching and mentoring are applied as developmental tools. Within OSCM, 'e-mentoring' refers mainly to the use of telephones but also involves some degree of e-mail contact.

There has not been much research into the effects of these different models of mentoring. It is probable, however, that the nature of the mentoring relationship varies tremendously between them. For example, it is fair to assume that there will be differences in relationship dynamics and power distributions between, say, traditional face-to-face mentoring that occurs on a one-to-one basis and e-mentoring or team mentoring. There might be individuals who are better able to benefit from some as opposed to other models.

E-mentoring in particular poses a number of challenges (see Table 4.1), since the visual element present in face-to-face contact falls away. It is much harder to pick up on emotions such as happiness, fear and anxiety when you are unable to see someone's facial expressions or body posture. E-mentoring might also increase the chances of conflict due to language misunderstandings, given that every individual has a unique way of using language. In face-to-face situations, differences in the use of language can be mediated through non-verbal signals or misunderstandings can be queried and corrected easily. This, however, is not possible when communicating via e-mail.

'Do-it-yourself' mentoring

In this mentoring model, individuals are asked to take on the responsibility for their own career development with the help of a range of formal and informal advisory relationships that they find and foster for themselves. The following quotation from Kerka (1998) summarizes the trends and issues facing mentoring in a time of organizational uncertainty:

> The combination of digital technologies and organizational changes is making individuals more responsible for their own learning and career development. Freelancing, consulting, and 'portfolio work' make it more difficult for people to connect with traditional sources of mentors in organizations. At the same time, teleworking increases physical

Table 4.1 Summary of possible advantages and challenges of e-mentoring.

Possible advantages	Challenges
✓ Mentoring contact becomes more flexible	✓ May be a poor choice for complex exchanges: e.g. lacks in richness as it is text-based and can lead to an increased number of communication difficulties such as overlooking subtle messages
✓ Viability of continued mentoring support for mobile workforces	✓ May prevent people who prefer face-to-face contact, from utilizing mentoring opportunities
✓ Making inter-team mentoring across shifts and sites possible	✓ May take longer to introduce than face-to-face mentoring schemes and require a lot more support on part of the organization in order to invoke attitudinal changes amongst employees
✓ International relocators can stay in touch with their previous/home mentor	✓ Effectiveness of mentoring relationships will vary greatly depending on people's attitude towards e-mentoring and their ability to discover and seize on its conversational flexibility
✓ Mentoring to stay in touch with women on maternity leave	✓ May impinge on employees' confidentiality, e.g. in companies where managers are monitoring e-mail exchanges
✓ Team mentoring might become more easy (especially if the e-mentoring also involves the use of notice boards on which individual can post development needs to be viewed by his/her team members)	

distance from the workplace and decreases the ability to acquire the tacit or craft knowledge that comes from interaction with experienced workers. For these reasons, mentoring becomes even more important for individuals attempting to develop an array of flexible skills and for organizations seeking to maintain institutional knowledge.

Do-it-yourself mentoring really does have a place in today's business world, even if it is only to complement one's experiences with a more formal mentor. It is particularly pertinent in organizations that cannot establish mentoring programs for reasons such as costs or an inappropriate organizational culture. Do-it-yourself mentoring might also be relevant for those organizational members who find it difficult to maintain regular contact with a mentor because of frequent international travel. These individuals are required to take care of their own development needs.

This concept of mentoring being an active development process driven by the mentee is well presented by Collins (1996), who argues that people in business (and especially entrepreneurs) should appoint a 'personal board of directors' for guidance and feedback. The suggestion is that the board should be composed of people one deeply respects and from whom one would like to learn. Collins goes on to observe that:

Personal-board members from outside one's profession or industry can help one overcome the limitations of conventional wisdom and remain true to one's goals. Perhaps the most significant contribution the personal board can make is to help one attain self-knowledge and, ultimately, self-actualization.

The degree of formality of the mentoring scheme/relationship

There is little doubt as to the fact that the degree of formality espoused by a program influences the degree of formality present in a mentoring relationship, and this in turn appears to influence the dynamics and outcomes the relationship. For example, if program co-ordinators ask of their participants to supply written records of everything (e.g. mentoring contracts, individual sessions and overall progress), the relationship will inevitably be limited to an extent by these procedures. Perhaps it is not going to be as spontaneous as others. Perhaps openness will suffer owing to the fact that program co-ordinators and/or others are monitoring the relationship so closely.

Even though these examples happen to be negative ones, there is still enormous doubt as to whether the degree of formality of a scheme influences outcomes negatively or positively. Opinions are divided between academics and practitioners – the latter being individuals involved in designing and running mentoring schemes. In short, academics typically claim that informal mentoring is more advantageous for the mentee than formal mentoring, whilst the reverse is suggested by practitioners.

Before trying to distil this somewhat arduous debate, we have to define what we mean by a formal and informal mentoring program/relationship. Formally organized mentoring schemes are those that create and support mentoring relationships. Informal mentoring occurs on a natural, sometimes *ad hoc* basis, where mentor and mentee find each other and decide (explicitly or not) to embark on a mentoring relationship. With informal mentoring, the involvement of the organization tends to be minimal or non-existent. If it is minimal, it probably amounts to no more than general encouragement to all employees to form mentoring relationships if and where they can.

Rather than viewing formal and informal mentoring as two disparate entities, it is probably more helpful if they are regarded as two ends on a continuum. Tables 4.2 and 4.3 illustrate this point.

Table 4.2 Spectrum of mentoring relationships

	Control by organization	Control by mentor	Control by mentee
Formal	Organization selects/pairs mentees and mentor	Mentor selects mentee with help from HR	Mentee selects mentor (with help from HR) from a panel of well-trained mentors
Semi-formal	Organization develops and trains pool of mentors and encourages relationships to happen	Mentor makes interest known to mentee	Mentee informs HR of selection; approaches mentor
Informal	Organization tolerates *ad hoc* mentoring	Mentor adopts mentee. Gradual evolution of relationship	Mentee makes interest known to mentor. Gradual evolution of relationship

Table 4.3 Formal versus informal mentoring – the spectrum of control

	Formal ──────────────────────→ Informal		
Measurement	For program review	For benefit of program and individuals	For benefit of mentor and mentee	No measurement
Recording	Activity logs open to HR	Activity logs kept by mentor/mentee	Activity logs used as discussion triggers	No activity logs
Agenda	Formal, agreed in advance	Formal, agreed on the spot	Informal, agreed on the spot	No agenda, random discussion
Program management	Official scheme coordinator	Organizational peer support group	*Ad hoc* support for mentors and mentees	No support for mentor and mentees

Which works better: formal or informal mentoring?

Given that you are probably right now either in the process of designing your own mentoring scheme or at least trying to accumulate information about formal programs, you will certainly want to know what degree of formality to aim for. Before finally presenting you with the 'evidence' on the value of formal versus informal schemes, we would like to make one point extremely clear: as yet, the proponents of neither formal nor informal schemes have succeeded in designing and conducting any truly convincing and high-quality studies. The results of both sides are highly biased, for reasons that we shall consider in a short while.

Informal mentoring

On the basis of research studies conducted mainly by American academics in American companies, it could be concluded that informal mentoring works better in that it appears to benefit the mentee more than formal mentoring. That is, academics including Kram (1983), Chao *et al.* (1992) and Ragins and Cotton (1999) found, in a number of comparisons between formal and informal mentoring, that informal mentoring appears to engender:

- Mentees who receive higher salaries and enhanced career development (Chao *et al.*, 1992), and greater sponsoring, coaching, protection and exposure as well as more challenging assignments.
- More satisfied mentees who perceive their mentors as more effective.
- Relationships that focus on the long-term needs of mentees rather than short-term career goals.
- More motivated mentors who possess better communication and coaching skills (although this observation is currently only supported by field work, and not by tightly controlled qualitative or quantitative studies).

Whilst informal mentoring overall appears to fulfil greater career functions than formal mentoring, there are studies that suggest there to be no differences in the fulfilment of psychosocial functions (Kogler-Hill and Bahniuk, 1998). Furthermore, for reasons to be considered in a moment, the apparently greater ability of informal mentoring to meet a variety of mentee career goals might also not be as convincing as it currently seems.

Formal mentoring

From the evidence existing to date, informal mentoring appears to benefit mainly the mentee. Formal mentoring, on the other hand, seems to promote a more equal balance between organizational and individual benefits. Furthermore, practitioners maintain that formal programs can provide a wider range of benefits for the mentor than informal programs.

On the basis of case studies, anecdotes and field experience, practitioners view the individual and organizational benefits of formal schemes as shown in Table 4.4. It can be seen that each of the points under the heading of 'organizational benefits' has a counterpart under 'individual benefits'.

Unfortunately, some of the points listed in Table 4.4 are still solely based on anecdotal information. This criticism relates mainly to 'performance', 'best use of talent' and 'opportunities to learn'. Notwithstanding this argument, these benefits have nonetheless been reported and/or observed and cannot be ignored.

Additional benefits of formal programs include:

- *Social inclusion.* Providing a structure can enable individuals who might otherwise find it difficult to access influence networks to overcome tacit or explicit barriers to commencing mentoring relationships. This means that a formal mentoring program is actually a vehicle for promoting organizational justice: with the help of program co-ordinators a larger number of employees are given the opportunity to benefit from mentoring relationships. This contrasts strongly with informal mentoring, which has a tendency to be highly selective and elitist: only those individuals who are

Table 4.4 Organizational and individual benefits sought through formal mentoring

Organizational benefits	Individual benefits
Retention	Career development
Performance	Skills development
Best use of talent	Opportunities for learning and gaining experience
Knowledge sharing	Knowledge acquisition
Safety valve for key staff to work through concerns	Having a sounding board and/or counsellor to prevent career moves

either courageous enough or who are being picked by a mentor will benefit from this type of relationship. Since mentors (if left to their own devices) tend to pick only successful individuals as mentees, those in greater need will be denied an important development opportunity. Inevitably, this kind of self-regulation will create perceptions of unfairness amongst employees.

- *Learning potential.* David Clutterbuck has observed that, left to their own devices, mentees will seek mentors who are either easy for them to get on with, or high-flyers who may provide a career towrope for their mentees. The disadvantage of the former is that there is a tendency towards creating relationships where similarity and comfort dominate whilst stimulation and challenge take a back seat. Furthermore, being satisfied with a mentoring relationship is not the same as achieving development benefit from it.

Shortcomings of the research

As pointed out previously, it is not clear yet how much credence can be given to the research conducted in the formal or in the informal camp. Let us take a look at the following shortcomings.

Distinction between the different degrees of satisfaction with mentoring relationships

It is obvious that mentoring associations will vary as to the degree of satisfaction experienced by mentor and mentee. At one extreme there might be dissatisfying or even dysfunctional relationships, and at the other extreme there might be highly satisfied pairs. It is logical to assume that there will be differences between these in terms of mentoring outcomes. However, to the best of our knowledge all but one previous empirical study has taken this distinction into account. When this factor was considered (Ragins and Cotton, 2000), it was revealed that satisfaction with the mentoring relationship had a stronger impact on career attitudes than whether the mentoring was formal or informal. The career attitudes measured included career commitment, job satisfaction, organizational commitment and intention to quit.

The implications of satisfaction

Many studies that compare formal and informal mentoring seem to yield the result that informal mentoring engenders greater satisfaction with the relationship. But what does this mean for the outcomes of a relationship? Earlier we pointed out that satisfaction with a mentoring relationship does not equate with the achievement of developmental benefits, although it might benefit career attitudes (see p. 129) – that is, for many reasons a mentee could theoretically be satisfied with a very comfortable and under-challenging association that does not provide any career functions at all. Even more to the point, some individuals may unconsciously seek dysfunctional work relationships as much as they seek dysfunctional personal relationships (Ragins and Cotton, 2000) – not aware of their dysfunctionality, they may nevertheless be satisfied with these. So the argument that informal relationships are somehow 'better' because they are more satisfying is to an extent questionable.

The proportion of failed versus successful mentoring relationships

The data presented in empirical studies seem to suggest that there is a greater number of unsuccessful (or, as it is usually called, 'dissatisfying') mentoring relationships amongst formal pairs. However, the evidence that might lead to this conclusion appears somewhat undermined by the following issue: it might be that formal relationships are more often characterized as less satisfying because:

- They are frequently the first pairing, and therefore the first relationship for either one or both protagonists within it.
- Mentors and mentees may not disband as easily as the pairs within informal relationships, even if the association is perceived as dissatisfying. This might be the case because they feel more obliged to try and make it work, since the relationship is being externally monitored.

People with successful informal relationships, on the other hand, may previously have had a whole host of unsuccessful attempts but have left them again very quickly. As Clutterbuck and Megginson (2000) put it: 'The question of how many frogs did you have to kiss first? is relevant here'. It would therefore be interesting to measure the proportion of failed attempts *vis-à-vis* successful ones in both formal and informal mentoring relationships.

Academic studies

It is probably fair to say that the academic studies conducted on the differences between formal and informal mentoring have an American bias. You might not perceive this as a 'big deal', but when you think back to the section in Chapter 1 regarding the different concepts of mentoring in America and Europe, you will appreciate the significance. Just to remind you, the American view of mentoring emphasizes protection and sponsorship, whilst the European view favours the mentee's insight and self-resourcefulness. To use the terms introduced in Chapter 1, Americans tend to utilize sponsorship mentoring whilst Europeans are more likely to embrace developmental mentoring.

These different emphases and the fact that most academic studies are actually carried out by Americans leads us to suspect that the research results might be rather biased and perhaps not all that applicable to European mentoring schemes. Upon examining the American studies in more detail, one finds ample corroboration for this suspicion: Ragins and Cotton (2000), for example, reported that their study showed that mentees received more career functions. When defining these, it transpires that the definitions are actually more relevant to American than European mentoring. To Ragins and Cotton, receiving greater 'Career functions' equates with receiving greater sponsorship, protection and coaching. Although coaching is important even in European mentoring terms, protection and sponsorship are not considered appropriate. In fact, mentors are actively discouraged from acting as sponsors within organizational contexts.

With regard to academic studies:

- Although many of the studies researching the outcomes of formal and informal relationships tended to confirm the view of better career development and enhanced salaries as a result of *informal* mentoring, others did not. For example, Fagenson-Eland and colleagues (Fagenson-Eland *et al.*, 1997) did not find a significant difference in career development functions between the two.
- Virtually all of the benefits of *formal* mentoring that are reported and documented are drawn from anecdotes, case studies or field experience. Notwithstanding the power of these, there ought to be empirical studies to corroborate the existing information.

How to resolve this dilemma

Considering the evidence in favour of formal as well as informal mentoring, together with the shortcomings of the ways in which the data were accumulated and interpreted, what should be done? First of all, despite the shortcomings of many of the studies on informal mentoring, their results should not be ignored. After all, they do repeatedly point towards the advantages of informal mentoring over formal programs.

However, besides the benefits that do seem to be associated with *formal* schemes (see p. 128), there is at least one other strong argument for implementing a formal mentoring program in organizations: at the very minimum, it is an efficient and fair way of helping a great number of employees to acquire mentors, and it is vital for the organization that this actually occurs. Why is this the case? Because numerous (quantitative, qualitative and other) comparisons between *mentored* and *non-mentored* individuals have shown that mentored employees are more 'positive employees'. For example, mentees tend to report greater career satisfaction (Fagenson, 1989), career commitment (Colarelli and Bishop, 1990) and career mobility (Scandura, 1992), and more positive job attitudes (Scandura, 1997). The caveat here is that the relationship must be a positive one, too. As Scandura (1998) found, dysfunctional mentoring may be destructive for the mentee – one more reason for monitoring relationships to an extent.

Furthermore, it can be seen from the study conducted by Ragins and Cotton (2000) that, under certain circumstances, the type of relationship (formal or informal) is irrelevant. In fact, Ragins now resolves the formal–informal dilemma by emphasizing that it is the *quality* of the relationship that matters, not whether it is formal or informal. And there is certainly the potential for high-quality relationships in both types of environment!

Combining formal and informal methods

Until valid and high-quality studies have been conducted, it might be a good idea to try and combine the best of formal and informal approaches. That is, wherever possible within your formal scheme you might want to emulate some degree of informality, which might enable you to reap the benefits of both worlds. Thus, apply the rule of creating a *formal framework* and promoting *informal relationships*.

Encouraging informal mentoring as much as possible within the program as well as throughout the organization could be achieved by:

- Making it public that the organization endorses *ad hoc* mentoring as much as formal mentoring.
- Encouraging mentees to approach potential mentors who may not yet be part of the formal scheme – mentors who are brought into the scheme by their mentees might have to undergo training once they have accepted the relationship.
- Allowing mentees to select their mentors (on their own or with the help of HR from a panel of mentors) and enabling the gradual development of a relationship – for example, it might be a good idea to ask pairs to meet a few times prior to deciding whether or not they wish to continue the relationship.

- Making it public that a no-fault-opt-out clause underlies the relationship.
- Encouraging mentors and mentees to continue their relationship on an informal basis once their formal relationship (i.e. the duration of the association as agreed under the scheme guidelines) has come to a conclusion.
- Making participation in the program voluntary so as to ensure commitment and motivation on part of the mentors; to ensure competency amongst mentors, this should be complemented by rigorous mentor selection as well as training.
- Keeping interference with the relationship by third parties to an absolute minimum – for example, although line managers should be involved in the association, they do not have to receive a report every week.
- Not forcing pairs to complete a mentoring contract; this does not affect outcomes as long as the pair possesses mutual clarity of purpose as well as mutual clarity about the appropriate behaviours.

Line versus off-line mentoring relationships

Just as formality can affect the mentoring relationship, so can hierarchy have an impact. In a hierarchical relationship between the mentor and mentee, i.e. one in which the mentor is the mentee's boss, the mentoring can lack openness, freedom and a developmental focus. Line mentoring is also less likely to be a power-free, two-way, mutually beneficial learning situation where the mentor provides guidance and shares experiences in a low pressure, self-discovery approach. This is because line mentoring relationships will always be influenced by the boss's focus on achieving results, and the mentoring might therefore not be solely mentee centred. Role confusion on part of the boss-mentor is another factor why most developmental mentoring schemes specifically avoid boss–subordinate pairs.

Another issue with line mentoring relationships is that bosses have a vested interest in maintaining a level of superiority over their staff, and hence genuine professional growth in the mentee can be perceived (and handled) as a threat. The risk to the boss is that the mentee's competence will undermine the mentor, or enable the mentee to seek a better position elsewhere. In either case, the underlying belief on the part of the boss might be that time spent mentoring is wasted time.

Fortunately, there are alternatives to the line mentoring relationship. The options include peers (the advantages of which have already been discussed under 'Models of mentoring relationships'), external mentors, and mentors from other departments.

Advantages of off-line mentoring

Besides what we have seen so far, there are also concrete advantages in having an off-line mentoring relationship. Having a mentor from another department, for example, seems to result in more satisfying relationships (and therefore at the very least more positive career attitudes) than having a mentor from the same department (Ragins and Cotton, 2000). This finding could be explained by assuming that restricting the selection of mentors to one department may also restrict the range of quality mentors available. Mentors from other departments might provide a different (and perhaps more valuable) set of learning experiences, including:

- Fresher insights.
- A broader organizational perspective.
- The possibility for lateral moves.
- The ability to see the mentee's career in broader terms.
- More effective support for their mentees because of, for example, a reduced inclination to want to manage mentees in terms of achieving departmental results.

To summarize, line managers should not be mentors because they are too results-focused and are responsible for helping others to do their job correctly. Therefore:

- They tend to adopt a telling style that creates dependency and promotes little initiative and problem-solving on part of the mentee (Brounstein, 2000).
- They are too influential over the mentee's career progression, and hence the openness and trust of the relationship might be affected.
- They are more likely to fall into a sponsorship role than a developmental one.
- Mentees might feel inhibited about breaking off the relationship, even if they feel ready to do so, because they will continue to remain under the influence of the mentor and do not wish to create a conflict-ridden atmosphere.

Differences in employees' perceptions of mentors and supervisors/line managers

It appears that many employees see the role of a mentor as different to that of a supervisor/line-manager. In a survey by Starcevich and Friend (1999), the majority of respondents saw mentors as being person-focused whilst supervisors were perceived as results/productivity focused – a role that may be incompatible with that of a mentor. In fact, this potential incompatibility was corroborated by an experiment that David Clutterbuck once conducted with several hundred Human Resource professionals. He asked them to name who they regarded as their most *frequent* and who as their most *intensive* source of learning at work. The findings were such that peers appear to be the source of the most *frequent* and mentors the source of the most *intensive* learning. Line managers, on the other hand, scored near the bottom of the pile on both criteria. Interestingly, these results have since been replicated with other groups of employees.

However, it is usual practice to inform line managers of any mentoring relationships that their direct reports are taking part in. Not only does this serve the purpose of keeping negative emotions at bay, but also involving line managers can enable mentees to make better use of the learning that occurs as a result of the mentoring relationships. For example, if mentees have learnt the value of participating in new projects, they might find it easier to be placed on a particular one if they explain to the line manager the rational behind this new desire. The topic of *how* to involve line managers will be covered in Chapter 11.

Spatial issues

Where can we meet? If meetings are to be held away from the workplace, then can we find a suitable environment that is quiet and private? The environment in which the mentoring session takes place will inevitably influence the level of openness adopted by mentor and mentee. If the meeting is conducted in a very noisy environment, concentration might also be affected. Since both openness and concentration are desirable characteristics of mentoring, organizations should encourage their mentoring pairs to meet in quiet and private surroundings. Where mentoring rooms are in short supply, an off-site venue may be appropriate.

Choice issues

Is it compulsory that mentor and mentee meet as part of a larger organizational or government-funded program? If so, then the mentoring relationship may become artificial and unrelated to the real needs and interests of mentor and mentee. This in turn will affect motivation and commitment and, ultimately, the outcomes of the relationship. The issue of compulsory versus voluntary participation in mentoring relationships will be discussed in detail in Chapter 8.

Internal factors

Gender

There are several ways in which the genders of mentor and mentee can influence the nature and outcomes of mentoring relationships, and various studies have confirmed this claim (e.g. Allen *et al.*, 2000). However, it must be remembered that gender issues are largely symptoms rather than causes. For example, sexual discrimination is the symptom of a deeply held stereotype – it is the result of mentor and mentee acting out these stereotypes, consciously or not. In fact, this applies to a wide variety of discrimination and harassment, whether due to gender, race or disability; the problems experienced by disadvantaged individuals are consequences of the person being trapped inside the stereotype. What then is a stereotype? According to Harre and Lamb (1986):

> Stereotypes are oversimplified, rigid, and generalized beliefs about groups of people, in which all individuals from the same group are regarded as having the same set of leading characteristics.

Stereotypes affect the disadvantaged individual externally as well as internally. Externally, they influence how other people think about and behave towards them, the end result of which may be occurrences such as discrimination. To be more specific, discrimination is the behavioural aspect of stereotyping: the tendency for people to change their behaviour as a function of assumptions they make about others (Thompson, 2000). Internally, stereotypes influence how the disadvantaged individuals themselves think and behave. For instance, they might think of themselves as 'low achievers' or as 'unworthy of being treated fairly' – thoughts that may well become a self-fulfilling prophecy. In their book *Mentoring and Diversity*, Clutterbuck and Ragins (2001) describe this awkward situation very aptly:

> Our assumptions create a framework of expectations, which can lead to self-fulfilling prophecies ... The adage 'behaviour breeds behaviour' is nowhere more valid than in dealing with stereotypes.

In a nutshell, the stereotypes held by disadvantaged individuals and by those around them influence *everyone's* thinking and behaviour. Although much of this may be subtle, suppressed, and even subconscious, stereotypes can cause the occurrence of symptoms such as discrimination and harassment. Within a mentoring program, it is therefore paramount to raise individuals' awareness of stereotypes and their potential effects. Mentors, mentees and program co-ordinators must all learn to question their assumptions, even if these appear to the individual to be rational and based on evidence. This should help to prevent many of the issues about to be described here, as well as in Chapter 11, from occurring.

Potential issues in cross-gender relationships

Sexual discrimination/harassment

Fortunately, cases of sexual discrimination and/or harassment within a mentoring relationship are extremely rare. Naturally, where either of these does occur, the impact on the mentoring relationship will be large. Not only is the mentoring relationship likely to malfunction, it is even more likely to be terminated by the victim. After having had such an experience, it is to be expected that the individual concerned will not enter into any future mentoring relationship – and if he or she does, the relationship is likely to be fairly constrained in terms of trust and openness.

The issue of sexual harassment in mentoring relationships can be viewed from two different angles: first, the angle of the mentor fearing that he or she might be incorrectly accused of sexual harassment – an allegation with potentially dire career consequences; and secondly, the angle of the mentor or mentee suffering sexual harassment at the hands of the other party. In some cases harassment has occurred prior to a mentoring relationship, but it still affects individuals' attitudes, leading them to stick with same-gender mentoring.

There are, however, a few actions you can take in order to ensure the carefree continuation of cross-gender dyads. These include informing everyone involved with the program of the

company's position with regards to discrimination and harassment (e.g. emphasizing the existence of a zero-tolerance policy)
and explaining the potential consequences for the perpetrator if
a case is brought to light. For further advice on how to deal with
these issues, refer to Chapter 11.

Personal involvement (or perceptions thereof)

As in any other professional relationship, the occurrence of
sexual involvement between two people in a mentoring relationship cannot be ruled out. If it happens, it is not necessarily a
disaster. The main point to remember is to have mechanisms in
place that help to manage this situation in positive terms. For
example, within a formal mentoring scheme participants should,
during training/briefing sessions, be encouraged to do the
following if they become personally involved with their
mentor/mentee:

- Talk about it openly between themselves – what are the
  consequences for their mentoring relationship and for their
  careers?
- Make the relationship public if it is to continue. This avoids
  the spreading of harmful rumours. At the same time, it is
  strongly advisable to discontinue the formal mentoring relationship, simply because others might fear that the mentee
  will now receive privileged treatment.
- Adhere to the organizational policies on dating other
  employees.

Other measures such as transferring one of the couple might
also be considered by the organization, depending on the
policies for involvement between employees.

The second issue relates to the risk of *perceptions* about inappropriate relations between mentor and mentee (Wickman and
Sjodin, 1997). Male–female mentoring relationships are perhaps
exposed to greater scrutiny than same-gender pairs, and this
may put extra pressure on both participants to emphasize
career/instrumental factors at the expense of genuine and legit-
imate psychosocial benefits.

If third parties (genuinely or not) perceive there to be a sexual
involvement between a mentor and mentee and act on their
unproductive feelings, the mentoring scheme and the organization can encounter difficulties. Such perceptions must not be
ignored but carefully managed.

Male dominance amongst mentors

A much higher number of women than men are part of cross-
gender associations, typically as mentees, simply because there

are many more male than female mentors around. There are several ways in which both men and women will tend to behave differently in cross-gender dyads than in same-gender ones:

- Both parties may assume stereotypical behaviours that could serve to reinforce those of the other party, including the ones typically 'working against' the person in corporate environments. An example of the latter would include women's tendency to access informal networking communities within the organization less frequently. If mentors, consciously or not, fail to encourage their mentees to take part in these, such behaviours are unlikely to change.
- A male mentor with a female mentee may also be more inclined to act like a protector and helper, demonstrating that he is powerful and dominant. Under some circumstances this might create over-reliance and dependence on the advice of the mentor, which would prevent the mentee from developing autonomy.

This might mean that women potentially receive a very different set of mentoring experiences to men. To provide equal opportunities to all participants of a formal mentoring program, it would be advisable to ensure that both male and female mentees experience a mix of mentors (in terms of gender) throughout their careers.

Mentee selection

According to a study conducted by Allen *et al.* (2000), mentors (both male and female) are biased towards selecting mentees based on their perceptions of the mentee's potential/ability rather than perceptions of his or her need for help. This means that the extent of a mentee's need for help is not as important a determinant in mentee selection as is his or her perceived potential to grow and develop.

Termination of mentoring relationships

Having multiple sequential mentoring relationships has been found to be a key ingredient in career development and organizational advancement (Burlew, 1991). In this respect it has also been suggested that men are more likely to terminate a relationship as soon as they have detected that it might not be useful anymore. Women, on the contrary, were thought to hold onto a relationship longer, sometimes past its usefulness (Ragins, 1989). For this and other reasons men are often viewed as having more mentoring relationships than women, which might again put them at an advantage in terms of variables such as career development. However, a more recent study on women's behaviour in relation to the termination of mentoring relationships did not confirm this view. Ragins and Scandura (1997) found that women did not differ from men in the number and duration of mentoring relationships, and that they also did not tend to hold different reasons for ending relationships.

Perceptions of power

These can influence how mentees treat their mentors, that is, their beliefs in what they can gain from the mentoring relationships will inadvertently affect how they will relate to their mentor (e.g. the choice of topics and the mentees' perception of how long they can see the mentor as being beneficial to them).

Gender, representation and access

Gender also plays a role in mentoring relationships in two other respects: *representation* and *access*.

Representation

The representation issue is that mentoring relationships in organizations are more frequently composed of middle and senior mentors working with junior mentees. In most large organizations the senior management population is still largely male, and therefore more career mentors are male than female purely on the basis of representation. Some authors (e.g. Kogler-Hill and Bahniuk, 1998) argue not only that female mentors are scarce and frequently seen as less powerful than male mentors, but also that men have easier access to the existing informal communication networks and therefore have easier access to supportive relationships with mentors or sponsors.

This issue will also emerge in the discussion of ethnicity. Establishing a mentoring program with the same gender or ethnicity in mentor and mentee may have some relationship advantages. The disadvantage is that mentors from 'under-represented' groups are by definition rare, or may not be as senior as (say) white male mentors. In this case, it may be better to have a 'blind' mentoring program that does not seek to match participants on the basis of ethnicity or gender.

Access

Some studies have revealed that women seem to have less access to mentors than men do. That said, the evidence regarding this point is contradictory and there are other studies that disagree. Yet where reduced lack of access for women *is* the case, it might be explained by the following reasons:

- Lack of encouragement for women to seek out mentors.
- Reluctance of male mentors (which, as we have seen before, still predominate in terms of numbers) to take on female mentees. This leads to a reduction of the numbers of mentors available to women. Again, this might be due to a combination of factors; people are subconsciously attracted to those who they perceive as similar to themselves, and male mentors might select male mentees because they can more easily identify with them. Furthermore, male mentors might be reluctant to enter into a cross-gender dyad for reasons discussed previously, such as fear of harmful rumours.

One of the clear advantages of mentoring schemes is that they have the potential to mediate some of these unpleasant effects. For example, formal schemes can not only encourage but also support female mentees in finding a suitable mentor. Moreover, male mentors might feel somewhat more relaxed about taking on a female mentee if this comes as part of a formalized program: they might perceive it as the necessary legitimation of their relationship.

Ethnicity/race

Once again, the issue of representation affects the choice of mentors for mentees from under-represented ethnic groups. There seems to be no clear evidence either way about the relative long-term effectiveness of same-group versus cross-group mentoring relationships. However, there is some support for the psychosocial advantages of same-group relationships (Kogler-Hill and Bahniuk (1998)):

Mentoring relationships have an even greater positive impact on career success for blacks than for whites. Both cross-race and same-race mentoring relationships provide career support. However, same-race relationships provide more psychosocial support and have shorter and easier initiation periods. Blacks tend to receive most of their mentoring support from other blacks, with other groups being less involved. There is also evidence that cross-race mentees are treated differently by mentors due to cultural stereotypes.

Similarly, mentors also need to be sensitive to different cultural perspectives or mentoring might be in danger of perpetuating institutionalized prejudices. Yet cross-race mentoring relationships can be very beneficial in other respects, such as helping both parties to build their skill repertory regarding their interaction with other cultures. Once again, it appears that seeking a mix of mentors throughout one's career is the best way to gain the benefits of all types of pairings.

Personality

In addition to 'demographic' issues of gender and ethnicity, mentors and mentees are also individuals with unique personalities. Some mentoring programs attempt to pair relatively junior and senior employees who are very much alike except for their experience levels, although some organizations find that matching people who are dissimilar maximizes learning opportunities because the resulting relationship might be more challenging and stretching.

The argument that mentees can benefit from having mentors with opposite personality types who can provide guidance where they need it most is balanced by other views. For an article Tyler (1998), for example, interviewed Barbara Glanz, speaker and author of CARE Packages for the Workplace: Dozens of Little Things You can Do to Regenerate Spirit at Work' disagrees with the notion of matching different personality types. She recommends:

> Some initial matching of talent, skills and interests on business and human levels [is desirable]. If I love golf and he happens to love golf, we'll have a lot more to talk about than if they give me a mentee who plays bridge ... Like any relationship, there must be chemistry, if there isn't, not much is going to happen.

However, this view seems to let mentors off their responsibility for relationship building. If a mentor understands the art of establishing rapport (for example, if the mentor offers trust, empathy, and wants to empower the mentee), and if there is a clear goal to achieve, people will find their points of similarity. In fact, every pair has far more points of similarity than dissimilarity!

Furthermore, matching opposites can be more beneficial than matching people who are too alike. Besides the fact that dissimilar individuals can get on very well, the learning in a dissimilar pair is going to be very stimulating indeed. The solution to the 'problem' of matching dissimilar or similar people seems to lie in the following: try to avoid *gross* differences and avoid matching people who would definitely *not* get on!

Time issues

When can we meet? How often? For how long? Limitations may result from mentor or mentee work and life demands, costs, or simply scheduling problems. In terms of the *frequency* of meetings, problems might arise if this is too low given the needs of a particular mentee and the stage of the relationship. In most mentoring programs, mentors and mentees tend to get together every 4–8 weeks. However, if a relationship is at its very beginning and/or the mentee requires a lot of support, this might not suffice. This is because it can be difficult to build a relationship from scratch when meetings happen only on very rare occasions. Reducing the frequency of meetings even more (e.g. to once every 2 or 3 months) is best left to the later stages of a mentoring relationship. Meeting too infrequently will also affect the speed with which development goals are achieved.

In terms of the duration of meetings, a duration of between 60 and 90 minutes is recommended. However, there can sometimes be exceptions where mentoring might take several hours – this is particularly true when the mentor is in 'coaching mode'.

Mentor's personal style

A mentor's 'personal style' is his or her own unique way of mentoring. That is, although mentors should adhere to best practice guidelines in terms of using the recommended mentoring techniques and processes (described in Chapter 6), they will always add their own 'slant' when putting theory into practice. Although it might often be difficult to describe someone's style, we will endeavour to give you some examples: some mentor's might adopt a more humorous style than others, and others might be more challenging than their fellow mentors. Yet others might question mentees much more than others in order to help them explore their own resourcefulness in making decisions. Irrespective of which styles mentors adopt, it is clear that this will influence the dynamics and outcomes of the mentoring. Picture it this way: it is unlikely that one mentee would develop exactly the same with one mentor as with another one.

Mentee needs

It is obvious that mentee needs will influence the *outcome* of a relationship. However, in addition to outcomes, mentee needs will also influence its dynamics. For example, can you imagine how different it would be to mentor someone who wants to become better at planning and organizing his or her job tasks than to mentor someone who wants to gain greater confidence in diverse work situations?

'In-between' factors

Besides some of the topics discussed above that have clear ethical implications (e.g. sexual harrassment), there are additional ethical issues surrounding mentoring relationships. For example, does it matter whether other people know that one of their colleagues is meeting a mentor? What about the ethics surrounding the fact that within a mentoring scheme not all employees can benefit from having a mentor? Mentees might be asking themselves these questions, which in turn could influence their behaviour. They might feel limited in the extent to which they can apply the learning gained in the mentoring relationship to work situations for fear of provoking envy in their non-mentored colleagues. To limit feelings of envy amongst non-mentored employees and to enable mentees fully to utilize the mentoring relationship, organizations have to safeguard their programs as much as possible. The most practical way to do this is to de-mystify mentoring relationships through, for example:

- Making public the rationale underlying the choice of mentees – it has to be one that will satisfy most employees in the sense that they will feel equally valued as a result.
- Informing non-mentored employees of the nature of mentoring relationships – i.e. what is their purpose and how do they work – and making explicit that mentors are not in the business of helping their mentees to get promotions and privileges, and, once again,
- Involving the mentee's line manager but not allowing collusion between him or her and the mentor.

Where possible, it would also be a good idea to offer alternative training and development options to non-mentored employees. This helps to reintroduce a sense of equity amongst those who might feel disenchanted with an organization's sense of fairness.

There are additional situations in which ethical concerns can influence the dynamics of a mentoring relationship: a fundamental aspect of the mentor–mentee relationship is that each has privileged access to the other. Mentees may be encouraged to disclose information about current or potential problems that could be damaging to their own career or reputation if widely revealed. Likewise, mentors might share a personal 'disaster' to help mentees anticipate and avoid a similar pitfall. In either case, both parties have a professional obligation to the relationship to not exploit the other's disclosures.

This is particularly true in the case of specifically appointed ethical mentors, who may be appropriate for individuals and organizations operating at the leading edge of science and technology, law, and medicine. In these cases the mentor is privy not only to business and career issues, but also to wider considerations that might impact upon the environment and society as a whole. There will inevitably be times when the mentoring relationship is stretched or even broken by the actions of one party being too extreme to remain within the confidentiality bounds of mentoring. For example, the disclosure of criminal activity by the mentee may result in the mentor being implicated as an accessory if he or she does not take action or oblige the mentee to take action to address or rectify the situation.

The obligations of mentors and mentees to each other are explored in subsequent chapters, and the issue of confidentiality in particular is returned to in Chapters 10 and 11. Overall, the literature is remarkably devoid of references to ethical issues in business mentoring. It is highly likely that this will be the focus of academic and practitioner concern in years to come as mentoring is established as a common framework for handling ethical dilemmas in business.

Summary

This chapter has given an in-depth account of the external, internal and 'in-between' variables of mentoring relationships. Although some of the variables mentioned (such as the formality of the scheme) will be the same for all mentoring relationships within a particular program, others (such as the mentor's style) will vary between pairs. Because of this and because we are dealing with human beings, no single mentoring relationship that you are part of or that is part of your program will be the same as another. Some of them will be more beneficial to mentees than others, and some of them will last longer than others.

In the face of so many variables that impact on the mentoring relationships in your scheme, you will have to accept a degree of powerlessness. Yet there are, of course, some measures you can take that go a long way towards ensuring that most mentoring relationships will be effective (else, we would not have written this book!). The two main points to remember when designing a mentoring scheme are:

- *Standardize the official environment for fairness.* Create the same environment for everyone – for example, apply the same selection and matching principles, the same rules of formality, and the same principles regarding monitoring and evaluation to every pair in your scheme.
- *Provide the mentor and mentee with freedom in their relationships.* Although a degree of monitoring and evaluation is important, once matched, mentoring pairs should be given considerable freedom with regard to how they relate to each other and how they conduct their meetings. The mentoring program should be seen as a framework that defines boundaries and certain rules, but within which the mentoring pairs can move freely and safely. Furthermore, if you are (or will be) running multiple schemes in the same organization, it is important to have some core principles that all schemes adhere to.

Acknowledge that, while you cannot control everything, creating a solid groundwork will considerably maximize the chances of your mentoring scheme being successful. Over the chapters to come, we will explore the foundations of mentoring schemes in greater detail.

References

Allen, T., Poteet, M. L. and Russell, J. E. A. (2000). Protégé selection by mentors: what makes the difference? *J. Org. Behav.*, **21**, 271–82.

Beech and Brockbank, 1999.

Brounstein, M. (2000). *Coaching and Mentoring for Dummies*. IDG.

Burlew, L. D. (1991). Multiple mentor model: a conceptual framework. *J. Career Dev.*, **17**, 213–21.

Chao, G. T., Walz, P. M. and Gardner, P. D. (1992). Formal and informal mentorships: a comparison on mentoring functions and contrast with non-mentored counterparts. *Personnel Psychol.*, **45**, 619–36.

Clutterbuck, D. and Megginson, D. (2000). The success of formal versus informal mentoring: making sense of the evidence. Paper presented at the European Mentoring Conference (no. 7).

Clutterbuck, D. C. and Ragins, B. R. (2001). *Mentoring and Diversity*. Butterworth-Heinemann.

Colarelli, S. M. and Bishop, R. C. (1990). Career commitment: functions, correlates, and management. *Group Org. Studies*, **15**, 158–77.

Collins, J. (1996). Looking out for number one. *Inc. Magazine*, **June**. At http://www.inc.com

Fagenson, E. A. (1989). The mentor advantage: perceived career/job experiences of protégés versus non-protégés. *J. Org. Behav.*, **10**, 309–20.

Fagenson-Eland, E. A., Marks, M. A. and Amendola, K. L. (1997). Perceptions of mentoring relationships. *J. Vocational Behav.*, **51**, 29–42.

Gregg, C. (1999). Someone to look up to. *J. Accountancy*, **188**, 89–93.

Harre, R. and Lamb, R. (1986). *The Dictionary of Personality and Social Psychology*. Blackwell.

Harrington, A. (1999). 'E-mentoring – the advantages and disadvantages of using e-mail to support distant mentoring'. Herts Tec. At: http://www.mentorsforum.co.uk

Kerka, S. (1998). New perspectives on mentoring. ERIC Clearinghouse on Adult, Career, and Vocational Education. At: http://www.peer.ca/Perspectives.html (Digest No. 194).

Kogler-Hill, S. and Bahniuk, M. H. (1998). Promoting career success through mentoring. *Rev. Bus.*, **19**, 4–7.

Kram, K. (1983). Phases of the mentoring relationship. *Acad. Man. J.*, **26**, 608–25.

Kram, K. and Isabella, L. (1985). Mentoring alternatives: the role of peer relationships in career development. *Acad. Man. J.*, **28**, 110–32.

Ragins, B. R. (1989). Barriers to mentoring: the female manager's dilemma. *Human Rel.*, **42**, 1–22.

Ragins, B. R. and Cotton, J. L. (1999). Mentor functions and outcomes: a comparison of men and women in formal and informal mentoring relationships. *J. Appl. Psychol.*, **84**, 529–50.

Ragins, B. R. and Cotton, J. L. (2000). Marginal mentoring: the effects of type of mentor, quality of relationship, and program design on work and career attitudes. *Acad. Man. J.*, **43**, 1177–94.

Ragins, B. R. and Scandura, T. A. (1997). The way we were: gender and the termination of mentoring relationships. *J. Appl. Psychol.*, **82**, 945–53.

Scandura, T. A. (1992). Mentorship and career mobility: an empirical investigation. *J. Org. Behav.*, **13**, 169–74.

Scandura, T. A. (1997). Mentoring and organizational justice: an empirical investigation. *J. Vocational Behav.*, **51**, 58–69.

Scandura, T. A. (1998). Dysfunctional mentoring relationships and outcomes. *J. Management*, **24**, 449–67.

Starcevich, M. and Friend, F. (1999). Effective mentoring relationships from the mentee's perspective. *Workforce* (Suppl.). **Jul**, 2–3.

Thompson, L. (2000). *Making the Team: A Guide for Managers*. Prentice Hall.

Tyler, K. (1998). Mentoring programs link employees and experienced execs. *HR Magazine*, **Apr**, 98–103.

Wickman, F. and Sjodin, T. (1997). *Mentoring*. McGraw-Hill.

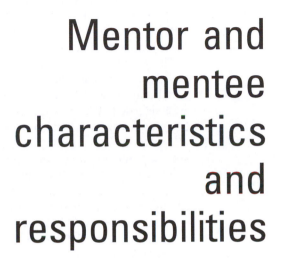

Mentor and mentee characteristics and responsibilities

Successful mentoring relationships require both the mentor *and* the mentee to possess a certain set of skills, qualities and attributes. For example, good mentees are characterized by their commitment to learning and their efforts to develop their own solutions. Furthermore, they must stick to agreed goals and show appreciation for the value of their mentor's time and effort. However, no mentee is perfect. The key criterion is that mentees *want* to be in the relationship and value their mentor's intervention. In many cases, learning how to be a good mentee is part of the journey the individual has to undertake. This may be another reason why some *first* formal mentoring relationships are less successful – such a relationship is a practice run for the mentee!

Similarly, to be a good developmental mentor certain prerequisites must also be fulfilled. Key competencies that a mentor should possess include well-developed communication skills, self-awareness and a genuine belief in the mentee's potential. For many mentoring relationships it is also important that the mentor possesses a substantial knowledge and experience base in the area he or she is mentoring on. Lastly, it is vital for the success of a mentoring relationship that the mentor has a positive attitude toward it – i.e. the mentor must genuinely desire to be one, and be willing to support the mentee in his or her quest for 'learning how to learn'.

The mentoring competencies described in this chapter are based on the work of Clutterbuck Associates, who have been collaborating with thousands of mentoring pairs over the past two decades. When you are reading through them, you will become aware of just how big a range of competencies an effective mentor must possess. This means that carefully selecting the mentors for your scheme is important. However, bear in mind that it is impossible to be perfect on all of these skills, and that they can be learned and developed over time. Mentee needs differ between individuals, and some of the characteristics presented below might be more important for some than for others. For example, for some a mentor's extensive business acumen might outweigh any lack of patience *if* the mentee feels that it is the mentor's business savvy that helps the mentee to achieve his or her goals and *if* this lack of patience does not prevent the mentee from doing so.

You might also occasionally stop and ponder over a specific characteristic, wondering why a mentor *has* to possess it. The answer to that will always be the same: all of the mentor characteristics described in this chapter are important to enable mentees to take charge of their learning. They are important to help mentees develop their own solutions, make their own decisions and become independent learners. To achieve this, mentors must be capable of:

- Fostering self-reliance, self-confidence and a belief in their own potential within mentees.
- Enabling mentees to identify their development needs and goals, write development plans and meet their goals.
- Helping mentees to solve problems by analysing, reflecting and enhancing their self-awareness.

The next section entails a description of effective mentor characteristics, which is mainly based on research conducted by David Clutterbuck over several years and involving many mentoring pairs (Clutterbuck, 2000). Following this, mentee characteristics and behaviours that help mentees to gain the most from developmental mentoring relationships are outlined. Destructive mentee behaviours will also be considered. The last section of this chapter takes a look at factors beyond mentor and mentee characteristics that also influence how much a mentee gains from a relationship.

Mentor characteristics

We will consider the following essential mentor characteristics over the next few pages:

1. Business knowledge and experience:
   - Negative experiences
2. Skills and abilities:
   - Self-awareness.
   - Behavioural awareness – understanding others.
   - Building and maintaining rapport/relationship management.
   - Commitment to the mentor's own continued development.
   - Communication competencies.
   - Conceptual modelling.
   - Sense of proportion/good humour.
   - Goal clarity.
   - Flexibility
3. Attributes:
   - Patience.
   - Self-confidence.
   - Encouragement.
4. Attitudes:
   - A strong interest in developing others.

Business knowledge and experience

The extent to which a mentor will need business knowledge and experience (as well as the nature of the acumen needed) is likely to vary greatly, and is determined by the mentee's development needs. For example, executive mentors are likely to need substantial amounts of business knowledge, not least to appear more credible in the eyes of the executive/director they are mentoring. In fact, many attempts to pair middle managers in large companies (the mentor) with entrepreneurs in small businesses (the mentee) have failed because the mentor has not had valid experience in the mentee's eyes. Peer mentors within graduate induction schemes, on the other hand, will require relatively small amounts of general business acumen. In addition, you must not forget the *aim* of mentoring, which is to foster individuals capable of managing their own learning.

Mentoring is not about presenting all the answers on a golden plate, but it is about helping people to find these answers through skilful questioning.

There is not a great deal that can be done to acquire business savvy in the short-term; there are very few shortcuts to experience and judgment. Even if a mentor has not yet acquired vast amounts of it, it is nevertheless possible to be a skilled mentor whilst in the process of expanding his or her own business acumen. This can be done because:

- Mentoring relies on people developing their own solutions.
- The acquisition of mentoring skills, techniques and processes can enable individuals to help many people reach their development goals.

However, as has been hinted above, the amount of business savvy required should be appropriate to the mentee's needs. To return to the above example, a chief executive is likely to benefit most from someone with equal or more experience, given the sheer complexity of their roles. Even if the executive mentor will not present the mentee with answers, he or she will at least be more capable of guiding the executive's learning in the right direction. That is, the types of reflective, probing or other questions asked by mentors are likely to be more purposeful if they are based on real experience. The mentor would also be in a better position to assess carefully whether or not the mentee is just about to commit a major mistake that might seriously harm the business. Through making the mentee reflect upon a proposed solution, the mentor might be able to avert potentially disastrous decisions.

An additional and highly important part of business mentoring involves having had negative experiences, i.e. having committed career mistakes and having learned from them. Showing mentees that the mentor's job life has not always been a smooth flow of events, but that mistakes were a vital part of their progress, helps mentees to reduce their fear of any mishaps and to begin seeing them as horizon-widening occurrences.

Whatever the extent of the mentor's knowledge and experience, this should be used to:

- Enable mentees to become self-reliant, to grow, and eventually to realize their aims.
- Question mentees skilfully and get them to reflect and develop their own solutions.
- Point mentees to sources of information, which they can seize on at their discretion.

- Explain his or her own coping strategies – this helps mentees to build their own.

In sum, the mentor's business savvy is more important for some and less important for other relationships. The extent and nature of business acumen needed for successful mentoring should be decided on the basis of the mentee's needs.

In many circumstances, factors other than business knowledge will be more important in determining the quality of a mentoring relationship. These include that mentors must possess a particular set of skills, abilities and attributes. Furthermore, they must be familiar with mentoring techniques and processes and possess the right attitude towards mentoring. We will take a look at all of these components in the following sections.

Skills and abilities

Self-awareness

Mentors need high self-awareness in order to recognize and manage their own behaviours within the helping relationship and to use empathy appropriately. The activist, task-focused manager often has relatively little insight into these areas – and indeed may actively avoid reflection on such issues, depicting them as 'soft' and of low priority. Such attitudes and learned behaviours may be difficult to break, and yet doing so is important for mentors. Why is that the case? To answer this question, let us take a closer look at what self-awareness is, what it involves and what its benefits are.

Self-awareness is *gained* by beginning to observe yourself objectively and by reflecting upon what you see. *Being* self-aware means being able to realize and analyse what you are doing (your behaviour), why you are doing something, and what impact this has on you, others and your goals. Self-awareness also means acquiring the ability to see patterns in your own behaviour. This provides you with the means by which to change your behaviour and, ultimately, your performance. Self-awareness is the essence of learning and taking control; learning about yourself and taking control of personal change.

Self-awareness is also the basis of learning about and understanding others. Finally it is, of course, one of the aspects that mentees are supposed to develop throughout a mentoring relationship. Being self-aware is essential for learning to occur. Given that the aim of mentoring involves helping people learn how to learn, it makes sense that mentors should foster mentees' self-awareness.

Behavioural awareness – understanding others

Like self-awareness, understanding how others behave and why they do so is a classic component of emotional intelligence. To help others manage their relationships, the mentor must have reasonably good insight into patterns of behaviour between individuals and groups of people. Predicting the consequences of specific behaviours or courses of action is one of the many practical applications of this insight.

Furthermore, understanding others also involves being sensitive to their moods, fears and anxieties. Gauging these types of emotions requires interpreting not only verbal messages but also non-verbal ones. Observing body language is a powerful way of understanding what someone is really thinking or feeling. If mentors sense negative emotions, they should respond appropriately. For example, if mentees appear to be depressed and/or self-conscious, mentors might want to counteract this by being positive and encouraging.

Building and maintaining rapport/relationship management

Although highly important, the skills of rapport-building are difficult to define. When asked to describe rapport, managers' observations can be distilled into five characteristics:

1. Trust:
   - Will they do what they say?
   - Will they keep confidences?
2. Focus:
   - Are they concentrating on me?
   - Are they listening without judging?
3. Empathy:
   - Do they have goodwill towards me?
   - Do they try to understand my feelings?
4. Congruence:
   - Do they acknowledge and accept my goals?
5. Empowerment:
   - Is their help aimed at helping me stand on my own feet as soon as is practical?

The importance of trust is central. Mentoring relationships are intimate and tend to deal with very sensitive issues, problems, challenges and even weakness on the part of mentees. They might initially be embarrassed to discuss these openly, and talking about them requires a substantial amount of trust. Without it, a mentoring relationship is not feasible.

In addition to establishing rapport with their mentees, mentors should also be capable of building rapport with individuals in general. This is because one of the roles a mentor fulfils is that of a networker/facilitator.

Networking with other mentors is important, too. It serves a variety of purposes, such as enabling the exchange of mentoring-related information. Mentoring as a profession is also still very much in its infancy, and staying in touch with the developments in this field is vital in order to operate under best practice guidelines. Forming networks with other mentors is also important in cases where a mentor is unable to help a mentee with a particular problem and the mentor wishes the mentee to consult fellow mentors.

Commitment to the mentor's own continued learning

Effective mentors seize opportunities to experiment and take part in new experiences. They read widely, and are efficient at setting and following personal development plans. They actively seek and use behavioural feedback from others.

Several reasons underlie this devotion to learning: first and foremost, it is because mentoring is all about learning – being capable of and subscribing to self-managed life-long learning is the philosophy on which mentoring is based. If mentors have not internalized this, two things are likely to happen:

- They will be poor role models for their mentees by not practising what they preach, and their credibility will be undermined.
- The success of their attempts to encourage self-managed learning in the mentees might be somewhat diminished.

Communication competencies

When we think about communication, we have a propensity to associate this term with written and oral messages. Effective communication goes beyond speaking and writing intelligibly; it includes:

- Listening: opening the mind to what the other person is saying.
- Allowing silence: not trying to fill in any pause in the communication – sometimes silences are where the best thinking occurs.
- Observing as receiver: being open to the visual and other non-verbal signals, recognizing what is *not* being said.
- Parallel processing: analysing what the other person is saying, reflecting on it, preparing responses.
- Projecting: crafting words and their emotional 'wrapping' in a manner appropriate for the situation and the recipient.

- Observing as projector: being open to visual and other non-verbal signals as clues to what the recipient is hearing/understanding, and adapting tone, volume, pace and language appropriately.
- Exiting: concluding a dialogue or segment of dialogue with clarity and alignment of understanding (ensuring message received).

Active listening in mentoring relationships

The first facet of communication listed above is listening. The exact type of listening a mentor engages in is usually known as '(pro-) active listening' or 'reflective listening'. Experienced mentors repeatedly name this skill as the key to successful mentoring. Active listening requires mentors to be extremely sensitive and to concentrate on the mentee for sustained periods of time – not an easy task!

The aim of this type of listening is to:

- Understand genuinely what the mentee is trying to say; this sometimes means being able to 'read between the lines' in order to discover the underlying issues.
- Be able to ask relevant questions that help to move mentees closer to understanding and achieving their goals.

The first step involved in active listening is making the learner feel completely relaxed. This means making the mentee feel safe and creating an environment in which judgment is suspended. The next step is to focus completely on what the mentee is saying by giving your undivided attention. This can only be done if you genuinely try to 'enter the mentee's world' and, so-to-speak, 'hold a space' for him or her. Whilst you are listening, there are a few things you might want to do as well as a few things you should and should not do:

- *'Might want to do'*: you might want to take notes of what the mentee is saying; this combats the problem of having spare mental capacity, which might tempt you to daydream. For some people, taking notes also enhances their understanding of what is being said. If you do decide to take notes, it is a good idea to advise the mentee on why you are doing it, otherwise your carefully created relaxed atmosphere might be destroyed again.
- *'Should do'*: whilst you are listening, you should try to summarize what the mentee is saying in your head. You should also, of course, reflect on what is being said and prepare appropriate responses, such as questions. You

should show the mentee that you are really interested in what is being said. You could do this in a variety of ways, such as maintaining eye contact, nodding, leaning forward, and verbally acknowledging that you are listening.

- *'Should not do'*: under no circumstances should you interrupt the mentee – interrupting a communication flow can be equated to suddenly pushing someone who trusted you across a room: it is certainly unexpected and can cause a lot of damage.

Once the mentee has finished speaking, it might *sometimes* be useful to either summarize or paraphrase what has been said, particularly when you are not sure that you understood correctly. You could use words such as: 'Is what your are saying that …'. Please note, however, that in the main you should not be summarizing for the mentee. Instead, it is regarded as best practice to get the mentee to summarize what has been said and learned! This activity is especially important at the end of a session.

That said, summarizing and paraphrasing, either by mentor or mentee, does not have to be done all the time. It should only be done if it fulfils a purpose, such as:

- Mentors trying to clarify for themselves that they have understood what their mentee said.
- Mentors wanting to help the learner understand an issue better.

When you do summarize or paraphrase (or get the mentee to do so), it should be done either after a whole dialogue or at least a section of a dialogue has been completed. Summarizing or paraphrasing after every few sentences is a little too extreme. If summarizing and/or paraphrasing do not seem necessary at all, you might want to go straight on to asking a question that moves the conversation to the next point.

Questioning skills in mentoring

Another important part of communication competence is the ability to ask the mentee appropriate questions at the appropriate time. Active listening and questioning go hand in hand, because the questions come as a response to the listening – that is, for most part the mentor chooses the next question having listened to and reflected upon the mentee's issues. The rule to remember when thinking about what question to ask is whether it is a helpful one. Is this question going to bring the mentee closer to achieving his or her development goal? Is it offensive? Or judgmental? Or am I simply going to ask it to satisfy my own curiosity?

The skills of questioning are widely covered elsewhere and therefore not dealt with in detail here. The most common distinction is between open and closed questions. *Closed* questions provoke only very short, sometimes one-word responses – for example, 'have you had a nice day?' or 'are you intending to write this e-mail?'. *Open* questions are types of questions that encourage fairly elaborate responses. The onus is on the respondent. Open questions tend to start with words such as 'how', 'why' and 'what'. Since this is the type that is mainly used by mentors, the different kinds of open questions are looked at more closely in Table 5.1 (Parsloe and Wray, 2000).

Conceptual modelling

Effective mentors have a portfolio of models that they can draw upon to help mentees understand the issues they face. These models can be self-generated (i.e. the result of personal experience), drawn from elsewhere (e.g. models of company structure, interpersonal behaviours, strategic planning, career planning) or –

Table 5.1 Types of questions used in mentoring

Type of question	Aim of question	Examples
Reflective	Get mentee to say more about an issue and to explore it in more depth	'You said ..., can you explain in more detail how you mean this?'
Hypothetical	Introduction of new ideas on part of mentor; making suggestions	'What about ...?', 'What if ...?'
Justifying	Obtaining further information on reasons, attitudes, feelings	'Can you elaborate on what makes you think that?'
Probing	Discovering motivations, feelings and hidden concerns	'What would you perceive as the cause of this?', 'When did you first experience that?'
Checking	Establishing whether the mentee has understood clearly	'Are you sure about that?', 'Why do you feel this way?'

at the highest level of competence – generated on the spot as an immediate response.

According to the situation and the learning styles of the mentee, it may be appropriate to present these models in verbal or visual form – or the mentor may not present them at all, and simply use them as the framework for asking probing questions.

Sense of proportion/good humour

Leaving aside the issue of definition – i.e. whether humour qualifies as a competence – seeing the funny side of things certainly has a place in mentoring relationships. Laughter, used appropriately, is invaluable in developing rapport, in helping people to see matters from a different perspective, and in releasing emotional tension. It is also important that mentor and mentee should *enjoy* the sessions they have together.

Goal clarity

Mentors must be able to help learners sort out what they want to achieve and why. This is quite hard to do if you do not have the skills to set and pursue clear goals of your own. Therefore, goal clarity seems to derive from a mixture of skills, including systematic analysis and problem solving, and the skill to plan and organize effectively. Being decisive is another factor that is significant in being able to pursue one's goals. Let us take a close-up look at 'analytical and problem-solving skills' and 'planning and organizing'.

Analytical and problem-solving skills initially help in analysing situations correctly and identifying problems. They also enable one to view issues from different perspectives and to devise a range of solution alternatives. Examining a problem from different angles also helps the mentor to:

- Create objectivity.
- Challenge the feasibility of the mentee's plans.
- Help the mentee choose the best option. Mentors should never dictate solutions to problems; instead, they should develop those skills within mentees that enable them to solve their problems independently. It is the aim of mentoring to create mentees who are self-reliant and can tackle problems in an autonomous manner.

Planning and organizing are closely associated with a mentor's job. For example, part of the mentor's task involves guiding the mentee in devising a structured and logical personal development plan (to be addressed again in Chapter 6). Besides diagnosing development needs, this means enabling the mentee to set timetables and objectives. The mentor should possess excellent organizing and time-management skills to support the mentee in specifying the development plan. Similarly, planning and organizing skills are also essential for the mentor's own continued learning and development.

Flexibility

Being flexible helps mentors to adapt to a variety of changes in their mentee's requirements. For example, although the mentee might most of the time require a 'hands-off' approach to mentoring, in which the mentor poses a lot of questions intended to help the mentee form his or her own solutions, a more 'hands-on' approach might sometimes be useful. This might be true in circumstances where the mentee would like to learn about a specific skill such as 'competency-based interviewing' or, indeed, 'active listening'. Under these circumstances, the approach of the mentor would have to move towards the coaching-facet of mentoring (see 'Integrated model' in Chapter 1). On other occasions, the mentor might have to use more of the 'guardian' or the 'counsellor' approach.

Flexibility is important in other ways within a mentoring relationship. For instance, even though mentees will set up personal development plans that entail certain timescales and objectives, these may need to be changed as the mentoring relationship develops. A rigid approach to mentoring will seriously compromise its value to the mentee.

Attributes

Attributes are types of personal qualities. Contrary to common wisdom, however, they are not genetically destined to remain at a certain level. Like skills and abilities, attributes can be developed.

Patience

Patience is one of the attributes most frequently associated with mentoring. For example, seeing mentees achieve results often takes much longer than mentors had originally envisaged. This requires mentors to stay calm and to understand that mentees have other day-to-day priorities, so they are often not in a position to invest as much time and effort into the mentoring agenda as many mentors might expect. In addition, mentees are typically not as knowledgeable and experienced in the issue of concern as the mentor, so it may take them longer to understand and 'see the light'. In short, the mentor's role can thus involve helping and guiding the mentee to focus on the real issues.

Self-confidence

It is not only mentees who expose themselves by disclosing their problems and weaknesses. Similarly, mentors can also make themselves vulnerable by sharing their wealth of experience with mentees, some of which may be humiliating. In order to expose failures and mistakes, mentors must possess a substantial amount of self-confidence.

Furthermore, mentors are only human. They are therefore prone to making the occasional mistake when advising their mentees. This, in turn, might result in criticisms from the mentee. A mentor must be able to accept these and other types of feedback in a non-defensive way, a reaction that is certainly promoted by a healthy self-confidence.

Being self-assured is also important, as it inspires trust in the mentee and adds credibility, albeit subjective, to the mentor's advice.

Positivity

Being positive and encouraging is a constant need in mentoring relationships. For example, mentees often reach a point where their self-confidence and drive fail, and faced with yet another challenge they may be inclined to give up. In these and similar situations, mentors must continue to build their mentee's self-belief. Mentors must persist in encouraging mentees, motivating them and supporting them to become independent, self-managing, and altogether more competent performers.

Attitudes

Although the knowledge, skills and attributes discussed above are essential for a successful mentoring relationship, initial gaps are not catastrophic. Knowledge can be acquired, and most skills and attributes can be learned and developed. However, the most important determinants of the quality of a mentor are his or her attitudes and beliefs. If these are incompatible with mentoring, the mentoring process runs a high risk of failure, leaving both parties deeply dissatisfied. The attitudes and beliefs that mentors should genuinely hold can be encapsulated as 'a strong interest in developing others'.

A strong interest in developing others

Effective mentors have an innate interest in achieving through others and in helping others to recognize and achieve their potential. This instinctive response is important in establishing and maintaining rapport and in enthusing mentees, building their confidence in what they could become.

Effective mentors manifest this interest in a number of ways, including demonstrating their commitment to the role and being enthusiastic about their mentee. It must be emphasized that entering into a mentoring relationship is a big commitment. It asks mentors to invest a lot of time and effort into someone else's development, sometimes for a considerable length of time. Mentors also have to be frequently available. All of this is only possible if a mentor is whole-heartedly committed to the role. Mentors who do not possess a committed attitude might find the obligation straining and invasive. Most importantly, not being truly involved in the mentoring relationship might compromise its quality and lead to its premature termination.

Enthusiasm for the mentee involves having a very positive attitude towards him or her, and having the mentee's best interests at heart. Mentors should genuinely believe in the mentee's potential to improve his or her performance. They must also take the mentee's problems, desires and aspirations seriously.

Mentee characteristics and behaviours

The potential of a developmental mentoring relationship to bring benefits to the mentee is influenced by a wide range of factors. Among these are the design of the mentoring program and the skills of the mentor. The extent to which a mentee displays certain characteristics and behaviours can also influence the capacity of the relationship to meet the mentee's needs. This means that there will be variations in the degree to which individuals benefit from developmental mentoring. That said, mentees, like mentors, come in all shapes and sizes, but contrary to mentors, for whom a set of specific characteristics exist, the presence of which is vital for the mentoring relationship, mentees have greater freedom of variation when it comes to characteristics.

For example, there is some evidence to suggest that mentees with an *internal* locus of control (i.e. people who see themselves as being in control of their environment and their life) gain substantially greater benefits from developmental mentoring than mentees with an *external* locus of control (i.e. people who believe that everything that happens to them is beyond their influence). To benefit from developmental learning, one must believe in taking charge, in the value of self-managed learning and in taking control of one's life. Because of this attitude, individuals with an internal locus of control might also be more easily able to attract and keep a mentor. Those with an external locus of control will also benefit from mentoring, but may appreciate extra support in taking charge of their own development. In a nutshell, mentees do not have to display all of the characteristics and behaviours described in Table 5.2 in order to benefit from a mentoring relationship. However, the more of them they do demonstrate, and the greater the extent to which they do so, the more value both mentor and mentee will get from the relationship.

Negative mentee behaviours

In contrast to the above, the following constitutes a list of mentee behaviours that do not promote effective mentoring:

- Being distant and consistently suppressing emotions.
- Being argumentative – for example, saying 'That's not what I was told by ...'.
- Being arrogant – for example, saying 'Who are you to tell me anything?'.
- Being uninterested – for example, saying 'Who cares?'.
- Being sloppy – for example, not attending meetings and persistently failing to pursue the goals that have been agreed upon.

Beyond characteristics

Besides mentor and mentee characteristics, there are other factors that influence the extent to which mentees can benefit from a mentoring relationship:

- The mentee's needs and the extent to which a *particular* mentor can meet these (irrespective of mentoring skills).

Table 5.2 Useful mentee characteristics and behaviours for developmental mentoring

Characteristics	Behaviours
✓ Internal locus of control	✓ Takes charge of the relationship, e.g. prepares meetings and sets agenda
✓ Positive attitude to mentoring and development in general	✓ Clearly expresses needs and helps to identify development goals
✓ Openness to feedback and mentor's ideas	✓ Actively seeks the input from the mentor
✓ Able to trust	✓ Demonstrates commitment through following up action-points set in meetings, making time, and attending meetings
✓ Respect for others	✓ Maintains confidentiality
	✓ Seeks to understand the mentoring relationship, e.g. roles, expectations and boundaries

Whilst some mentoring experts argue that a skilled mentor should be able to develop any mentee (irrespective of the mentee's needs), we do not categorically subscribe to this view. Take the example of a fairly young employee, who might be supervisory or junior management. Although this employee might be a great mentor for certain mentees, he or she would be hard pressed to act as a traditional executive mentor. Also, irrespective of skills, the differences between the departments of a company can mean that a particular mentor cannot fulfil a mentee's needs as well as another one could. This scenario is illustrated in the following quotation (Antal, 1993):

The first time the (mentoring) program was run the training consultant tried to mix people from different cultures: she tried matching a mentor from a 'hard' department with one from a 'softer' area in the administration, but found that the cultures of the departments were so different that the people could not understand each other's problems:

- National cultural differences. A variety of research studies have highlighted differences between countries in the extent to which they accept and benefit from mentoring as a developmental approach. Table 5.3 and the following comments will explain this statement in more detail (Laurent, 1981, 1983; Hofstede, 1991; Trompenaars, 1993, 1994).

The national differences described in Table 5.3 could affect people's ability to benefit from developmental mentoring in the following ways:

1. *High uncertainty avoidance*. Mentees are less likely to take readily to *developmental* mentoring. In effect, personal change is not cherished and 'things are fine the way they are'. *Sponsorship* mentoring, on the other hand, may be welcomed. *Low uncertainty avoidance*. Mentees are open to the opportunity for change, so development and progress through mentoring is likely to be welcomed.
2. *Manager as expert*. Anyone of greater seniority, influence or authority than the mentee is perceived as the expert. Thus, a mentor, like a manager, might also be viewed in this way, which means that knowledge is absorbed passively. This stands at odds with the central tenet of developmental mentoring. *Manager as facilitator*. Mentees are likely to give greater legitimacy to learning and development. They are willing to seek and share information with a mentor, as well as welcome the psychosocial functions of the relationship.
3. *Acceptance of input from outside the hierarchy*. Mentees are likely to be open to entering a developmental mentoring relationship with a mentor who stems from any environment – perhaps from another department or external to the company. *Adherence to hierarchy*. Mentees are likely to seek input from people who are in a more or less direct line relationship with them – e.g. their line-manager or his or her boss. Developmental input from an external source is unlikely to be accepted.

Summary

Business knowledge and experience, the right attitude, nine types of skills and three types of attributes: although a mentor

Table 5.3 A sample of national differences on organizational dimensions

Source aspect	Difference	Implications	Relevant countries
Propensity to change	Low versus high uncertainty avoidance	The extent to which people try to control their environment through predictable ways of working	*Low uncertainty avoidance*: Western European countries (e.g. Sweden; the UK; the Republic of Ireland; Norway; and the Netherlands) *High uncertainty avoidance*: European Mediterranean countries (France, Italy and Spain)
Leadership perception	Manager as expert versus facilitator	The extent to which managers are seen as expert knowledge givers	Germany, France and Italy have a high manager-as-expert orientation. Sweden and the Netherlands are relatively low
Communication flow	Acceptability outside the hierarchy versus adherence to hierarchy	The extent to which people are conditioned to seek information, knowledge and views outside the organization	Insufficient data currently available to accurately distinguish between countries

should ideally possess all of these characteristics, some will always be more important with regard to specific mentees than others. Furthermore, mentors are not perfect and must be given a chance to grow into the role of 'people-developer' over time. Mentor characteristics are in part important for mentor *selection*. However, when choosing mentors for your scheme, you cannot expect each of them to score 100 per cent on all of these factors. Therefore, concentrate on the most important selection characteristics. These are that mentors should:

- Possess the knowledge and experience that matches the mentee's needs – in fact, the importance of this particular criterion in mentor selection cannot be over-emphasized.
- Have an interest in and the skills for developing others; be committed to their mentees.
- Be able to build rapport.
- Possess goal clarity and be able to focus others.

Apart from these characteristics, additional criteria for mentor selection will be discussed in Chapter 8.

To benefit from mentoring relationships, mentees also need to display a range of characteristics and behaviours that enable this to happen. These include an internal locus of control and its behavioural manifestation of taking charge of the mentoring relationship. Furthermore, an interest in developing themselves and the ability to respect confidential information are also important.

That said, like mentors, no mentee is perfect either. In selecting mentees for your scheme, it is therefore pivotal to be on the lookout for *negative* mentee behaviours as well as the positive characteristics – be cautious about choosing mentees who display too many of these to too great an extent!

In the last part of this chapter we also highlighted factors other than mentor and mentee characteristics that influence the extent to which a mentee benefits from a mentoring association. Thus, experience–needs match between mentor and mentee is a vital contributor to a mentee's gains, as is (potentially) their membership of a particular national culture.

References

Antal, A. B. (1993). Odysseus' legacy to management development: mentoring. *Eur. Man. J.*, **11**, 448–54.

Clutterbuck, D. (2000). Ten core mentor competencies. *Org. People*, **7**, 29–34.

Hofstede, G. (1991). In: *Mentoring in Mainland Europe and the Republic of Ireland* (J. Walton, ed.). At: http://www.mentorsforum.co.uk

Laurent, A. (1981). In: *Mentoring in Mainland Europe and the Republic of Ireland* (J. Walton, ed.). At: http://www.mentorsforum.co.uk

Laurent, A. (1983). In: *Mentoring in Mainland Europe and the Republic of Ireland* (J. Walton, ed.). At: http://www.mentorsforum.co.uk

Parsloe, E. and Wray, M. (2000). *Coaching and Mentoring – Practical Methods to Improve Learning*. Kogan Page.

Trompenaars, F. (1993). In: *Mentoring in Mainland Europe and the Republic of Ireland* (J. Walton, ed.). At: http://www.mentorsforum.co.uk

Trompenaars, F. (1994). In: *Mentoring in Mainland Europe and the Republic of Ireland* (J. Walton, ed.). At: http://www.mentorsforum.co.uk

CHAPTER 6

Mentoring methods, techniques and processes

There is no one best way of mentoring. The methods, techniques and processes outlined below are merely guidelines for conducting a formal/semi-formal one-to-one mentoring session. We aim to identify those elements that are identical in most mentoring relationships, irrespective of their environment. However, with time, every mentor will adopt his or her own unique style in using the methods, techniques and processes introduced here.

This chapter is divided into five sections. The first section explains what can be done prior to the first meeting and outlines the important elements of a 'typical' *first* meeting. The second section does the same for the second and third meetings, whilst the third section depicts those elements that apply to *all* mentoring sessions. Together the first three sections provide an outline of the mentoring process, and the methods and techniques that tend to be employed within it. The fourth section explores the topic of roles and duties of mentors and mentees in more detail, whilst the last one briefly considers the ways in which the mentoring process changes over a long period of time.

In order to put the next four sections into perspective, let us take a look at a model (based on one by Parsloe and Wray, 2000) that illustrates the mentoring process on a *micro*-level (Figure 6.1).

When reading through the following sections, you will see in more detail what will happen at each of the four stages.

Before entering the first sub-unit it is necessary to emphasize that whichever style a mentor eventually adopts when running the mentoring sessions, he or she must never be autocratic. Mentors should never dictate the agenda of the meetings, let alone the issues to be discussed. The focus has to be on the mentee: it is the mentee's needs that ultimately determine the content and order of the meetings. In short, the mentor's role is to:

- Help the mentee to identify and raise their issues and needs.
- Support the mentee towards goal achievement.
- Provide guidance so as to keep the meeting focused and productive.
- Enable them to become an independent, enthusiastic learner.

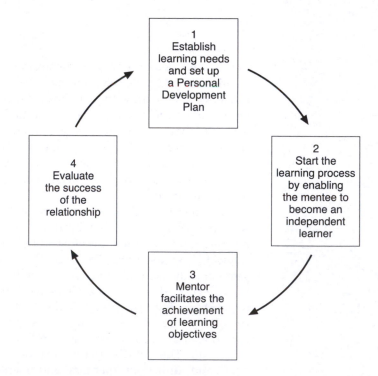

Figure 6.1 Model of business mentoring.

The first meeting/the mentoring relationship

Preparing the first meeting

If you are running a formal mentoring scheme, you will ideally be training your mentees and mentors prior to their first meetings anyway. However, even if this is being done (but particularly if it is not), it is always good for mentors – as well as mentees – to prepare the first meeting. For example, you could encourage them to think about their goals and their mutual expectations in advance. Perhaps they might want to note them down so that the first meeting can become really focused on a discussion of these points, without either party running the risk of forgetting the most important ones. Unless they have not done so already, mentees could also be encouraged to begin thinking about their development needs.

Guidelines for the first meeting

The main purpose of the first meeting is to establish the ground rules for the mentoring relationship and to exchange relevant information. The following points could become part of the process.

Introduction

The first meeting has three main goals:

1. Establishing rapport.
2. Establishing a sense of common purpose.
3. Building an understanding of what each should expect of the other.

To this end, mentors should make every effort to put mentees at their ease. Furthermore, it is useful if they gather as much information about their mentee, the mentee's career and (if appropriate) the mentee's company as possible. Understanding mentees and their situation is vital because problems can only be correctly identified, and tailored development plans designed, when the context is clear.

Mentors might want to ask mentees about:

- Their current job: what tasks are involved, what relationships are important, and how they feel about their role.

- The current climate within the team/department/overall business.
- Their career plans.

Expectations, roles and duties

This is the most vital part of the first meeting, and mentors should invest a lot of time in this. Being clear about the purpose of mentoring, expectations and responsibilities is import-ant in order to eradicate any discrepancies and thereby to pre-vent disappointments. If the mentee has had either training or a brief-ing note or both, mentors can pick up on the relevant information. If the mentee has had neither, the mentor should assume total ignorance and discuss every aspect of the relationship in detail. In doing so, the aim of mentoring should be emphasized and the way in which this is to be achieved explained.

Naturally, expectation management is a two-way process and, like mentors, mentees must be afforded an equal chance to explain what *they* expect from the mentoring relation-ship and from the mentor. Mentees and mentors should also talk about roles and duties. The mentor, for example, might benefit from pointing out that the mentee must make decisions alone and that the mentor does not bear any responsibility for these.

Sometimes expectation management will already have taken place during a training session, which mentors and mentees may even have attended together. However, this will have been on a general level, involving *all* the mentors and mentees who are part of the scheme. It is therefore necessary to resume this topic again in a private environment, where mentor and mentee can exchange their personal opinions regarding their expectations.

Identification of learning needs, goals and objectives

Although mentees may already have mentioned some of their problems, aims and objectives when detailing their expectations, these topics should be discussed in more detail. It might be the case that mentees are not yet clear about what aims they seek to achieve. Identifying these is, of course, an ongoing process, which does not only occur during the first meeting.

Needs and objectives might emerge in various ways: first, the mentee might have worked them out as a result of reflecting upon current performance; secondly, the mentee's line manager or team leader might have been substantially involved in determining these; thirdly, the mentor, through careful questioning, might prompt the mentee to evaluate his or her personal and professional situation, and potential needs and objectives could surface this way. This process could be supplemented through the use of one or two self-assessment questionnaires such as the Myers–Briggs-Type Indicator, a personality inventory. Lastly, through being mentored mentees might discover other aspects of themselves that they would like to develop.

Throughout the first session, you might want to make notes of the development needs and goals put forward by the mentee. If there is to be a formalized personal development plan, these can help to specify goals and objectives.

Identification of learning styles

As explained in Chapter 1, learning is the process of acquiring new knowledge, skills and understanding. However, the way people embark on this process varies greatly. According to Honey and Mumford (1983), who based their model on work by Kolb (1984), there are four disparate types of learning styles: activist, reflector, theorist and pragmatist. Each of these learning styles is associated with a particular stage in the continuous learning cycle (Figure 6.2). The learning cycle illustrates the different phases people go through in order to learn from experience. That said, not all people in every situation will make use of all four phases of the cycle: first, it is possible to enter the cycle at any stage – it has neither beginning nor end; and secondly, people might skip stages because of lack of opportunity to engage in it.

Activists are people who prefer to learn at the 'doing' stage, i.e. at the point where the experience actually happens.

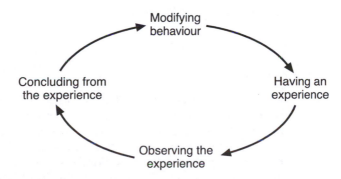

Figure 6.2 The learning cycle.

Reflectors prefer to review what happened, theorists prefer to conclude and develop models or theories, and pragmatists plan for an experience in which they can try out these models.

For mentors to be successful in developing their mentees, it helps to know a mentee's learning style and adjust their developmental efforts to these. Adapting to the mentee's learning style means helping the mentee to identify those learning opportunities from which he or she is likely to benefit most. These would be mainly such that they correspond to the mentee's preferred style. For example, activists might learn best in situations in which they are simply confronted with a new task, such as taking on a role in an usual project without preparation. Adapting to the mentee's learning style also means adapting the way in which the mentor communicates with the mentee. However, the mentor should also encourage the mentee to use the other learning styles, particularly the one least preferred; this is because the best learning occurs only when an individual passes through all four stages of the learning cycle.

Table 6.1 presents some of the characteristics associated with each learning style.

Details of meeting

The frequency of meetings, which could be once a week or once a month, should be agreed upon. Furthermore, the place of the meetings has to be arranged. However, mentoring relationships should be characterized by a certain degree of flexibility in terms of the frequency and duration of meetings. Different arrangements and events may necessitate more or less frequent and longer or shorter meetings. Lastly, an agreement about the etiquette for electronic mentoring (used between face-to-face meetings) should be made.

Exchange of contact details

As a mentor, it is important to demonstrate a willingness to be contactable by providing the mentee with a range of alternative means of getting in touch. This is necessary because mentoring relationships are of a supportive nature, aimed at helping people to cope with their problems. Sometimes urgent problems might arise unexpectedly and need to be dealt with immediately, perhaps by telephone.

Table 6.1 Characteristics associated with the four learning styles

Activists	Theorists
Positive about learning. Use opportunities for development. Are unlikely to plan.	Excellent at identifying underlying causes. Set high standards.
But	*But*
Dislike preparing for and reviewing learning. Can dominate because of their enthusiasm.	May complicate issues and fail to accept the obvious and so fail to get action. Less interested in emotions and feelings.
Reflectors	**Pragmatists**
Not dominating. Prepare well. Good at pulling out learning.	Positive, anticipate improvement. Like practical solutions support relevant learning.
But	*But*
May fail to encourage risk. Do not always grasp opportunities. Sometimes a direct request for help might fail.	Dislike concepts and theories. May not encourage longer term activities. May look for solutions to fit the current culture.

Guidelines for the second/third meeting

The diagnostic plan

During the second meeting, more effort should be put into the further identification of the mentee's development needs through:

- The mentee's own analysis and self-insight.
- The mentee's manager's or team leader's suggestions.

- The mentor's analysis and insight.

If appropriate, a diagnostic plan can emerge based on this analytic process. This is not to be confused with a personal development plan (PDP). Diagnostic plans only serve to describe the mentee's issues and problems in detail and to provide ideas for the personal development plan (see below).

Personal development plan

Many successful mentoring relationships have a very informal approach when it comes to documentation and articulating goals. They might initially focus on rather vague objectives, such as the mentee's ambition to 'get to understand how the organization works'. For these kind of relationships, a deeper developmental agenda may emerge much later in the relationship. The point here is that having a personal development plan from early on is not always necessary to engender a successful relationship. That said, it is not a disadvantage to produce a PDP, and we will now look at how this can be done.

On the basis of the diagnostic plan, mentees can put together their own PDP. In this respect it is important to allow mentees the freedom to take on the responsibility for this process. Try to resist the temptation to point to needs and goals in an attempt to speed up the process. This is vital if you want to send out consistent messages: after all, the learning relationship is supposed to centre around the *mentee's* agenda, and from start to finish the mentee ought to be in control. That said, if the mentee asks for your help because he or she is really stuck, you can of course help out, particularly with:

- The identification of development needs through, for example, self-assessment questionnaires and/or careful reflective questioning.
- Ensuring that the development goals are SMART: specific, measurable, achievable, realistic and timescaled. So, if your mentee suggests as a development need that he or she wants to become the world's most efficient futures and options trader, you might want to ask the mentee to be a little more specific than that: how does he or she define 'most efficient'? What knowledge, skills and abilities does this entail? How does the mentee compare to this ideal at present? What steps does he or she need to take to reach this goal, and when by?

It is very likely that a PDP will have been developed by the end of the second, third or, at the latest, fourth meeting. The plan details the needs of the mentee, the objectives, the agreed means for achieving these and the envisaged timescales. To show you what a simple PDP format looks like, we have included a standard template (Figure 6.3). Feel free to add your own elements to it, though!

Guidelines for *all* meetings

Implementing the personal development plan

Supporting the mentee to realize his or her PDP through learning and development is, of course, the mentor's main task. The following paragraphs, particularly the section on 'Techniques', will give you some insight into how you can help the mentee to achieve this.

Note-taking

Both mentor and mentee could take notes of the issues that are being discussed or mentioned during the meetings. These can be used in the ongoing review of the mentee's progress, but also to diagnose new needs. The written record of the meetings can be used in evaluating the benefits and successes (or difficulties) of the mentoring program. Note-taking is a particularly useful tool for new mentors because it helps them to develop their active listening skills: note-taking aids concentration and focus on what the mentee is saying.

Note-taking is also a useful method to prompt the mentee to keep track of problems that occur between meetings. For example, the mentee might encounter various difficulties whilst managing a particular project, but some of these can be quickly forgotten if not written down.

Techniques

Review of progress

The mentee's progress and the state of his or her development needs should be monitored at regular intervals. In very formal relationships, this would be done at the beginning of each session by looking at the extent to which the mentee has achieved the *action points*, which were set at the end of the previous meeting (see 'Action points', below). After having

Development goal/s:

How will goal/s be achieved? (Add dates to individual steps if appropriate)

Start date:

Meetings/development reviews:

Completion date:

Signed: Signed:

Date: Date:

Figure 6.3 Personal development plan template.

reviewed the action points, the mentee would then set the agenda for *today's* meeting. However, as pointed out in Chapter 4, the degree of formality varies between schemes and pairs and, depending on the rules of your program, mentoring partners will use different versions of this process. Figure 6.4 is a template for a progress/development review.

The aim of a progress review is to see whether the objectives are being met using the suggested means. Monitoring also serves to assess whether the timescales are being adhered to wherever this is vital. Lastly, reviews also involve evaluating whether new or additional goals/objectives have to be set.

To be consistent with the mentor's role of encouraging and motivating mentees, it is crucial that the mentor avoids pointing out mentees' shortcomings. Instead, mentors should mainly draw mentees' awareness to what they have already achieved. In terms of mentees' failures, it is important to help them learn useful lessons from their mistakes. If mentees persistently fail to reach objectives, you could eventually explore with them why – i.e. try to find out why they have chosen not to do something at all or to delay it and, if they still want to achieve a goal, find out what is stopping them. Try not to judge mentees: perhaps they were not aware of procrastinating, or perhaps a certain goal has become obsolete and could be replaced by a new one, or perhaps they are facing major obstacles in its achievement.

Action points

At the end of each meeting, mentees should come out with a list of action points. These should be aligned with mentees' goals and support their achievement. Creating action points is a stepping-stone approach to achieving mentees' final goals; they are designed to move mentees gently forward, allowing them to make accomplishments as they go along. Creating such short-term successes is a good means by which to build mentees' self-confidence and motivation. They also function as measures to monitor mentees' progress.

Pro-active listening and questioning

These are the most important techniques in mentoring. Approximately 80–90 per cent of a mentoring meeting should be spent on listening actively, summarizing or paraphrasing (if appropriate) to reflect back the mentee's thoughts, and question-ing. The remaining 10–20 per cent of the meeting should be spent sharing and discussing ideas, and might also involve the mentor making some suggestions if appropriate – for example, if

Date:

Agenda items:

Issues discussed:

Action points:

Date of next meeting:

Figure 6.4 Progress/development review template.

the mentee is really stuck or in danger of committing a seriously harmful mistake.

Feedback

Providing feedback, negative as well as positive, is another important technique that a mentor has to master. Feedback is highly important for learning to occur because it helps mentees to evaluate their current levels of performance and to understand what needs to be done to shift their performance to a higher level.

The caveat in this connection is to avoid giving unsolicited negative feedback. Uninvited negative feedback can come as a big shock to the recipient, and people are likely to react very defensively. In mentoring relationships, which are very much based on trust and respect, unsolicited negative feedback might – rightly or wrongly – be perceived as a breach of the ground rules.

If you are in a situation where you happen to feel that negative feedback should be given, you might want to ask yourself the following questions prior to stating the feedback: why do I feel that I have to say this to my mentee? Is it really going to be helpful, or is it me assuming the role of a scolding parent? Do I want to tell my mentee because I really have his or her best interests at heart? Really examine your intentions behind your urge to provide negative feedback. If there is any doubt whatsoever as to whether your feedback is well-intentioned and helpful, we suggest you hold back.

If you do decide to give unsolicited feedback, it is best if you start off by asking the mentee whether or not he or she would like to hear what you think about a particular event or behaviour. Should the mentee decline the offer, respect their decision. It might simply not be the right point in time for the mentee to receive negative feedback because he or she might feel emotionally very vulnerable. When giving feedback, it is also important to remember that, as a mentor, you will most likely have acquired the data on which to feed back actually from the mentee (feedback based on observations at work is a method of traditional coaching), and what the mentee is saying may well be a somewhat distorted account of reality. This means that careful questioning in order to establish objectivity is crucial for giving feedback.

Encouraging self-management

The mentor's role in the relationship is not to create dependencies by dictating problem-solving techniques and decisions to their mentees. In order to teach their mentees to be independent, mentors could:

- Encourage mentees to manage the achievement of their objectives themselves.
- Provide their experience as a source for ideas, but let mentees choose and decide.

However, if mentees get stuck in their pursuit of their aims, the mentor might want to:

- Help identify the range of factors that need to be managed in order to achieve the objectives.
- Support mentees in identifying the causes of any difficulties they might experience.

Setting the rules for the relationship: roles and duties of mentors and mentees

In the previous section, we mentioned that discussing mutual expectations is highly important for both mentor and mentee. This process defines the ground rules for the relationship, and is a vital means by which future disappointments can be avoided. Knowing about roles and duties also plays an important part in maintaining a mentoring relationship. This section is devoted to taking a close-up look at the roles and duties of mentors and mentees.

Enhancing learning

For some mentees, the objective of a mentoring relationship may well be *learning to learn*. In this case, mentors must enable them to acquire this skill by, for example, motivating them and opening their eyes to all the different learning opportunities surrounding them. However, many mentees are already very good at learning *per se*, but they do require a source of greater and/or different experience to tap into.

Positive environment

The mentoring relationship should seek to release mentees' potential and motivation so that their performance will be enhanced. This can be achieved by creating a trusting, encouraging and open atmosphere. Most importantly, the mentor must genuinely believe in the mentee's abilities.

Ethical and moral values

Besides asking mentors about business problems that can be solved analytically, mentees tend to discuss ethical issues with their mentors. It is on these occasions that mentors can contribute to the health of society: they should raise mentees' ethical and moral sensitivity. They ought to demonstrate the value of ethical behaviour for business success and depict the downside of unethical actions.

Independence

It is the mentor's role to evaluate whether the mentee shows signs of becoming dependent on the mentor. If this turns out to be the case, mentors must reassess their methods and apply those that encourage independence and self-reliance.

Responsibility

The nature of the mentoring relationship resembles that of friendship. It is (or should be) a voluntary relationship in which the mentor functions as the trusted friend who listens, guides and enables through skilful questioning and, if appropriate, making direct suggestions. Under no circumstances has the mentor any responsibility for the mentee's success or failure. Mentees are solely accountable for decisions and their outcomes.

Failures and mistakes

Besides occasionally sharing their success stories with mentees, mentors might also want to reveal failures and mistakes they have made. This provides mentees with a more realistic view of certain business situations. They are then in a better position to appreciate the problems they might encounter whilst pursuing a goal.

Goals and objectives

Mentors should support mentees in the diagnosis of their developmental needs. Based on these, mentors can then assist mentees in the development of a PDP *if* – once again – this is considered desirable by either the mentee and/or the organization hosting the mentoring program.

Review

Challenging, questioning, and discussing actions are important means of managing performance. In all this, the mentor's role involves stimulating this ongoing review of the mentee's progression towards goal achievement. Mentor and mentee should discuss what the mentee did and why. They should also jointly evaluate whether actions were effective and identify whether outcomes were as expected – i.e. meeting the set objectives.

Options versus direction

If mentees are really stuck in finding a solution to a problem, mentors might want to help them explore a variety of options. However, this should not be done in a directive manner; effective mentors refrain from stressing one solution in particular.

Privacy and confidentiality

Mentoring relationships are of a voluntary, trust-based nature. Both parties often share very personal thoughts and experiences with each other. Mentor and mentee should therefore protect one another's reputation by respecting the confidentiality and privacy of the meetings.

Extended commitment

Mentors must be willing to accept that mentoring relationships transcend the normal office-hours and status distinctions. That is, even if meetings have been scheduled in advance, spontaneous meetings, e-mails or telephone conversations might also be necessary. Mentors should be prepared occasionally to make an extra effort, which might extend beyond what one would consider normal. Such actions go a long way towards making mentees feel valued and reinforcing their self-confidence. On the other hand, mentees must also respect their mentor's privacy and only contact them in a sensible manner.

The mentoring process on a macro level

Having examined the detail of the mentoring meeting, it is appropriate to consider how the mentoring process changes over a long period of time. The main work in this area has been conducted in the 1980s by Katherine Kram (Kram, 1983). She suggested that the mentoring relationship moves through four disparate stages: the start of the relationship (stage 1), the middle period (stage 2), dissolving the relationship (stage 3), and restarting the relationship (stage 4). Kram has since revised her initial definitions of these different stages. Furthermore, it was recognized by European mentoring practitioners and academics that Kram's four stages are not fully representative of what happens during developmental mentoring. For this reason, you will find below a brief description of the stages of American as well as European mentoring. For a more detailed account of these, please refer to *Everyone needs a mentor* (Clutterbuck, 2001).

Stages of mentoring relationships within sponsorship and developmental mentoring

Stage 1: the start of the relationship

Sponsorship mentoring:

- Stage 1 usually lasts for the first 12 months of the relationship.
- In most cases, the mentee tends to idealize the mentor; strongly identifies with him or her, and draws emotional support from the relationship.
- In some cases, the mentor fails to gain the mentee's respect or takes a long time to do so.
- The mentor also feels very rewarded.
- At the end of the first year, rapport is built and confidence created. The relationship can now progress to arrangements for learning.

Developmental mentoring:

- Stage 1 usually takes up to 6 months.
- *Rapport-building* and *direction-setting* are the two main components of this first phase: rapport-building means learning how to work together, building respect and trust; direction-setting means establishing desired outcomes and ways of achieving these.
- Although rapport-building somewhat precedes direction-setting, it is by no means as lengthy and intense as in sponsorship mentoring: deep friendship is not required; mutual respect, goodwill and relevance of experience are important.

Stage 2: the middle period

Sponsorship mentoring:

- Stage 2 usually lasts from year 2 to year 5 of the relationship.
- It is regarded as the most rewarding for both parties: the mentor coaches and promotes the mentee, creates opportunities and helps the mentee to define his or her sense of identity; the mentor gains most satisfaction from knowing that he or she was instrumental in the mentee's development.
- Development goals and career paths are frequently only clarified during this phase.

Developmental mentoring:

- Stage 2 begins at the latest after 6 months, and typically lasts for about 18 months as a formal, supported relationship.
- The mentor is solely a sounding board and has no other role to play in the projects and tasks the mentee undertakes.
- Probing, challenge and analysis characterize this stage.
- The mentee begins to develop greater independence from the mentor.
- Mentors learn as much as or more than the mentee from the mentoring dialogues.

Stage 3: dissolving the relationship

Sponsorship mentoring:

- The mentoring relationship usually draws apart after 2 to 5 years. Reasons include that the mentee has gained new autonomy and has assumed more responsibility for his or her own career objectives. The mentoring relationship might have become superfluous as the mentor has taught all that he or she knew.
- Depending on whether the mentee was prepared for this change or not, he or she will either react with anxiety or will begin to enjoy the newly gained freedom.
- Even after separation has occurred, most mentors will continue to encourage their mentees to advance in their careers. Very occasionally, a mentor might not do so because he or she resents the mentee's greater career opportunities.

Developmental mentoring:

- The winding down phase begins after 24 months, and might last for approximately 6 months.

- Since the primary purpose of developmental mentoring is to foster self-reliance, dissolving the association tends to be less painful than in sponsorship mentoring.

Stage 4: restarting the relationship

Sponsorship mentoring:

- The mentor and mentee continue to interact, albeit on a more casual basis.
- The mentor and mentee now regard each other as equals, and maintain contact on the basis of mutual advantage.
- Occasionally, adjusting to the new peer relationship may involve hostility and aggression on one or both sides.

Developmental mentoring:

- The transitions are similar to those occurring in sponsorship mentoring. However, they tend to be somewhat gentler.
- Mentor and mentee continue to meet but informally, i.e. without agendas and organizational support. They regard each other as equals, as useful sounding boards, as valuable persons in their networks and as a learning resource.
- The relationship tends to transcend into a friendship.

Summary

The mentoring process roughly consists of four stages: identifying development objectives and confirming a personal development plan; encouraging the mentee to implement the plan self-sufficiently; *enabling* the implementation of the PDP; and evaluating the success of the relationship. To facilitate completion of this process (or *cycle*), mentors can utilize a range of techniques and methods – beginning with some preparation prior to the first mentoring meeting. Thus, writing a briefing document for the mentee is a good way to set the scene for a relationship.

The main emphasis of the first meeting is on managing mutual expectations and clarifying roles and duties. In developmental mentoring, these would mainly be such that mentees are responsible for managing the relationship and that mentors support mentees by, for example, focusing them, sharing experiences, and exploring options. The second and third meetings typically focus on consolidating the PDP, and all the following sessions on implementing it. Important techniques that mentors can apply to enable the mentoring process to happen include setting action points, reviewing the mentee's progress, and listening actively.

In the last part of this chapter, we reviewed the phases through which mentoring relationships typically pass. We suggested that there are four distinct phases, the nature of which appear to vary depending on whether it is a developmental or a sponsorship mentoring association.

References

Clutterbuck, D. (2000). *Everyone needs a Mentor*. CIPD.

Honey, P. and Mumford, A. (1983). *Using Your Learning Styles*. Peter Honey Publications.

Kolb, D. (1984). *Experiential Learning*. Prentice Hall.

Kram, K. (1983). Phases of mentoring relationships. *Acad. Man. J.*, **26**, 608–25.

Parsloe, E. and Wray, M. (2000). *Coaching and Mentoring – Practical Methods to Improve Learning*. Kogan Page.

Paving the way for your scheme – the implementation proposal

Formal as opposed to informal mentoring programs involve (Murray and Owen, 1991):

> A structure and series of processes designed to create effective mentoring relationships, guide the desired behaviour change of those involved, and evaluate the results for the protégés, the mentor, and the organization.

By virtue of being facilitated and regulated, formal mentoring schemes promote the attainment of objectives much better than informal programs can. Formal programs can also help to avoid many of the pitfalls associated with informal mentoring relationships, such as the exclusion of employees who find it difficult to network.

Setting up and sustaining a formal mentoring scheme can, however, be an immense task that requires much thought, preparation and determination. This chapter will highlight practical ways of carrying out initial steps in the design and implementation of a scheme. We will consider methods for assessing the organizational *need* and *readiness* for mentoring, and offer suggestions for drawing up a proposal for the mentoring program. Ultimately, this chapter is designed to help you to influence the decision-makers who will either enable or obstruct your plans to run a mentoring scheme. The extent of their buy-in will depend on the quality of your implementation proposal as well as the way in which you present it. Before drawing up your proposal and approaching the potential sponsors on a formal basis, this chapter will encourage you to gather the following information:

- Whether and why your organization might need a mentoring scheme.
- Whether your organization is ready to support a mentoring scheme.
- What potential benefits mentoring holds for the company and its employees.
- What objections you might face with regard to the program.

Part I: Striving for mentoring

A long-lasting and effective mentoring scheme requires putting in place internal structures and systems that support and reinforce the initiative. Furthermore, unqualified support is needed from all those involved. These include top management/the program's sponsors (note that here we will usually equate the sponsors of a scheme to a company's senior management, although we do realize that there are other parties who might sponsor a program, such as the government or Trades Unions), the boss of the mentee, and mentees themselves. Unfortunately, many development initiatives are introduced with little or no prior planning. Even if preparation does occur, inadequate attention is often given to important factors – frequently resulting in programs that fail to realize their objectives.

The two parties who help to ensure the success of a mentoring program from the early stages are:

- A competent and committed mentoring champion, and
- Supportive senior managers.

We will now take a look at each of these two parties, the reasons for their importance, and their role in the program's initiation process. In the following sections we will cover the research and documentation that is necessary to gain a positive response to your proposal. The last part of this chapter will consider the contents of the implementation proposal.

The mentoring champion

The mentoring champion is important because it is his or her task to carry out comprehensive analyses, plan thoroughly and provide the appropriate direction for the scheme. The nature and scope of the champion's role is likely to vary based on the size and preferences of an organization. So, for example, an organization of five people may cede responsibility for the entire process, including implementation and evaluation, to one individual. In a company of 20 people, responsibility for the process may lie with the champion, but with opportunities to receive input and assistance from others. In large organizations with employees that number in their hundreds or even thousands, the ability of one person to fulfil the range of roles in the entire process is likely to be limited. In these situations, there is often one formal champion, supported by several other people in the organization. Very often, the role of the program champion will later evolve into that of the *program co-ordinator*, the person bearing the main responsibility for the implementation and running of a mentoring scheme (this role will be described in more detail in Chapter 8). For the purpose of this book, we will assume that the champion *will* later become the program co-ordinator and *will* be responsible for driving the further implementation and evaluation of the scheme.

Let us now consider Table 7.1 to obtain a more thorough understanding of the role of the mentoring champion.

The champion's role is perhaps the most important in the design and implementation process, so mentoring champions should be (Nilles, 1998):

- Self-motivated and enthusiastic about the program.
- Familiar with mentoring/mentoring schemes.
- Excellent at project management.
- At a fairly high level in the organization – although the mentoring champion does not have to reside in the uppermost management levels, he or she should possess enough clout and experience to get things done.
- Willing to put in the time to make the program work, even if this might be in addition to his or her other duties.
- Sufficiently diplomatic so that the planning and implementation can proceed with minimal friction.

Table 7.1 Information required for the implementation proposal

✓ Whether and why your organization might need a mentoring scheme
✓ Whether your organization is ready to support a mentoring scheme
✓ What potential benefits mentoring holds for the company and its employees
✓ What objections you might face with regards to the program

- Sufficiently well-connected to be known and respected across the organization.

Senior management support is vital

The drive for an organization to adopt mentoring may come from a range of sources. It may be based on the desires or needs of employees, the requests of the training/HR function, or the wishes of shareholders. Whatever the impetus for mentoring, a characteristic of today's business is that senior management and executives typically carry the decision-making power. They can permit the scheme to take place and provide the necessary monetary resources. Senior management can also provide their personal backing, including showing commitment and enthusiasm, which influences other organizational members to accept and support the scheme. Their attitudes and behaviour are extremely powerful determinants of the evolution of a scheme for better or worse.

Part II: Preparing the implementation proposal – conducting the necessary research

Before you can dive into writing your proposal for the implementation of a mentoring scheme, you should embark on a research campaign. The aspects you need to obtain information about are:

- Organizational readiness for mentoring.
- Organizational need for mentoring.
- The benefits of mentoring schemes.
- Potential objections to the scheme.

Why is it necessary to conduct this kind of research? The overriding purpose is to evaluate the fit between your organization and a mentoring scheme, and to gather evidence that corroborates your argument in favour of its implementation. Whoever is going to sponsor this program is not likely to do so if they perceive your rationale as poor and cannot see sufficient organizational benefits resulting from its implementation. The information acquired during your research phase allows you to assess and express the business consequences of progressing or not progressing with a mentoring scheme. So, if you are serious about this project, conducting the research that qualifies its establishment is vital.

Additional reasons for conducting preparatory research include that it will:

- Provide you with a framework for the design and implementation of the scheme. For example, by researching the needs of your employees, you will find it easier to set effective program objectives and to identify your mentee target group.
- Enable you, the mentoring champion, to evaluate the risks to your reputation associated with pressing ahead with the scheme. For instance, an organizational readiness analysis that reveals that your culture is not conducive to a mentoring program will prompt you to stop your efforts and rethink. This may save you from great potential embarrassment!

We will now take a good look at the four research areas mentioned above, starting with a diagnosis of organizational readiness.

Research stage I: organizational readiness for mentoring

The idea for establishing a mentoring scheme rarely ever appears out of the blue, and you will probably have a fairly good idea of why your organization might need such a program. However, before you devote your time to verifying this need, and certainly before you begin to implement a program, you should research whether your organization would be able to sustain a mentoring scheme. Primarily, this means assessing whether top managers and executives are likely to sponsor the program both financially and by showing general goodwill and commitment. We both know from our experiences in setting up mentoring schemes and from interviewing the organizations that contributed case studies to this book just how influential management support can be. This sentiment is excellently summarized in a statement made by Nick Holley, who at the time was Personnel Director at Lex:

> The most important facilitator of mentoring in Lex has been the strong commitment of top management. The top team value mentoring as a means of growing the strategic competence of the business, and all have been actively involved as mentors. They were the first people to use the process, they have seen the benefits, and are now able to give credibility to mentoring and act as role models for this form of management development.

Coincidentally, this quotation also highlights one of the key tests to apply in order to evaluate your management's likely support: ask them whether they would be prepared to act as mentors themselves. If not, they probably do not really understand the value of the scheme, and are therefore also unlikely to commit to it on a large scale.

Conducting an organizational readiness analysis also means assessing whether your employees would want to be mentored. Some individuals may harness fears and concerns that prevent them from entering into mentoring associations – for example, they may not believe that confidentiality will be kept. Furthermore, in some organizations there may also be a more widespread disinclination to engage in mentoring relationships. This is often based on the view that mentoring is a 'sign of weakness' (i.e. you get a mentor if there is something wrong with you). Lastly, you need to find out whether training and development are generally valued within the organization.

Company support is vital; without it, no mentoring scheme will work. In summary, your organizational readiness analysis must provide answers to the questions in Table 7.2.

Depending on the extent to which you are familiar with your organization's culture and its HRD philosophy, you should be able to answer the majority of the above questions yourself. You could also consult with a few select colleagues, such as those in the HRD function, as well as representatives of senior management levels.

If you feel at any time that there are strong objections to the scheme, assess how valid they are, who they come from, and what impact they will have. In any case, you must deal with them by speaking with the individuals voicing their concerns. Later on in this chapter, we will look at commonly occurring objections and ways of addressing these.

Table 7.2 Questions to establish organizational readiness for mentoring

Value attached to human resource development (HRD) in general?	Viability of a *mentoring* scheme (as opposed to other training and development approaches)?
✓ Does management view HRD as a priority?	✓ Would a mentoring scheme fit with the organizational culture?
✓ Do managers allow time for their employees to engage in training and development activities or are other tasks always more important?	✓ Would top and middle management embrace it wholeheartedly, i.e. would they act as mentors themselves, would they support it?
✓ Are financial resources readily available for employee development?	✓ Are employees likely to be receptive to mentoring? Will they be interested in taking it up or would it not appeal to them?
✓ Is the management philosophy to grow talent as opposed to buying it?	✓ Does your culture encourage personal change and development, and value initiative and risk-taking?
✓ Do employees value development opportunities?	✓ Would you be able to recruit sufficient numbers of *volunteer* mentors?
✓ Are the people who develop others recognized for this?	✓ Will there be sufficient numbers of off-line mentors avilable?
	✓ Are your potential mentors able and willing to persist with the relationship for its entire duration?
	✓ Will you be able to find the right people for the design, implementation and running of the scheme?
✓ Is the organization generally committed to and supportive of the evaluation of development activities?	✓ Will it be possible to integrate mentoring with the total program of employee training and development?

Research stage II: organizational need for mentoring

The *purpose* of researching a company's need for mentoring can be summed up in the following questions:

- Does your company have a business need that requires training and development attention?
- What exactly is this need, and amongst which employee groups does it exist?
- Is mentoring the best method for addressing this need, or would other (existing) training and development approaches be more suitable?

If your research reveals that you do need a mentoring program, you then have the basis for a strong argument to implement the scheme. Having established the need for mentoring in your organization means that your program objectives will follow naturally, and that the whole process of designing the scheme will be somewhat simplified. There are three main ways of identifying whether your organization does have a need for mentoring, and these are illustrated in Figure 7.1. Although these methods are described as disparate, this is not entirely true since they do contain some over-lapping elements. For example, all of them require you to consult with top management.

Over the following pages, we will explain all of these methods individually. However, before you move on to reading these explanations, we must point out to you the assumptions

Figure 7.1 Methods to establish an organization's need for mentoring.

underlying the *organizational needs analysis* (ONA). As it is described here, carrying out an ONA is only relevant if your need for mentoring is related to business needs that can be met through specific improvements in employees' competencies and experience. For instance, when mobile telephone manufacturers Ericsson realized that they needed to develop the global management capability of their young managers, they had both a specific business need and a need for mentoring that could be translated into competency requirements. That is, their managers lacked certain types of knowledge and skills that could be fostered through mentoring. However, organizational needs for mentoring can also be of a nature different to that – for example:

- The need to retain staff.
- The need to create greater awareness of women's issues amongst senior management.
- The need to motivate certain employee groups.

With these needs, it is not necessarily human competence that is deficient. Even if it is, it is not a particular set of knowledge and skills deficits that apply to the entire employee target group – it might be entirely different deficits for different people. Should your need for a mentoring scheme fit better with the latter category, an ONA will probably not apply to you. It is more likely that you will have established your mentoring objective through organic means (see below).

An organic establishment of need

Sometimes organizations choose not to go through the rather formal process of an organizational needs analysis. Most of the time this is because they already have a very firm idea that their organization needs a mentoring scheme. This idea is often based on the observations of management in relation to business goals.

Although it has its advantages, an organizational needs analysis cannot be forced upon top management, and trusting that they know their business and its employees has to suffice. As pointed out above, an ONA is also often not applicable when, for example, the need for mentoring cannot be translated into specific competency requirements. However, if appropriate, you might want to suggest conducting a training needs analysis (see below) on the group of people identified by management as the mentee target group. This enables you to verify that they really do need development support in order to acquire the competencies they are supposed to possess. If they did not, you might decide not to set up a mentoring scheme after all, or to do it for a different reason, such as motivating employees and showing them that you value them.

The organizational needs analysis

The stages of an organizational needs analysis (ONA) are as follows:

- Stage 1: consulting with senior management about business goals and needs.
- Stage 2: translating business needs and goals into human resource development needs.
- Stage 3: assessing the people.
- Stage 4: so there is a need for development, but is there a need for *mentoring*?

Before exploring the individual stages of a needs analysis, we would like clarify that not all companies conduct such research in order to establish their mentoring needs. Some of them will simply determine their needs organically, i.e. by observation and consultation with top management. Even if organizations do carry out a needs analysis, there will be variations in the extent to which this is done. The following factors will typically direct your decision as to how deeply you wish to delve into this activity:

- *Senior management's judgment.* If the impetus for your mentoring scheme came directly from top management, then there may be already a very firm idea of what business needs would be addressed through mentoring. This will limit or even obviate the necessity for any lengthy and formal needs analysis. Yet it is still a good idea to *verify* their judgment, even if this only means checking some succession planning data or putting the idea to relevant people such as division heads, function heads or team leaders. Verifying management's perception of the need for a mentoring program simply serves the purpose of determining whether organizational resources will be put to best use.
- *Your observations.* Depending on your role in the organization, you may have a very clear idea of why a mentoring program may be useful. You may also be a very influential person who can approach and convince (other) senior managers of the value of mentoring. If you are fairly sure that your perception

of a need for mentoring is accurate, you may again decide to limit your organizational needs analysis.

- *Finally, the HRD budget.* Sometimes budgetary limitations will determine the extent to which you can engage in an ONA.

So, depending on the above three factors, you may engage in one, two, or all of the stages of an ONA.

Stage 1: consulting with senior management about business goals and needs

Asking senior management about their business plans for the near and far future, as well as gathering their views on the business's needs, will go a long way towards identifying a need for mentoring. Involving them at this stage also serves the purpose of gaining their buy-in to the scheme: perhaps they had not analysed their needs and goals for a while? Perhaps they never realized the existence of a particular need? During this consultation, it is up to you to facilitate and structure managers' thinking – in essence, you will be acting as their team mentor during this activity.

To inspire and guide managers' thinking, you might want to ask them the following questions:

1. What are senior management's short-term and long-term plans and goals?
2. What factors could impact on the business in the near/far future?
   - *External*:
     New technology?
     Changes in customer behaviour?
     Activities of competitors?
     Changes in legislation?
     Changes in the economy, e.g. market deregulation?
   - *Internal*:
     A planned merger or takeover?
     Strategic changes?
     Structural changes?
     Process/operational changes?
     Cultural changes?
3. Based on the above, what business needs do currently exist? Are they likely to change and when?
4. Which factors might hinder the achievement of goals?

The end result of stage 1 should be that you have gained a clear picture of what business needs there are as well as an idea of which employee groups might be most important for achieving these. These employee groups, by the way, could be your potential mentee target group.

Stage 2: translating business needs and goals into human resource development needs

You have now defined your business needs and gained an idea of the group of employees that requires attention, in order to address these. Equipped with this, you can move on to determining whether business needs can be translated into specific human resource requirements. This means attempting to translate them into competencies, their underlying components (knowledge, skills and attitudes), and experience. The following questions will help you to translate business needs into HR needs:

1. What people do we need in order to achieve our business goals? Which employee groups/company divisions are the most crucial?
2. Which competencies, knowledge, skills and attitudes, and experience do they have to possess in order to support the company in achieving its goals? Now/in the future?

You could at this stage also hazard a guess at whether the employees you have selected as the target of your development efforts already possess the necessary competencies and experience. However, this guess should definitely be verified, which is the task of stage 3. Answering all of these questions should again be done in collaboration with top management.

Having answered all stage 1 and stage 2 questions in collaboration with senior management will mean that you have gained a good idea of which employee groups might require development – if indeed any. Thus, a certain company division and/or a particular group of employees, such as the graduates or managers within a division, might have evolved as the target group. Fortunately, it will therefore be unnecessary to conduct a stage 3 needs analysis of *all* job families/*every single* employee in the organization.

Stage 3: assessing the people

The main objective of stage 3 is to establish whether your employee target group already possesses the competencies and experience required for business goal achievement. Even if you are fairly sure that it does not, you should conduct a thorough analysis in order to identify the exact elements on which it requires development and the extent of the support needed.

This type of information will help you accurately to answer later questions, such as whether mentoring is the best method for addressing your employee's needs.

The main way to determine to what extent your target group already possesses the required competencies involves conducting what is commonly known as a *training needs analysis* (TNA).

TRAINING NEEDS ANALYSIS

What is a TNA? Once you have determined what competencies and experience you would like to see amongst your employee target group, you have to determine the extent to which the group possesses these. This is precisely what a TNA does: it is a process by which one identifies the gap between individuals' actual and required performance (Hackett, 1997). By the end of a thorough needs analysis, you should have a very clear picture of both group and individual deficits with regard to competency requirements. These results can then feed into whichever training or development approach you choose – and thus individuals may obtain a personalized learning plan, which promotes setting targeted development objectives.

How to conduct a TNA: Before we look at the individual steps associated with conducting a TNA, we would like to emphasize that this task should not be conducted in solitude – that is, for each of the following steps, you should consult as many relevant people as possible rather than working alone. The parties to involve include, once again, senior management, but also those knowledgeable about the job role you are investigating – e.g. job incumbents, line managers/team leaders, function heads etc. In addition, when assessing your employee target group against the set criteria (see below) you should make every effort to involve the individuals concerned. Refrain from only asking their team leaders or managers to identify whether these individuals possess/do not possess the required competencies.

Involving the actual target group in making the needs assessment has two major advantages: first, it will make your assessment more accurate because you will have the opportunity to speak with people directly and observe for yourself; secondly, it will mentally prepare them for the fact that they will be offered some form of training and development soon. Whatever development approach you are going to select in the end, the employees will perceive it as more relevant if they have been given a chance to be active in diagnosing their needs.

So, what are the steps associated with conducting a TNA?

1. Define your competency requirements in detail:
   - What exactly are these competencies?

- What behaviours are associated with each of these? If, for example, one of your competencies is 'customer responsiveness', the behaviours associated with it might include: reacts to client needs in a timely and effective manner; clarifies client expectations; checks for satisfaction; prioritizes client needs; anticipates client needs.
- What knowledge, skill and attitude components does any one competency consist of?
- To what level would you like to see individuals displaying these competencies? Boydell and Leary (1997), for example, distinguish between three levels of performance: implementing – doing things well; improving – doing things better; and innovating – doing new and better things.

2. Decide which employees you wish to assess against the competency requirements: do you want to assess all of them, or just a representative sample? If your target group is very large, the latter may be the more feasible option.

3. Assess your employee target group against the defined competencies. Among the methods that can be used to establish the extent and nature of training needs are:
   - Interviews and/or questionnaires that can be administered to your target group as well as to their team leader/manager.
   - (360 degree) performance appraisals involving interviews, questionnaires, and existing performance data.
   - Assessment/development centres involving role plays, case studies, group exercises, in-trays and/or presentations.
   - On-the-job observation.
   - Psychometric tests such as personality or aptitude tests.

Before we move on to stage 4, one last comment about the potential outcomes of your people analysis: what do you do if the people you thought destined for a particular role require *too much* development? What if they demonstrate such extreme competency deficits that it seems more efficient to recruit alternative employees? The answer to these questions will entirely depend on you – more specifically, it will depend on your organization's commitment to grooming its own talent. If you believe that your employees have potential and that competency deficits could be erased through mentoring, mentoring is certainly more cost- and time-effective than recruiting.

Stage 4: so there is a need for development, but is there a need for mentoring?

Let us assume that your TNA has revealed that your employee target group is not up to speed with its competency requirements and will need some form of development. How do you decide which one? Is mentoring best? Perhaps a combination of approaches is needed? The best way to find a solution to this problem is to begin by critically examining your list of development needs. In relation to these, try to answer the following questions:

1. By when does the target group have to have acquired them, and to what standard?
2. What is the available budget?
3. How many people require training and development?

When you have answered these questions, write down the whole range of training and development approaches available to you (e.g. mentoring, traditional training courses, self-study etc.). Next, list the benefits and limitations of each approach and, when doing so, consider the answers you gave in response to the above questions.

Completing these steps should already have given you a fairly good idea as to what approach (or which combination of approaches) is best suited to fostering the desired competencies amongst your target group. However, in order to get a professional answer to the question of whether and how mentoring could help, you might want to consult with someone who is highly knowledgeable in this field. For example, in Case study 3.2, the District Audit case study, we mentioned that David Clutterbuck was commissioned to evaluate whether mentoring could help them to meet their business needs.

If and when your organizational needs analysis finally reveals that it is mentoring you should aspire to, you can slowly begin to design your program – slowly, because first there might be some additional research to do.

Succession planning

Another way to establish whether there is a need for mentoring involves consulting first with the people responsible for a company's succession planning. This would typically be the HR/HRD department, but speaking to department heads can also be worthwhile. Jointly, they should be able to provide you with insight into your organization's supply and demand situation. Their databases ought to contain information about:

- The number of people needed with regard to certain job groups.
- The point at which these people are needed (if at all).

- What competencies and experience the job roles require of the jobholder.

Considering this information will enable you to see which job groups and individuals might need mentoring support to prepare them for or help them to adapt to their new roles.

The succession planning approach assumes that you have not yet spoken to (other) senior managers about their perceptions regarding the company's need for mentoring. It means:

1. Considering employee data first.
2. Noting demand: which job roles will require to be filled, by when and with how many people? What competencies and experience is required of them?
3. Assessing supply: who within the organization might be able to fill these roles? Do they already possess the necessary capabilities?
4. Devising strategies for providing supply: will we train and develop our talent to fill these roles, or will we buy in? If we develop our own talent, which method should we use? Could mentoring be the most effective way to prepare people for these roles?

Using succession planning data in order to establish a need for mentoring goes much further than these four steps; you must always also talk to management about the organization as a whole – what plans and goals do we have for the organization? What internal and external factors will affect the organization in the near/far future? What factors could affect the group of employees we would like to develop? So using the succession planning method to identify an organizational need for mentoring does not obviate management input; it simply delays it to a later point. Once you have discussed your data and ideas with management, you might actually find that your plans have changed – for example, an employee group different from the one you had envisaged might require mentoring more urgently.

As with the 'organic method' of establishing a need for mentoring, the succession planning method should ideally be supplemented through conducting a training needs analysis. Again, this is to *verify* whether your employee target group does need development, to what extent it needs it, and on what competencies.

In the rest of this chapter we will assume that your research so far has revealed that there is a need for mentoring in your organization, that your organization is 'ready' for it, and that you will now want to go ahead with designing and implementing the program.

Research stage III: the benefits of mentoring schemes

What benefits do mentoring schemes typically bring to mentors, mentees and organizations (see Chapter 2)? What specific benefits could it bring to your organization? Would it be a cost-efficient, effective and targeted development approach? Would it help to achieve desired business goals? Would it enhance the organizational image in the eyes of the customer? What other positive impact might it have on the organization? It goes without saying that potential sponsors will be more likely to commit to a program that has clear and tangible benefits for them and the business. To find answers to the question of what benefits mentoring might have for your organization, you could:

- Consider the research findings presented in Chapter 2.
- Locate new research.
- Look at case studies of mentoring schemes.
- Speak to (and learn from) colleagues and contacts who have implemented a mentoring program.

Research stage IV: potential objections to mentoring

Whichever method you chose to establish an organization's need for mentoring, it will in the very least have involved a discussion with senior management. Perhaps you also conducted a training needs analysis, or simply chatted to some organizational members about the forthcoming mentoring scheme. Either way, you will probably have gained a good idea of how people feel about this whole project, including their concerns.

Identifying and dealing with individuals' concerns regarding the mentoring scheme is equally, if not more, important than emphasizing all its benefits. This is because the people with concerns that are left unattended are the ones most likely to spoil your plans – be they potential financial sponsors, potential participants, or those who are not allowed to enter the mentoring scheme because they do not fit the mentee target group. It is therefore in the best interests of your scheme to identify all concerns and to deal with them as soon as possible. Beware that many concerns may only be voiced when you are proposing to the potential sponsors of the scheme. Since you will not always have the opportunity to hear about all of them in advance, you can use the notes below to prepare for the most commonly expressed worries.

Before considering these concerns, however, we would like to introduce you to a generic six-point strategy for dealing with objections (Maurer, 1998).

Handling concerns and objections

1. *Embrace and acknowledge objections*. Encourage people to express their concerns and the reasons behind them. This approach enables you to understand why the initiative is being opposed, and to deal with this in more concrete terms. By embracing and acknowledging objections, you will be able to establish whether they are:
   - To the idea.
   - To the way the initiative is to be implemented.
   - To you, the champion.
   - To the timing of the announcement/adoption of the initiative.

2. *Listen to people with an open mind in a climate of trust and mutual respect*. This way, you are creating a positive environment for dealing with objections. Make a special effort to avoid attacking others' views, maintain a clear focus, and use information to seek common ground. Behaving like this is beneficial because you are setting an example – you are determining the tone of engagement between you and them, which most people will tend to adopt.

3. *Be honest in communicating the elements of the initiative*. You may not be able to answer all questions and concerns at once, but they must be acknowledged and not simply glossed over. As the situation becomes clearer, employees should be kept informed openly and honestly. Perceptions that you are bluffing or being evasive are likely to generate negative responses.

4. *Emphasize mutual benefits*. Much of the resistance to new initiatives (including mentoring programs) is based on a perceived lack of benefit for certain people, and they will want to know what they stand to gain. It is therefore important that you pay special attention to answering the 'what's in it for me?' question. However, you should also point out the benefits for you (e.g. the organization) as well as the *combined* benefits, i.e. the joint benefits for mentors, mentees, line managers, the organization, and you, the mentoring champion. This will provide people with a clearer understanding of the need for the initiative.

5. *Establish all the issues first and then embark on finding solutions*. If at all possible, try to collate the total amount of objections prior to addressing them. This provides you with a clearer overall picture of what these issues are. Furthermore, it will prevent you from involuntarily solving one problem at the expense of another. As an example, take the hypothetical scenario in which top management object to a mentoring

initiative on cost grounds, insisting on a cheaper scheme. Your potential mentors, on the other hand, object on time grounds. If you deal with these as they arise, you might exacerbate the situation with one of the parties. Thus, if senior management voice their concerns first, you might promise them immediately that the scheme will become more cost-effective by obliging mentors to take on five mentees instead of one. Whilst this approach might please top management, it is likely to leave you with next to no mentors.

In addition to collating the total range of objections, you should also endeavour to involve people in finding solutions. Ask them, for example, how they would like to see the issue addressed.

6. *Accept that not everyone will come on board.* Schneider and Goldwasser (1998) emphasize that, even when objections are addressed effectively, there is no guarantee that all employees will go along with the initiative. The advice is to avoid giving entrenched objectors too much attention, as this typically reinforces the problem behaviour. Proceeding despite them and being willing to 'let squeaky wheels squeak' may be the last resort!

Having considered the above six-point strategy for dealing with objections, let us now examine their nature in more detail: what are the most commonly voiced concerns when it comes to the implementation of mentoring programs?

Common concerns about mentoring programs

It is unlikely that the fears described below will materialize for your particular scheme. Still, they must be taken seriously and addressed to the satisfaction of the relevant parties. We emphasize strongly that most of the fears described below are the result of distorted conceptions about the nature of mentoring. Providing *all* organizational members with thorough information as to what mentoring entails will counteract the occurrence of most of them.

Let us now take a look at the objections:

'What if the mentor actively sponsors the mentee so that the mentee will be promoted and I will not?'

There is a whole range of measures you can take to minimize or erase fears such as this. First of all, educating all of your employees with regard to the role of a mentor is highly important – sponsoring employees is not an aspect of a mentor's role, at least not in a European context. It is equally effective to advise your employees that adherence to this role is taken very seriously within the scheme: point out that mentors and mentees will know what is expected of them because they will undergo an effective training session. In addition, you could point out that mentoring relationships are monitored (if this applies to your scheme). Secondly, removing the influence of the mentor over the mentee's promotion as much as possible will also reassure people. Thus, having off-line mentoring relationships and possibly matching mentors and mentees from different departments is going to support this endeavour.

'What if the mentor helps the mentee to carry out his or her work tasks?'

Other employees may be concerned about this – jealous, in fact. However, given the nature of mentoring, this is an unrealistic fear that you can once again reduce through informing all organizational members about the nature of mentoring. Advise everyone of the mentor's and mentee's roles and responsibilities. Emphasize in particular that mentees are supposed to use their learning to perform their work, and not to get the mentor to do it. Besides, most mentors would neither want to nor have the time to assist mentees in carrying out their job.

'What if a mentoring relationship turns into a personal relationship?'

Since we have previously touched on this topic, you will probably remember that occurrences of this kind are very rare indeed – so to begin with, you can reassure those concerned of this fact. To back this up, it would be good if you found research evidence or anecdotal reports from other companies or divisions that run mentoring schemes. Next, you should also formulate program guidelines stating that sexual relationships between mentors and mentees are prohibited, and that the onset of such a relationship will lead to the immediate termination of the mentoring association.

'What if there are going to be cases of harassment or discrimination?'

Again, you can reassure everyone that this is highly unlikely. However, should it occur, it will be taken very seriously and dealt with by the company's existing policies and procedures concerning such matters.

'What if the mentor infringes on my (the line manager's) territory?'

First, make clear to both line managers and mentors where the boundaries of a mentoring relationship lie – i.e. mentors are not to interfere with work tasks given by the line manager; they are not to discuss the line manager with the mentee in negative terms; and they are not to get involved in conflicts between the line manager and the mentee. Emphasize that competing against the mentee's boss is certainly not one of the mentor's roles; instead, it is to complement the opinions of the line manager and to assist the mentee in developing a better relationship with his or her manager and team. It may be appropriate to involve the line manager in the relationship, and, once again, demystify what mentoring is – really ensure that the line manager knows how the mentor's role differs from his or her own role, and point out the benefits to be gained from having an employee who is being mentored.

'What if the mentoring will lead my employee to neglect his or her usual work tasks?'

In everything you say or write about the mentoring scheme, emphasize that mentoring should be undertaken in addition to (and not at the expense of) daily work tasks. Point out that mentees are being trusted to maintain their responsibilities to the organization. In addition, monitor the mentoring relationships so that issues such as the neglect of daily work tasks can be flagged up.

'If I receive mentoring, will people think that I am incompetent or inferior?'

Programs that are specifically geared towards supporting organizational minority groups may arouse these concerns amongst mentees. The ideal way to overcome this would be to offer mentoring schemes to other employee groups so that it becomes clear that mentoring is not 'something for the weak'. Thus, running several mentoring schemes (some of them for high flyers and some for senior people) would be a good way of eradicating this prejudice. Furthermore, whatever publicity you engage in with regard to a minority mentoring scheme should be phrased as clearly and positively as possible. It is important to show that mentoring has benefits for everyone, and asking some top managers to talk about their experiences as mentees might be a good way of demonstrating its true value.

'What if I am essentially grooming the mentee to take over my job?'

Although mentors might be afraid that their input into the mentoring relationship means that the mentee will overtake them in ability and therefore take on their job, this fear should really be very rare in a formally organized scheme. This is because the mentor should not be the direct line manager of the mentee. It is also important to ensure that your processes for advancing employees are generally clear, fair and objective, in order to prevent perceptions of unfair advantage.

'What if our HRD/training department feels threatened by the mentoring program because they believe that their role in employee development has been diminished?'

It is highly important to involve your human resource/training personnel in the scheme: they could be made responsible for integrating the mentoring with other training and development activities. Thus, explain to them that mentoring is not meant to replace other methods, but that it is a complementary facility, which has to be co-ordinated with others. HRD/training could also, as is often the case, take on the responsibility of managing the scheme (for example, the program co-ordinator might be the head of training and development).

'What if the program does not lead to any bottom-line benefit, such as improvements in employee performance?'

Although there is a paucity of statistical evidence for mentoring improving work performance, there is substantial anecdotal information from mentors and mentees. Generally, mentees find that mentoring helps them to improve their performance – they learn to adapt to new roles more rapidly, and they tend to gain specific skills through mentoring, such as managerial skills. Furthermore, mentees report that mentoring has helped them to gain promotions and generally to be more successful at work. Furthermore, mentors often tend to improve their people development skills, and there is certainly a lot of evidence that mentoring improves motivation and satisfaction for both mentors and mentees. Notwithstanding the fact that there is no *direct* relationship between these two variables and performance, it makes good logical sense to assume that extreme *de-*motivation and *dis-*satisfaction at work will have a negative impact on performance. So, if nothing else, mentoring will at least have a positive *influence* on performance.

To convince your sceptics, you might want to revisit some of the evidence presented in this book (in the forms of both case and research studies). In Chapter 2, for example, we emphasized that mentoring is typically associated with many organizational benefits. To remind you, this included:

- Better recruitment and retention of key staff.
- Reinforcement of culture change.
- Increased productivity.
- Communication across boundaries.
- Developing two for the price of one.

Many of these will have an effect on overall company performance, even if this is indirect and can only be seen over the long term. Furthermore, some companies have started to compare mentees' appraisals year-on-year with those of their non-mentored peers. Mentees make greater progress than others on the competencies that they have worked out with their mentors.

Conduct your own research – there is always fresh evidence (both anecdotal and statistical) coming out. Perhaps you can gather information from personal accounts of mentors and mentees, and complement this with evidence from mentoring schemes run in other organizations/divisions. Lastly, but very importantly, be honest and clear about why you would be implementing the program in the first place: often this is not *directly* to improve performance, but to address another need instead (e.g. managing organizational diversity or helping women returning from maternity leave to adjust). In this case, looking for performance improvements (when this was not the reason for implementing the program) seems unwarranted.

Part II: The implementation proposal

To recap, you should by now have accumulated the following data:

- Information on whether and why your organization might need a mentoring scheme.
- Information on whether your organization can sustain it.
- A list of the potential benefits of mentoring for your company and its employees.
- Insights into potential objections to the program and responses to these issues.

In gathering these data, you should already have spoken to one or several of the individuals who you will soon officially approach as the scheme's sponsors. This preparation means that you will be ready to embark on writing a powerful proposal for the establishment of a mentoring scheme. However, be prepared to adapt the contents of your proposal; it is rarely the case that a proposal will retain 100 per cent of its original contents. When approaching sponsors with the proposal, you should be prepared to *present* on the topic as well as providing them with a written version of the proposal. For many sponsors a presentation may be more convenient, and it has the added advantage of having greater impact than a written document. Three general tips with regard to the proposal are:

1. *Estimate costs and returns.* If possible, try to provide quantitative information on both costs and returns associated with the scheme. You will find that calculating costs is certainly the easier part – naturally these will, at this stage, only be estimates. The difficulty in calculating financial returns will vary depending on the objective of your scheme, but generally the following points are well worth converting into monetary terms:
   - Costs saved on training or other expensive and perhaps inappropriate developmental activities.
   - Costs saved on recruitment and the enhanced retention of key staff – this cost estimate should include the avoidance of expenses for recruiting and training new hires to replace those who have left, and costs saved on not having someone in place for a period.
   - Increased income from sales and productivity gains.
   - In the case of Equal Opportunities, avoidance of regulatory fines and access to government approved supplier lists.
   - The value of knowledge-sharing with regard to, for example, innovation and the transfer of good practice.
2. *Summarize your research.* All research findings that you will present in your proposal should be summarized and made comprehensible (i.e. jargon free).
3. *Customize your proposal.* Design the proposal with the audience you will be addressing in mind. What are they like? What is the best way to approach them? What information would interest them in particular? Can they be better influenced with more or less data?

The following checklist sums up the points you will want to address in an implementation proposal:

1. The main purpose and the subsidiary objectives of the scheme:
   - Why is the program needed?
   - Who would be the mentee target group?
   - What is it aiming to achieve? (For example, to 'foster globally competent managers'?) Subsidiary objectives could include familiarizing (young) managers with the imperatives of an international firm, helping them to develop the essential networks, or raising their ability to think globally.
2. The value of the scheme to the business:

- Why should the organization support a mentoring scheme?
- What direct and indirect benefits does the program bring to the organization?
- How will mentoring assist in achieving business objectives?
- How will it contribute to fostering an organization that can compete today and tomorrow?
- How will it raise the organization's profile in the eyes of customers and shareholders?
- Why is mentoring better suited to addressing the set objective(s) than other training and development approaches?
- How does it find with other currently used training and development approaches?
- What are the benefits for line managers? For mentors? For mentees?

3. The viability of the scheme within the company:
   - Would the organization be able to sustain a mentoring scheme?
   - How would it fit with and support the company culture?
   - Would we be able to recruit sufficient mentors, and who would these be?
   - Would there be a positive response amongst the mentee target group?

4. Resource needs:
   - What human, spatial, temporal and material resources will be needed to design, implement and run the scheme?
   - How much money is needed to cover the expenses associated with the program?

5. Estimates of returns:
   - What savings will we make through running the mentoring scheme?
   - What financial returns can we hope to gain through mentoring?

6. Implementation strategy:
   - What is the timeframe for designing and implementing the mentoring program?
   - What are the individual stages involved in designing and implementing the scheme? (see Chapter 8)
   - How are you going to communicate the scheme to employees?
   - Who would you like to involve in the design and implementation phase, i.e. who would your steering committee consist of? List all the different roles associated with the implementation of the scheme (see below), and make temporary suggestions as to who you would like to fill these; emphasize that the scheme's sponsors should also form part of the steering committee.

- What is the role of the steering committee?

7. Measurement of objectives:
   - What are the objectives of the scheme, and how can they be measured?
   - What evaluation criteria should we apply?
   - When should the evaluation take place?
   - What methods should we use?

8. Risk factors and contingency plans:
   - In the worst-case scenario, what could go wrong with a mentoring scheme?
   - What would you need to do to put things right?
   - How can you prevent potential pitfalls from occurring?

9. Recommendations:
   - What type of mentoring model would you like to employ – one-to-one, team, reverse mentoring, or a combination of different models?
   - Should the program be formal or informal?
   - Would it be best to start off by running a pilot scheme?
   - What is the envisaged scope of your pilot scheme/the subsequent mentoring program – how many mentor and mentee pairs would you like to have enrolled at any one time?
   - When should the scheme commence?

Part III: The steering committee/implementation team

In the above checklist, we mentioned that you should explain the function of the 'steering committee' or 'implementation team' (as it is also sometimes called) to the audience you are proposing to. In addition, we suggested that you advise the scheme's sponsors, to whom you are proposing, on the roles typically associated with it, and that you encourage them to join the committee.

Steering committee and implementation team – what is the difference?

Before we consider the roles that are typically associated with the steering committee or implementation team, we would like to draw a distinction between these two terms for future reference. Although *steering committee and implementation team* are usually applied to the same entity, we will break this tradition in this book for the purposes of clarity: the steering committee will from here on be taken to mean the implementation team *plus* the scheme's (financial) sponsors. In contrast, the implementation team only consists of those people who are involved *hands-on* in implementing a mentoring scheme. This is not to say that the sponsors do not help to implement the program, but their support usually concentrates more on overseeing its progress and acting as a sounding board and feeder pool for ideas and suggestions (as well as, of course, financing the scheme). Since the sponsors are typically a company's top managers, time constraints tend to prevent them from carrying out 'real' (hands-on) implementation activities such as designing marketing strategies and recruitment plans, producing relevant documentation, and organizing training.

The implementation team

In its entirety, the implementation team could consist of the following members:

- Program champion.
- Program co-ordinator.
- External consultant.
- Trainers.
- Relationship supervisors.
- Administration staff.

The time to assemble the implementation team would ideally be *prior to* researching and designing the implementation proposal. This is has two main advantages: first, a proposal that comes from a group is often more believable; and secondly, you can share the preparation work if you are working as a team rather than on your own. If the team was not formed prior to drafting the implementation proposal, this should be your first task after it has been passed.

The steering committee

The role of the steering committee is typically that of a guiding council in the implementation of a mentoring program. Once your sponsors have accepted the proposal, you should encourage them to join the steering committee. When doing so, ask them to define the role they would like to play in the mentoring scheme; this will prevent future disappointments and role confusion on both your part and that of the sponsors. Throughout the entire design and implementation phase, you must ensure that you involve the sponsors regularly by updating them on all developments and seeking their input.

Summary

To obtain the go-ahead for your scheme, you cannot simply dive into approaching potential sponsors. If you are serious about getting the implementation of a scheme accepted, you must do your homework first and ensure that:

- You have a convincing rationale for implementing a program that has been corroborated by your needs assessment. Needs can be established organically, through the succession planning method, or through an ONA. Whichever method you choose, the needs assessment should always involve a consultation with senior management, not least to gain their buy-in to the program. It should also be complemented by a readiness analysis.
- You have evidence for believing that your organization would sustain a program. In particular, this means ensuring that senior management completely support the program and that employees would be enthusiastic about taking it up.
- You know the benefits that mentoring can bring to your organization and its people, and you have sufficient evidence to back up any claims regarding these. This evidence could stem from case studies, anecdotes and published research data.
- You are aware of the objections to the mentoring initiative and have devised strategies for addressing these. In particular, you will have dealt with/will deal with those of senior management, the mentor and mentee target group, and colleagues of the mentee target group.
- You have a clear idea of what and how to evaluate later on in the scheme.

Equipped with the information collated in the above steps, you can then draw up an implementation proposal. This proposal can be presented and/or given to potential sponsors in writing. Typically you would do both, but the main factor to bear in mind when trying to influence sponsors is to aim the proposal at their unique preferences – you must analyse your audience and try to assess what information would convince them the most, and in what package it needs to be presented.

References

Boydell, T. and Leary, M. (1997). In: *Introduction to Training* (P. Hackett, ed.). CIPD.

Hackett, P. (1997). *Introduction to Training*. CIPD.

Maurer, R. (1998). From resistance to support. *Executive Excellence*, **15**, 16–19.

Murray, M. and Owen, M. (1991). *Beyond the Myths and Magic of Mentoring*. Jossey-Bass.

Nilles, J. M. (1998). *Managing Telework. Strategies for Managing the Virtual Workforce*. John Wiley and Sons.

Schneider, D. and Goldwasser, C. (1998). Be a model leader of change. *Man. Rev.*, **87**, 41–5.

Implementing the mentoring program

By now the program champion should have received the 'go-ahead' from the program's sponsors (see Chapter 7). The scheme's objectives should either have been established by agreement with the main stakeholders and/or through an organizational/ training needs analysis. This means that you are now in a position to commence with the actual implementation of the program, and to consider ongoing support and maintenance.

This present chapter is organized into three main parts:

- Part I: implementing the mentoring scheme – an outline of the individual steps that need to be taken.
- Part II: globally implemented schemes – a case study and brief discussion of internationally organized mentoring programs.
- Part III: Templates to be used in mentoring schemes.

As mentioned previously, it is vital to gain input from significant others (e.g. the prospective mentors and mentees) throughout the design and implementation phase, as this input ultimately affects the success of the scheme. The scheme's participants will view the initiative as much more relevant to them and will be more happy to take up this opportunity if they had a say in designing it. However, if the occasions on which to involve participants were limited during the phase of designing the proposal, you should make every effort to involve them more during the implementation phase. This means that some of the issues tackled during the design of the proposal will need to be revisited, and some decisions altered.

In this chapter, we endeavour to provide you with a complete overview of the main steps involved in implementing a mentoring program – so we will be covering some familiar territory. It is also necessary to understand that these implementation guidelines will not exactly map onto every organization. The chapter is intended to provide you with sufficient insight into what is involved in implementing a mentoring scheme, and with both the confidence and the know-how to customize the approach to your own needs. We will work on the premises that:

- *You are having to implement the program from scratch* and will remain involved with it for a long period of time.
- *You are probably working for a medium-sized or large organization* (be this as a full-time/part-time employee or a consultant). That said, this chapter, and indeed the whole book, is highly relevant to mentoring schemes in small firms too.

There is plenty of information here to help you tailor materials to your individual needs, whatever your circumstances. This chapter once again assumes that you are the person who has the main responsibility for the scheme.

Part I: Implementing the mentoring scheme – an outline of the individual steps that need to be taken

The steps tackled in Part I are as follows:

1. Founding the implementation team.
2. Marketing: providing information and inviting feedback.
3. The statement of strategic objectives and long-range plans.
4. Parameters of mentoring schemes.

5. Drawing up a recruitment plan, selecting and recruiting.
6. Training.
7. Matching mentors and mentees.
8. Drawing up mentoring agreements.
9. Implementing the agreement.

The above steps are relevant irrespective of whether you are first running a pilot scheme, i.e. a mentoring program involving only very few participants, or are launching the 'main' scheme straight away. Throughout the course of a scheme you might have to revisit and amend some of the above points, taking into account any feedback you have received. For example, good practice stipulates that you should evaluate your scheme occasionally (see Chapter 10). With a pilot scheme this seems obvious, but main schemes should also be evaluated regularly. The feedback gathered during these evaluations can then be used to improve the scheme, and the changes should be reflected in any publicity campaign. For example, should the selection criteria and methods for mentors and/or mentees change, this needs to be brought to the attention of all relevant parties.

Before we move on, one last comment with regards to pilot schemes. Preceding a main scheme with a pilot is an extremely good idea, particularly if you are intending to run a very large scheme overall. Pilots are essentially a trial and error run; they help you to avoid many a pitfall that, if occurring on a larger scale, could be very costly and/or have negative repercussions for you and the scheme. Besides helping you to avoid mistakes, pilots are also a great way of boosting your confidence in approaching the larger scheme. If the scheme is a pilot, this should be made explicit, because it will help to alter others' attitudes – if those who are not part of the scheme hear that they might be able to participate at a later stage, they are more likely to turn their energy into making the scheme work rather than spoiling it.

Founding the implementation team

If you did not already found your implementation team prior to designing the implementation proposal, you should certainly do it now. In the previous chapter, we agreed to use the term 'implementation team' to refer to those people who are actively involved in implementing the scheme. In contrast to that, the 'steering committee' is the implementation team *plus* the scheme's (financial) sponsors, who, although involved with the program, do not usually help to design marketing strategies, recruitment plans and training plans. Besides financing the scheme, their involvement usually concentrates on overseeing its progress, and acting as a sounding board and feeder pool for ideas. Let us now remind you of the different roles associated with the *implementation team*:

- Program champion.
- Program co-ordinator.
- External consultant.
- Trainers.
- Relationship supervisors.
- Administration staff.

Although the above list shows a total of six different types of roles, the number of people required is highly variable. For a start, the program co-ordinator and the relationship supervisor often tend to be one and the same person or persons if your scheme is so extensive that it requires several program co-ordinators. It can also happen that the roles of program champion and program co-ordinator are filled by the same individual. Administration staff might also not be necessary, depending on the structure and scope of your scheme. That is, relationship supervisors and/or program co-ordinators might well be capable of undertaking all administrative tasks without the help of extra support staff.

In addition, it may be necessary to involve selected individuals on a temporary basis in order to obtain their input into the program design. These may include representatives from different organizational functions who can offer an objective view of program policies and procedures. Lastly, to ensure that things run smoothly and are ethically correct, you will of course have to consult with the scheme's stakeholders (e.g. financial sponsors and line managers) on a regular basis throughout the implementation process. However, these two groups are not usually considered part of the implementation team itself.

Responsibilities of program co-ordinators, relationship supervisors and trainers

Let us now look at the responsibilities associated with the program co-ordinator, the relationship supervisor and the trainer in more detail.

The program co-ordinator and the relationship supervisor

The program co-ordinator's role is essentially one of manager of the entire scheme. This person is *the* point of contact within a scheme, perhaps not the first one for everyone, but certainly the one who should really know what is going on in and around the program. Although it is not always feasible, having a co-ordinator who possesses substantial experience with mentoring and/or running mentoring schemes will be a great advantage for any program. As with all roles within mentoring schemes, the exact duties and responsibilities of the co-ordinator will vary slightly between organizations, but Table 8.1 summarises the tasks of most.

In terms of the number of program co-ordinators that are required, it is difficult to apply an iron rule. Typically, mentoring programs tend to have one co-ordinator who is responsible for the overall management of the scheme. However, depending on the scope of the scheme, there might well be variations to this; for example, it is sometimes necessary to assign one or two assistant co-ordinators. These individuals do not bear as much of a responsibility as the main co-ordinator, but can significantly help to ease his or her workload by taking over some of the tasks such as selecting and matching mentors and mentees. Furthermore, if the program is one that has been implemented across many cities or even countries, you might want to appoint one co-ordinator per region. If you do choose to appoint several co-ordinators, you must, however, ensure close collaboration between them so that the scheme is standardized or at least unified where appropriate. (We will consider the subject of implementing mentoring internationally in Part II of this chapter.)

Not every program has *relationship supervisors*, and sometimes the program co-ordinator will fill this role. This all depends on the scope of the program and, again, on your organization's preferences and resources. In larger programs, relationship supervisors are highly valuable: they ease the workload of the co-ordinator by taking over some of his or her responsibilities with regard to 'managing' the mentor–mentee pairs. Even if the program co-ordinator could in theory supervise all the pairs of the program, the relationship between a pair and a supervisor will always be more personal and perhaps more trusting because the supervisor can provide every single pair with much more quality time and attention than the co-ordinator could. Depending on the size of your scheme, recruiting supervisors could be a good idea. For example, if there are up to 10 pairs in a scheme who meet once per month, the program co-ordinator might be able to manage them. However, if there are

Table 8.1 Summary of responsibilities of co-ordinators and supervisors

Program coordinator	Relationship supervisor
✓ Managing *most or all* stages of the program: implementation proposal design, implementation maintenance and evaluation	✓ Providing mentors and mentees with the contact details of the other
✓ Leading the implementation team and liaising with all other parties involved in the program (e.g. ensuring that all stakeholders are kept well informed and involved where appropriate)	✓ Attending the first meeting to clarify any issues and to provide help with documentation such as mentoring agreements and personal development plans
✓ Overseeing *or* taking charge of marketing	✓ Acting as the first point of contact for mentors and mentees for any questions or problems liaising with the program coordinator about problems
✓ Overseeing *or* taking charge of all selection and recruitment needs (e.g. mentors, mentees, trainers, supervisors)	✓ Periodically monitoring the progress of the relationship
✓ Overseeing *or* taking charge of matching mentors and mentees	✓ Collecting, taking a look at or creating documentation such as progress reviews
✓ Managing the briefing/training including overseeing the training design and delivery – in some cases such as in small organizations the co-ordinator might well conduct the training themselves	✓ Within the bounds of confidentiality, keeping records of relationships and/ or informing the program co-ordinator of the status of associations
✓ Trouble-shooting the program; seizing on evaluation data by feeding it back into the program	
✓ Managing relationship conflicts where appropriate	
✓ Overseeing *or* taking charge of part/all of the administration	

any more than that you might want to consider the help of a few supervisors. If you are wondering what kind of person to recruit for this type of role, you might want to consider the following options (Lacey, 1999):

- A training facilitator.
- A previous mentor.
- An experienced human resource facilitator.

Either way, supervisors should not be in a line relationship with any of the participants assigned to them. The responsibilities of the supervisor are summarised in Table 8.1.

The trainers

There are usually two types of trainers within mentoring schemes: external facilitators/consultants who train program co-ordinators and relationship supervisors; and trainers (internal or external) who are responsible for equipping mentors and mentees with the knowledge, skills and attitudes necessary to make relationships a success. To make things simpler, we will typically use the term 'trainer' to refer to both types, but will make it clear, whenever a further distinction is necessary.

Although not automatically the case, trainers may also become involved in briefing other stakeholders of the program (such as line managers) with regard to scheme facts and their role within it (see Chapter 9). The role of the trainer could be occupied by a variety of people. Naturally, the individual(s) responsible for it ought to be competent in the art of training. Possessing mentoring experience is also an advantage. In addition, the mentoring champion and/or program co-ordinator as well as other groups will contribute to the training *design* and *delivery*.

To return to the question of who might occupy the role of the trainer, we suggest the following options:

- Your own in-house trainers if they are familiar with mentoring training.
- A manager (from, for example, the HR department) who knows a lot about mentoring/mentoring schemes and who has either done training before and/or could be effectively trained for the role – please note that this manager might be the program co-ordinator.
- External trainers, who are professional trainers specializing in mentoring.

It is vital for the success of your scheme to provide mentors, mentees and other relevant parties with first-rate mentoring training. In fact, the absence of such is a characteristic of many a scheme that has failed. Unless you have in-house trainers with substantial experience in mentoring and mentoring training, it is best to use external trainers who specialize in this area. Due to their experience, they will be more capable of answering questions and better equipped to respond to challenging situations.

In terms of the responsibilities of the trainers, they will be conducting some or all of the following tasks, depending on how much pre-work has been done for them:

- *Training design*: familiarization with the topics in general and the scheme in particular, collaborating with the program co-ordinators and others who can feed into the design stage, researching training needs, setting training objectives, grouping the trainees, choosing appropriate activities and materials, organizing venues.
- *Training delivery*: facilitating learning and transfer of new material.
- *Training evaluation*: ensuring that learning and transfer have taken place. That said, the assessment of the transfer of new knowledge and skills might not be the trainer's responsibility any more, depending on who the trainer is and to what extent he or she is involved with the program. Instead, it might be taken over by the program co-ordinator, who might choose to evaluate the skills status of trainees at a later stage as part of the overall evaluation of the mentoring program.

Recruiting members for the implementation team should be your top priority when implementing a mentoring program, since you could not implement and maintain a program without their support – particularly where it is a large-scale scheme. Recruiting for the implementation team is going to be one of your most vital tasks, as the success or failure of the mentoring scheme depends on this group especially. These people have to be both competent and motivated, as well as fitting with the mentoring culture you seek to establish. In order for you to attract people with the right kind of attitude and values, you must provide them with accurate information about the program and about their roles in advance. However, for practical purposes, this information may be a shortened version of the one to be given to the rest of the organization.

Collating and disseminating the information necessary to

inform the whole organization is likely to involve a lot of time and effort. It also requires the input of people with different kinds of expertise and knowledge. It is for these and other reasons that you will urgently need the help of your implementation team.

Marketing: providing information and inviting feedback

Prior to implementation, it is essential to inform organizational members about the forthcoming mentoring program. In doing so, the implementation team might want to consult with representatives of the various groups that will be affected by the mentoring scheme – such as mentors, mentees and line managers. Meet up with them and hold focus groups in which the forthcoming scheme can be introduced and feedback gathered.

The distribution of information is yet another vital step towards the success of the scheme. Not only does it serve to educate people about the mentoring program; it also serves to sell the initiative. And what is more, the dissemination of information about the scheme helps to prevent problems that might arise as a result of misconceptions of mentoring. For example, those precluded from the scheme (because they do not match the mentee target group) must also receive sufficient information about it so that they:

- Fully understand why they are not part of it, and
- Obtain an accurate understanding of what mentoring involves.

This will demystify the nature of mentoring – a vital step in avoiding the build-up of irrational fears and jealousy.

Options for disseminating information about the program

There are an enormous number of options in presenting such information. For example, you might want to print a brochure, introduce the program during team briefings, put up signs or posters on notice boards, write memos and/or personalized letters. In marketing their mentoring scheme, the retail department of BP UK has chosen to complement traditional methods such as posters with a special intranet site. Coincidentally, this is also where they tend to keep brief descriptions of their mentors so that mentees can look at these and select their mentors. Whichever means you choose, the information should provide organizational members with a good program overview, the elements of which are listed below:

- The nature and purpose of mentoring.
- The specific reasons for introducing it in the organization (e.g. the overall value to the organization, the objectives it is aiming to achieve).
- Roles within a mentoring scheme (e.g. who the backers are, the program co-ordinator, supervisors, administration staff, mentors and mentees).
- Vacancies within the mentoring scheme.
- A preliminary indication of the mentee and mentor target groups, including an outline of the most important selection criteria.
- The different foci, benefits, rewards and risks for mentors and mentees.
- A description of eligibility, screening processes and suitability requirements for becoming mentors and mentees.
- The level of commitment expected (time, energy, flexibility).
- An overview of different mentoring systems and their associated objectives.
- A summary of program policies, including written reports, interviews, evaluation and reimbursement.
- Logistical issues, such as the date the selection process commences, how to apply, dates for the start of the mentoring program etc.
- Contact details of members of the implementation team – individuals must be provided with an opportunity to ask questions and provide feedback.

The statement of strategic objectives and long-range plans

This is an elaboration of the objectives established in the implementation proposal on the basis of either a needs analysis or the client's (perceived) needs, and should now include long-term plans, and address:

- Goals, objectives and timelines for all aspects of the plan.
- Who, what, where, when, why and how activities will be performed.
- Funding and resource development plans.

Parameters of mentoring schemes

Having established the overall objectives for the program as well as more specific mentee needs, you and your team are now in a position to select the appropriate parameters for your mentoring scheme. As a reminder of the dimensions along which programs can vary, take a look at the following Table 8.2.

If your organization is very large and it has been decided that you want to offer mentoring to a range of different mentee target groups, it would be a good idea to assess whether these groups might benefit from differently organized schemes. Thus, if you want to introduce mentoring for different business divisions or departments, you might have to vary the design of the scheme along the above dimensions. The extent and nature of this variation would depend on the objectives that were set for each mentee target group, and on factors such as mentor availability. For example, one mentee group might benefit most from team-to-team mentoring and a more formalized scheme, whilst one-to-one based reverse mentoring might be best for another group. Customizing schemes to the different groups within an organization will make people feel valued as individuals, and will further increase the acceptance of the program.

In choosing one or several types of program, you will again have to take into account the views of all stakeholders. It is

Table 8.2 Summary of parameters of mentoring schemes

Parameter	Explanation
Objectives of the scheme	'Socialization' in a graduate/induction scheme or 'career advancement/ competency development' in a system geared towards developing high-potential employees (Chapter 3)
Degree of formality	Informal, semi-formal or formal (Chapter 4)
Mentoring models	For example, one-to-one or team mentoring; reverse mentoring or peer mentoring (Chapter 4)
Characteristics of mentors	For instance, a peer versus a senior member; a line-manager versus another manager; an older person versus a younger one
Choice of participation	Forced versus voluntary participation (Chapter 8)

likely that the scheme's sponsors (financial or other) will once again have the greatest impact on the decision of what type(s) of mentoring scheme to choose. However, if their choices appear to be inconsistent with the *dominant* organizational need for mentoring, the program is unlikely to be accepted! It is your task to marry together the different interests and to introduce a system that will satisfy the main players (i.e. the financial sponsors, the mentees' line managers, the mentee target group and the mentors). This will induce the greatest commitment from all parties, and will therefore support the longevity and success of the program.

The way in which to define the parameters of a program would ideally be the democratic one, involving everyone who is directly associated with it. In many a situation this may unfortunately be a practical impossibility due to factors such as the predominance of the sponsors' interests and/or the size of the organization. Furthermore, people who have limited knowledge of mentoring options may make achieving consensus difficult. Therefore, in trying to define the parameters for your scheme (or schemes) you should:

- Focus on the needs and characteristics of the mentee target group(s) and have their best interests at heart.
- Consult with the scheme's sponsors.
- Consult with representatives of the mentee target group(s).

Drawing up a recruitment plan: selecting and recruiting

You should start off designing the recruitment plan in a very broad manner – that is, begin by deciding on the approximate number of participants (mentors and mentees) that you intend to recruit initially. This number will be determined by a variety of factors, including:

- The budget allocated to the mentoring program.
- The size of the company.
- Whether it is a pilot program or a full-scale scheme.
- The objectives of the scheme and, therefore, the mentee target group.
- The number of suitable mentors available.
- The number of suitable mentees available.

Next you might want to stipulate the roles that need to be filled within the implementation team. As mentioned previously, these involve the program co-ordinator, potentially one or several external consultants, one or several trainers, relationship supervisors, and administration staff.

Having decided on the vacancies that need filling, determine the number of people needed for each role. This should be done in accordance with the number of mentees and mentors you are planning to recruit. Then you can draw up job descriptions and selection criteria for each of the vacancies. With regard to the selection criteria for trainers, relationship supervisors and (if still necessary) the program co-ordinator, please refer back to 'Founding the implementation team' and Table 8.1.

Once the implementation team is in place, recruitment should first focus on the selection of mentees before turning to the selection of mentors. The reason for this lies in the fact that mentoring is set up to benefit mentees (employees with certain learning requirements). In order for mentors to develop these employees, their needs must be ascertained first, and then mentors matched to them. Let us now consider mentor and mentee recruitment in more detail, starting with the mentee.

Recruiting mentees

The first step in the recruitment of mentees involves the identification of *who* the mentee target group is – that is, which segments of the organization constitute potential mentees. Chapter 7 discussed the methods of arriving at an explicit answer to this question. However, even if you know who your mentee target group is, some narrowing down might nevertheless be required. Let us take the example where the mentee target group is the *junior management level* of a particular business division. If your budget is limited, or there are not enough mentors, or you are implementing a pilot scheme, you might not be able to select all of these managers. You will therefore have to decide whether you only want to choose, for instance:

- The high-flying junior managers.
- Those in most need of development.
- Only minority group junior managers.

Minimizing your mentee target group should, of course, be guided by the primary objectives of the mentoring program. Sponsors, line managers, team leaders and HR could be consulted in narrowing down too large a mentee group.

Options for recruiting mentees

Once the criteria for minimizing the mentee population are set, you can begin to recruit *specific* individuals. There are a variety of options for doing this, and the option you need to use will, once again, be closely determined by the objective of your scheme. Mentee recruitment methods are summarized below:

- *Recommendation*: sponsors, line managers, team leaders and HR/training might be able to suggest potential mentees.
- *Marketing/open to all*: if the scheme is to be made available to *all* members of a particular employee group (e.g. all new hires of the sales division or the whole of the sales division), you will probably be offering it to them through appropriate marketing strategies and waiting for the mentees to approach you. Thus, it could be introduced on an induction/team building/training day, line managers could promote it and/ or e-mail circulars could be used.
- *Human resource data*: performance appraisals, results of Assessment and Development Centres, and reviews of coaching sessions could also provide you with useful insights into who in particular you could approach.
- *Part of training and development initiative*: if the mentoring is part of a larger training and development initiative for which employees have already been recruited, approaching specific individuals will be a fairly straightforward task.

If you utilize the recommendations of others to recruit mentees, they also must be well informed regarding the program objectives and the mentee selection criteria. This prevents a lot of unqualified candidates from being put forward. However, if your initial informative campaign has been carried out thoroughly, this should not be a problem!

Another issue warrants attention with regard to mentee recruitment: choice of participation.

CHOICE OF PARTICIPATION

Should the system be voluntary, compulsory or subtly coercive? Neither mentors nor mentees should be forced to partake in a mentoring scheme. This approach is likely to attract people with the wrong attitude and/or no motivation into a relationship, thereby benefiting neither the organization nor the mentors and mentees. However, when conducting your initial publicity campaign regarding the forthcoming scheme, you should have made it attractive enough to be of interest to many potential mentors and mentees. To make the program attractive you could, for example, emphasize the benefits both mentors and mentees would receive from their participation in the program.

Although we strongly recommend *voluntary* participation, it does have a downside: you may attract wrongly motivated people. For example, you might attract *mentors* who only want to take on this role to enhance their standing in the organization, rather than wanting to help another person. However, a great way of weeding out poor participants (mentors in particular) is *training*, which can be used as an informal measurement centre. In general, wrongly motivated participants can also often be caught out during the selection process by carefully assessing their intentions.

Mentee selection criteria

Once you have determined the mentee target group you will be in a position to establish mentee selection criteria, which can then be entered into the mentee eligibility screening process (see below).

As pointed out in Chapter 3, mentee selection criteria vary so greatly between schemes that it is virtually impossible to generalize about them. They are determined by the objectives of each program. Yet there are a few characteristics that you could look out for when recruiting your mentees, and these include:

- Being keen to learn and develop themselves.
- Actively seeking challenging assignments.
- Initiating career development themselves and frequently wishing to participate in learning, training and development opportunities.
- Being goal-oriented.
- Being receptive to feedback and coaching.

Mentee eligibility screening

A formal screening of mentees' eligibility is by no means a feature of all programs. Often candidates are hand-picked or are assumed to be mature enough to determine their own eligibility. Yet in very large programs a formal screening process can have practical advantages. For example, if the number of places is too small for the number of individuals wanting to enter a scheme, utilizing methods such as application forms can simplify this issue.

If you do choose to have a formal screening process, begin by evaluating employees' application forms for participation in the program (for a template of an application form, please refer to the end of this chapter). This means, for example, checking the mentees' suitability against specified criteria and examining whether the candidates fit the mentee target population.

After this, candidates' eligibility can, if you wish, be further investigated through:

- Conducting face-to-face interviews.
- Reference checks.

Having vetted an applicant and determined his or her suitability for participating in the mentoring program, the mentee recruitment is not over yet. You will have to collect as much information as possible about the mentee. This information will then be drawn upon in the mentor–mentee matching process and is intended to support the creation of a successful relationship. Such information could be gathered from one or all of the following sources:

- Mentee personality profile.
- Learning styles assessment (could be done during a training session).
- Preliminary assessment of the mentee's learning and development needs. Creating an initial development plan will be one of the most invaluable types of data with regard to matching mentors and mentees. Data regarding the mentee's development needs could initially be collated from, for example, the mentee's self-assessment and/or the assessment of his or her immediate supervisor or manager.
- Identification of relevant knowledge, experience and skills, as well as the mentee's gender, age, career interests, career goals, motivation for being a mentee, and academic standing (if applicable).

Recruiting mentors

This part of the recruitment process should be paid a lot of attention. After all, mentors are the linchpins of the program! You must therefore take great care to identify and recruit the right kind of mentors.

Important mentor selection criteria are depicted in Table 8.3.

To further ensure that you recruit the right kind of mentors, you can employ a variety of additional strategies:

1. Use a mentor application/recruitment form (refer to the back of this chapter for a template).
2. Try to use volunteers as much as possible. Again, in order to save you time you should have made the program objectives, time commitment and key selection criteria public in your initial information campaign. If you have not done this, you

Table 8.3 Mentor selection criteria

✓	Skills-needs match	Examining the development needs and objectives of the mentee target group, will guide you when specifying the mentor selection criteria, at the very least in terms of the skills, knowledge and experience prospective mentors must possess.
✓	Experience in developing others	
✓	Attitudinal fit	A willingness to assume accountability and willingness to grow and develop others and to pass on knowledge, skills or experience.
✓	Able to share credit	
✓	A strong people-orientation	
✓	Successful and *regarded* as successful	
✓	Espouses the organization's culture and is familiar with the company	
✓	Possesses an extensive network of resources	
✓	Possesses mentor characteristics	Displays many of the characteristics discussed in Chapter 5.

will find that there will be a lot of unqualified candidates asking to act as mentors, simply because they do not know what is involved. Making program objectives and mentor selection criteria known organization-wide is also important for recruiting mentors in alternative ways, such as by executive nomination or mentee nomination.

3. When describing the mentor role, take great care not to create unrealistic expectations – that is, do not make the mentor's responsibilities sound overly exciting and glamorous. Instead, you ought to describe it in the most factual and realistic way possible.

4. Depending on the size of your organization, advertising might be an important feature of the mentor recruitment strategy. You might want to place advertisements in any one or all of the following media:
   - Daily bulletins/e-mails.
   - Periodic newsletters and communications.
   - Union newspapers and publications.
   - Trade publications.
   - Management reports.
   - Training catalogues.
   - Desk-drop leaflets.
   - Intranet/Internet communications.
   - Notice and bulletin boards.

Furthermore, you could also attempt to rely on word-of-mouth delivery of the mentor recruitment process. Make it easy for volunteers or nominators to respond to your advertisement/ request for mentors – you might want to devise and hand out simple forms for them to fill out and return to you, stating clearly where they are to be submitted.

Another point to remember in mentor selection is that the mentors you want to recruit might be very different from each other, requiring distinct job descriptions and selection criteria. This is due to the fact that the mentor target groups (and their associated criteria) are determined by the organization's and the mentees' needs and objectives, as well as by the mentoring schemes that were selected.

Mentor rewards

Should there be any rewards or incentives? Well, preferably not. Consider, for example, the desirability of any reward and its compatibility with your mentoring scheme. If rewards are highly desirable and therefore encourage the wrong people to enter the program as mentors, the consequences for mentees may be extremely negative. Mentors may not be genuinely interested in them and not committed to the relationship, rendering the whole experience rather disappointing for mentees.

All-year marketing

A last point to mention with regard to your recruitment campaign is the importance of continued marketing. All-year publicity is important to keep the program going by ensuring the influx of new mentors and mentees.

Training

After having selected mentors, mentees and other program staff, they will have to receive some form of preparation regarding the mentoring program and their role in it. Training is a vital part in making schemes successful, and owing to its importance we have devoted the whole of Chapter 9 to this topic.

Matching mentors and mentees

After mentors and mentees have been selected, their profiles established and they have undergone their pre-match training, they can now be matched. In Chapter 9 we will explain how training can be used effectively to aid the matching process. This relates to the fact that you can train mentors and mentees jointly on some aspects. During this session, they can get to know each other and you can observe them interact. Afterwards mentees can, for example, be asked to indicate their preferences with regard to which mentors they might want to have and, even more importantly, which mentors they would absolutely *not* want to have. Avoiding the latter (i.e. attending to negative preferences) is often more feasible than granting the former (i.e. attending to positive preferences).

Materials to help you with the matching process include:

- A form that asks mentees to indicate their positive and negative preferences with regard to mentors – this could be specific people, or merely a statement of most versus least preferred characteristics.
- A form that asks mentors and mentees to indicate their general preferences on dimensions such as career experience, age, gender, ethnicity and interests.
- The mentor and mentee application forms.
- Learning styles, communication styles and personality questionnaires.

Possible criteria for matching mentors and mentees are listed in Table 8.4.

Table 8.4 Possible criteria for matching mentors and mentees

✓ Power over mentee	For reasons mentioned before (see Chapter 4), the mentor should not be too close to the mentee in terms of a power relationship. Thus, the mentor should not be the mentee's line manager. Rather you might want to select someone who is either a peer, from another department or external to the company. Having mentors who are more than two levels above the mentee often constitutes too great a power-distance in which mentees feel uncomfortable
✓ Compatability between the needs of the mentee and the experience of the mentor	As you can imagine, this matching criterion is of the greatest importance. After all, getting on like a house on fire will not benefit the mentee over the long-term if the mentor cannot match this with an ability to address the mentee's needs
✓ Details such as age, gender, and ethnicity as well as an indication of preferences on these dimensions with regards to the mentoring partner	
✓ An indication of interests	
✓ Geography/ location	
✓ Personality	Personality should only be taken into account in order to avoid impossible matches, i.e. those who would not work. You should steer clear of utilizing it to match very *similar* people (as many organizations do) because it can be equally – if not more– beneficial to have a mentoring pair consisting of opposites. Opposites can get on very well and the ensuing dialogue is likely to be more stimulating and certainly more challenging!

Drawing up mentoring agreements

Written mentoring agreements *can* be useful in facilitating successful mentoring relationships by outlining and therefore managing expectations and responsibilities. However, they are by no means compulsory. In fact, evidence suggests that if a number of mentor and mentee pairs are given the choice to agree on whether or not they want to use a written agreement, the outcomes for all of the pairs will be the same irrespective of whether or not they chose to set up a formal contract. That is, both types of relationships – those with and those without a written agreement – were equally successful. Naturally, if there is to be no written mentoring contract, expectations, roles and responsibilities have to be managed verbally.

So, the ideal way to handle the issue of mentoring agreements in your scheme would be to make the use of a *written* one optional to pairs. If you choose this method, you must, however, ensure that the pairs who decline to set up a written agreement really do negotiate their terms and conditions orally. Should you choose to make written agreements obligatory, it is probably a good idea to make the rationale underlying this decision very explicit and to make it positive, too. Otherwise, the individuals who would personally prefer to keep matters informal will be even more resistant to this idea. When using agreements, you should provide standard forms to each pair (there is a sample template at the end of this chapter). However, do leave some room for personal additions. Ideally, the relationship supervisor should ensure that agreements are made available to mentors and mentees prior to their first meeting so that both parties can read the terms and conditions in advance. The agreement should then be signed during the first or second meeting.

Implementing the agreement

Ensuring that the agreement is executed is also part of the implementation and maintenance of a mentoring program. Although the responsibility of the mentor and the mentee, it is also the task of the relationship supervisors to monitor whether the agreement is being carried out. There are broadly three stages in the execution of a mentoring agreement:

1. The mentoring relationship begins (the mentoring processes, particularly the first few meetings, have already been discussed in Chapter 6). As you will remember, one of the most important parts of the early stages of a relationship

involves diagnosing the mentee's development needs and establishing a personal development plan.
2. The relationship develops (the different phases of the relationship were discussed in Chapter 6, on both a micro and a macro-level).
3. Closure of the relationship. Ending a relationship *can* be characterized by activities such as exit interviews, and *should* be accompanied by an evaluation. Chapter 10 is devoted to all matters surrounding evaluation, and the proper closure of a relationship is covered in Chapter 11.

Naturally, the program implementation phase does not end here. However, the factors that should still be covered are more intrinsically linked to the maintenance of the program, and will therefore be covered in the Chapter 9.

Part II: Globally implemented schemes

A case study and brief discussion of internationally organized mentoring programs

Case study 8.1

A global mentoring scheme for managers in the consumer products division, by Malin Boultwood of Ericsson

Ericsson is the world's leading supplier of telecommunications with the largest customer base, including the world's top ten operators. Four out of every ten mobile calls are handled by Ericsson equipment. The company has been in business since 1876 and now operates in more than 140 countries, employing 100,000 people. Ericsson is split into five business divisions; one of these is known as the Consumer Products Division and presents the focus of this case study.

During the 1990s Ericsson was expanding rapidly, and in the spring of 1997 the management team of the Consumer Products Division decided that its managers, who were very young and therefore lacking in experience, required support. Mentoring was chosen as the preferred method of providing this support, and the first scheme, implemented on a global basis, began to run in September 1997. By 2000, Ericsson had run four such schemes with participants from Australia, Brazil, China, Finland, Germany, Hong Kong, India, Malaysia, the Netherlands, New Zealand, Singapore, Sweden, Switzerland, Taiwan, the UK and the USA.

The objectives of the scheme entailed the following:

- *Developing global leadership capability for the future.*
- *Increasing the understanding and knowledge of the consumer business.*
- *Increasing the awareness of Ericsson Mobile Phones' culture and values.*
- *Creating a global internal network among young managers.*

The program was championed by Lars Akeson, the HR Director of the Division, and its global implementation was co-ordinated by Malin Boultwood, Manager of Competence and Culture. Boultwood is still responsible for managing the scheme, which means that she matches mentors and mentees, organizes the training, and carries out evaluations. The scheme is funded partially by the participants' departments and partially from the central HR budget.

The scheme has been marketed through company websites and invitation letters. Half of the mentors recruited for the program were internal to Ericsson and typically recommended by senior management. The other half, the external mentors, were recruited with help from the business school IMD – they supplied a range of individuals who committed to mentoring on a voluntary basis. In the recruitment of mentees, Boultwood received assistance from HR and line managers in other countries, who nominated candidates. Selection criteria for mentors included that they had to be:

- *Strongly people-oriented.*
- *Good listeners and communicators.*
- *Interested in the development of people.*
- *Interested in learning from younger individuals.*
- *Prepared to devote time.*
- *Able to give constructive feedback.*
- *Well organized.*
- *A respected person with a good reputation.*

The mentees were chosen according to the following criteria:

- *Individuals with high potential.*
- *30–40 years old.*
- *An academic background.*
- *2–3 years of management experience.*
- *Received basic leadership training.*

Once a list of participants existed, the matching process began. One of the criteria applied in matching was whether mentees preferred external or internal mentors. Says Boultwood:

In general, since Ericsson is a Swedish company, the people from Asia and the US wanted internal mentors to learn more about the company culture and the Swedish culture. The people from Europe have in general been more interested in external mentors.

Furthermore, it was ensured that mentor and mentee pairs were in an off-line relationship.

Since its start in 1997, approximately 120 mentees and 40 mentors have passed through the scheme – on average, mentors take on the responsibility for three mentees. Ericsson gathered the entire mentee and mentor group three times per year. In the first scheme, which commenced in autumn 1997, Ericsson did not prepare any specific mentoring training for mentors and mentees, but realized later that this was needed. With the start of the second scheme in 1998, training was provided at the first and the third meetings – these took place in Sweden and Singapore respectively. IMD helped Ericsson to organize the second training session, which, apart from mentoring training, also involved a general management development session. The scheme's mentors were invited to attend this second module as well. Expectations of the mentoring, the mentor and mentee roles, and the question of who should drive the relationship were touched on in the mentoring training sessions. Following these three annual gatherings, Boultwood kept in touch with the participants for another year to see how the mentoring was progressing.

There were huge differences in terms of the frequency with which pairs met, ranging from every 5 weeks to every 4 months. This variation may well be due to the scheme spanning several countries. As Boultwood says:

Since it is a global program, it has been hard to find and match mentors and mentees that are based in the same area. When you have the travelling aspect to consider as well, it is harder to meet frequently.

Besides person-specific development needs, some recurrent themes also emerged from amongst mentees' learning needs. These included:

- Career management.
- Balance of life issues.
- Developing self awareness.
- Managing people.

Overall, the scheme has been a great success. Boultwood remarks that:

The scoring has been very high among participants. The success of the mentoring relations has of course varied from case to case. Some are keeping in touch several years after the program. Others didn't make it past a year.

What she would like to improve, however, is to ensure that those who accept the task of being a mentor really are committed to it.

The benefits for mentors, mentees and the organization were as follows.

Mentors:

- *'The satisfaction that the mentee appreciates our relationship'.*
- *The enjoyment of a frank exchange on future career concerns.*
- *Gaining a different perspective of business issues.*

Mentees:

- *'Someone is there when the need arises'.*
- *Having an independent source of information and advice.*
- *Learning to balance life and career.*
- *Hearing an external view; being able to check ideas and thoughts.*
- *Mentors sharing their experience and management skills.*
- *Being able to talk to someone with senior management experience.*
- *Receiving support and understanding, and being listened to.*
- *Gaining insights into issues.*
- *Structuring the career planning process.*

The organization:

- *A better network within Ericsson.*
- *The managers who have been involved in the program have in general a better perspective on different issues; inexperienced managers have someone to talk to.*
- *More motivated managers.*

Conclusions regarding international mentoring schemes

What struck us most when reading the case studies of globally implemented schemes such as the one presented above or the cases of BAT and Allianz (Case studies 3.5 and 3.8) is the fact that their implementation and maintenance is not actually that different from nationally organized programs. They can still be centrally controlled by one person, the program co-ordinator, who guides the design and implementation process. In Malin's case, this includes matching mentors and mentees, organizing the training, and leading the evaluation of the scheme. In the case of Allianz, it was two people who managed the entire scheme – quite remarkable, given the number of countries it had been implemented in.

The main point on which nationally and globally implemented schemes diverge is one of extent (or scale):

- The extent to which one requires support from other employees at local sites (e.g. help from local HR/management in recruiting mentors and mentees, or publicizing the program), and therefore
- The extent to which the program co-ordinator needs to collaborate with others and delegate tasks
- The scale of the budget needed
- The scale of the overall scheme (i.e. the numbers of mentors, mentees, line managers and relationship supervisors).

Part III: Templates

Below you will find standard templates for:

- A mentee application form (Figure 8.1)
- A mentor application/recruitment form (Figure 8.2)
- A generic mentoring agreement (Figure 8.3)

Please note that these are only examples, and will need to be amended by you to fit your company's circumstances and preferences.

Name:		
Age:	Sex:	Ethnic background:
Job title:		Division/department:

Company contact details:

_____

Line manager's name:

_____

How did you hear about this program?

_____

Why do you want to join this program? – Please be quite specific detailing your development needs and the objectives you are hoping to attain.

_____

Why do you think mentoring can help you to achieve these objectives/meet your development needs?

_____

What training and development have you taken part in over the last 5 years?

What other learning opportunities have you sought in this time period?

What are your views on self-managed learning?

Hobbies/interests:

Figure 8.1 Mentee application form.

Name:

Age: Sex: Ethnic background:

Job title: Division/department:

Company contact details:

How did you hear about this program?

Why do you want to join this program? – Please be quite specific in terms of what you feel you personally can contribute to this scheme.

Have you trained/developed employees before? – Please specify what training and development methods you applied, under what circumstances and what the outcomes were. Please be sure to highlight in particular any mentoring experience you have had.

Have you yourself received mentoring support?

What are your views regarding your own continued professional development? How do you practise it?

What are your views on employee development in general? How important is it for this company?

Hobbies/interests:

Figure 8.2 Mentor application/recruitment form.

Name of mentee:

Name of mentor:

Name of relationship supervisor:

Name of program co-ordinator:

I. The purpose of the scheme

The scheme intends to match a person with relevant experience (the mentor) with a member of staff who can benefit from this experience (the mentee). The objective is to (*state the objective of the scheme. If the objective requires the mentee to acquire specific types of knowledge, skill and/or experiences, you might want to list these here too*).

II. The mentoring program

Mentors and mentees as well as line managers, relationship supervisors and the program co-ordinator must undergo training. Mentors and mentees must attend this prior to being matched. Profiles of mentors and mentees are used to match pairs. Mentees are given several options to choose from and preferences with regards to particular mentors are taken into account.

III. The mentoring relationships

In this scheme, mentoring is a (*specify nature of relationship, e.g. one-to-one*). They are expected to last for (*specify duration of the relationships*) and pairs are meant to meet on a (*weekly/fortnightly/ monthly/bi-monthly*) basis. The *relationship supervisor* (program co-ordinator) will supervise the mentoring relationship. S/he is the first point of contact for mentors and mentees should there be any queries/problems. S/he is also responsible for providing feedback to the program co-ordinator regarding the success of the relationship.

The *program co-ordinator* will provide feedback to the steering committee. Apart from this general feedback, the relationship is *strictly confidential* and its contents must not be discussed with any outside individuals.

Within the relationship, the *mentee* is obliged to

✓ (e.g. honour confidentiality and attend meetings regularly)
✓
✓

Within the relationship, the *mentor* is obliged to

✓
✓
✓

Within this scheme, the *relationship supervisor* is obliged to

✓
✓
✓

Within this scheme, the *program co-ordinator* is obliged to

✓
✓
✓

IV. Liability disclaimer

Mentors cannot be held responsible for any loss, damage, costs, and/or expenses incurred by the mentee as a result of/in connection with the mentoring relationship.

V. Signatures

If you have read and understood this agreement, please sign in the appropriate space below.

Signature: Dated:

Signature: Dated:

Signature: Dated:

Signature: Dated:

Figure 8.3 A mentoring agreement.

Summary

To begin with, implementing a mentoring scheme might seem like a huge and perhaps very difficult mission, particularly if this is the first time you have done it and/or it is an international scheme. Scary as it may seem, it is not an insurmountable task and can be split up into many little steps. Whether you are introducing a pilot or a main scheme, you will, in a nutshell, typically begin by assembling an implementation team (i.e. people who can assist you throughout the design, implementation and running of the scheme). If you do not need or want an implementation team as such, you should at least consult with a few colleagues who could give you useful tips and assist you in other ways too.

Either way, you are not alone in this venture: you can discuss all ideas and actions with others, and get input from experts in the field (i.e. mentoring scheme consultants). The steering committee (the implementation team *plus* sponsors), which has to be kept up-to-date at all times, constitutes a further source of ideas and inspiration, as do other stakeholders such as future mentors, mentees and their line managers, and colleagues. External input and assistance can be extremely reassuring, particularly if you are tasked with implementing a large-scale scheme such as an international one.

Once the implementation team is in place (and/or in parallel to assembling it), you should explicate in detail the objectives and long-range plans for the scheme, and begin to specify concrete actions for areas such as the parameters of the program, recruitment, training, matching, and mentoring agreements. Next you can think about an effective marketing strategy to inform organizational members of the forthcoming scheme.

By this stage you will typically already have an idea of all of the above issues, since you will have had to advise the sponsors on them when vying for their support; however, the implementation phase serves to finalize and consolidate initial ideas. What is more, this phase should involve all stakeholders as much as possible in order to create a scheme that will be supported and accepted.

Once you have drawn up a *plan* that considers all the steps of the implementation phase, you are ready to embark on the task of 'doing' it, i.e. implementing the program. You should begin this stage by marketing the scheme to the entire organization, but particularly to your mentor and mentee target groups. Next, we recommend that you hold focus groups involving all stakeholders, in which you can introduce your plans and gather feedback. This feedback should be considered seriously and, if appropriate, used to change your plans.

In general, the key to implementation is *flexibility*: to put together a successful scheme, you must involve others, take on board their suggestions, and generally be prepared to change your approach. The goals to aim for regarding the ultimate *Gestalt* of the program are that it must be:

- An excellent match with your corporate culture, and
- A satisfying balance between the needs and wishes of its stakeholders (i.e. mentors, mentees, line managers, the steering committee, and everyone else affected by the program).

References

Lacey, M. (1999). *Making Mentoring Happen: A Simple and Effective Guide to Implementing a Successful Mentoring Program.* Business and Professional Publishing Pty Ltd.

Training for mentoring schemes

Within informal mentoring relationships, the subject of training does not really surface. This is hardly surprising when you consider that most of the time the participants may not even know that a mentoring relationship is occurring between them. Even if third parties are aware of the existence of the mentoring association, they do not usually have any power to interfere. In that sense, informal mentoring can be regarded as organic, typically free from any outside input such as training and evaluation. However, where mentor and mentee have *previously* been trained for a formal mentoring relationship, the informal one is likely to be more formal and achieve more.

In formal mentoring schemes, it is essential to provide all those involved in a scheme with the right type of preparation for them to perform their roles successfully. A recent survey of 34 organizations that are hosting mentoring programs (CMSI, 2001) revealed that 96.1 per cent rated the thorough preparation and provision of training as important with 65.4 per cent giving it the highest rating possible, indicating *prime importance*. Most of these organizations (57.7 per cent) spend more than 16 hours on the development and delivery of mentoring training (the average lay at around 13 hours). Typically, mentoring training involved three or more people in the tasks of preparation and delivery.

Aside from this one small study, research on this subject is quite scarce. However, anecdotal evidence and case studies confirm that training does play a crucial role in ensuring the success of a mentoring scheme. For example, Nadine Klasen once conducted a training course for mentees at the Institute of Cancer Research. Prior to the training, mentees were very concerned about learning how to 'be a mentee', how to get the most out of the relationship, and what they could expect from their mentors. Evaluation at the end of the session showed that mentees felt much better equipped to use the relationship, and that they were less anxious and more willing to take charge of the association.

Training quality is more important than quantity. People need:

- A clear conceptual model to follow.
- An understanding of roles and responsibilities.
- An introduction to the relevant skills and techniques of mentoring, with an opportunity to practice and reflect on their performance.

Throughout the case studies presented in Chapters 3 and 8, it was notable how important these companies perceived training to be. Firms that did not originally train their mentoring population later felt that this had been a mistake and introduced it soon after in order to create more effective future mentoring relationships. Formal training may only be a small part of the investment – in some cases as little as 3–4 hours. Frequent, facilitated discussion sessions may provide ample opportunity for mentors to go through the full learning cycle: do, reflect, theorize, plan.

Why is mentoring training necessary?

Training helps to direct, support and enhance the potential for positive mentoring experiences. The word 'positive' cannot be over-emphasized; training within mentoring schemes *is* something positive – it is not a chore. It is something intended to help people understand their roles better so that they can contribute to the program's success and gain a lot from it in return. With regard to mentors and mentees, the objective of training can perhaps best be summarized as follows (Gibson, 1999):

> The objective of the training is not mastery of all the skills, but to equip them with the confidence to begin the relationship, the insight to recognize how it should be managed and the tools to identify where the relationship is being least effective and most importantly, how to take appropriate action.

Without training, mentoring schemes are likely to be less successful. Consider the following quotation by David Clutterbuck (1998):

> A rough estimate is that alliances put together without any training will deliver meaningful results for one or both parties in perhaps three out of ten relationships. If the helper is well trained, the success rate rises to around seven out of ten. If the learner is also trained, both parties are likely to record significant benefits in nine out of ten relationships. If third parties are also trained to support the relationship, the success rate may be even higher.

Although not quantitatively proven, this estimate is based on David Clutterbuck's experience with hundreds of mentoring schemes. Its main message is that the impact of well-designed training can be quite remarkable. We will now consider additional reasons for providing this type of support. Through training, mentors, mentees and other people involved in the program will:

- Not only be willing to participate, but also be capable of doing so. A typical pitfall associated with volunteer programs is that they sometimes attract people who are indeed highly motivated but who do not possess the competencies required for a particular role. In very rare cases no amount of training can rectify this situation, but most of the time training can provide people with the knowledge and skills necessary to perform well.
- Acquire realistic expectations of themselves, colleagues and the organizations with regards to the program.
- Gain insight into the appropriate as well as potentially harmful behaviours of the participants of mentoring relationships.

- Attain knowledge of problems that can potentially occur in mentoring relationships and programs. Training should equip them with appropriate resolution strategies so that problems do not escalate but can be managed positively.
- Be in a position to achieve maximum gains from and for the program.

Between mentoring schemes, a fairly wide range of training practices exists. This wide range is caused by factors such as the different sizes of programs and organizations, and varying budgets as well as diverging training philosophies. At one extreme there are those that provide mentors and mentees with programs stretching over several days, and at the other are organizations that provide only an information pack to participants. In most cases, we recommend an 'in-between-approach' – that is, although information packs are important and we suggest you use them, they should supplement a specific training program. Generalizing about the *duration* of a training program is difficult – perhaps impossible – as this will depend on the following factors:

- The needs of your trainees (e.g. mentors, mentees and relationship supervisors).
- The number and type of trainees.
- Your budget.

Initial mentoring training might involve a minimum of 3–4 hours per trainee group – usually $1-1\frac{1}{2}$ days for mentors and 1 day for mentees. Whatever the duration, by the end of this chapter we will have covered many of the options regarding training for mentoring schemes. So this chapter should help you to customize mentoring training to your needs, and to make a significant start on training design. On the other hand, you will also appreciate why it is so difficult to generalize about training provisions in terms of duration, trainee needs, training content and so on without a good understanding of your specific needs and aims.

In essence, this chapter should provide you with a thorough understanding of what *could* be important for your own mentoring training. You are then free to choose, pick and mix in order to design a program that best matches your requirements.

What else can you expect from this chapter? We intend to provide you with our advice on best practice in mentoring training. We also endeavour to cover all aspects of the subject of training. To this end, we will address the following topics:

- Who should receive training?
- Who is responsible for organizing the training?
- Who should conduct the training?
- Training needs analysis.
- Who should be trained with whom?
- The contents of training programs.
- The timing of training.
- Training methods.

When we use the word 'training' in this chapter, we do not only mean practical *skills* training. Whilst important this is only one facet of training, the other one being *briefing* – i.e. the passing on of factual information about the mentoring scheme. So from now on, whenever we use the word 'training' we are referring to both the skills and the knowledge component. However, when we focus on the knowledge component, we will use the word 'briefing'.

Who should receive training?

The simple answer to that question is 'ideally everyone involved with the mentoring program'. The concerned parties and the training that they might require are summarized in Table 9.1.

Equipped with the right knowledge, skills and attitudes, all of this will help to make the scheme a success. Thus, mentors and mentees are of course the main players in the scheme, holding the predominant influence over creating positive or negative mentoring experiences. Program co-ordinators, relationship supervisors and administration staff are the people responsible for the smooth running of the scheme. They have to plan and organize, select and match participants and deal with any problems that might arise. The scheme's sponsors will of course also pave the way for an effective scheme by providing money, the permission to run the scheme and emotional backing.

In reality, providing every one of these parties with training is not always feasible. Consider, for example, the case of senior management, who typically sponsor a mentoring scheme both financially and in terms of goodwill. Although they should receive a detailed briefing on scheme facts together with other scheme participants, time constraints might prevent them from taking this up. They might prefer to receive their own short version of a briefing, which is separate from that of others. If

Table 9.1 Trainee groups within mentoring programs

Trainee group	Training potentially required
Mentors	Skills training and briefing
Mentees	Skills training and briefing
Relationship supervisors	Skills training and briefing on scheme and role
Program co-ordinator(s)	Skills training and briefing on scheme and role
Assistant program co-ordinators	Briefing on scheme and role
Administration staff	Briefing on scheme and role
Scheme sponsors such as senior management, line managers and external clients	All: briefing on scheme. Line managers only: briefing on role

they can attend a briefing session jointly with the scheme's participants it helps to make the program more credible and more attractive. It signals to participants that the scheme is important to the whole organization and that it is a privilege to be part of it. Furthermore, where top management does invest the time to participate in the full training experience, it sends a powerful positive message.

The special case of the program co-ordinator

In most mentoring schemes the program co-ordinator is either the mentoring champion or has at least been working on the design and implementation of the scheme from very early on, so he or she will have received a very early and personalized briefing. This implies that the program co-ordinator will be highly familiar with the scheme already, and any further briefing superfluous. In many schemes it is the program co-ordinator who conducts the briefing for participants, for example through 'lunch and learn' sessions. Hence, this chapter will assume that the program co-ordinator of your scheme does not require further briefing, either on the scheme or on the role. However, we will assume that some *skills* training is necessary, the nature of which will be described later on.

In Table 9.1 we listed the mentee as requiring training, and you might wonder why this is necessary at all. The mentee's role in the mentoring relationship is often thought of as being easy – after all, mentees are receiving help, advice and support from mentors who are suitably equipped to 'do mentoring'. This view is supported by a concept of the mentee being similar to a student in a teacher–student relationship. In reality, mentees hold the key to successful mentoring equally with mentors. They are not empty vessels into which mentors pour information and advice; rather, mentees are thinking beings, with the choice to enter into the relationship in the first place and the power to steer and direct it.

Successful relationships require mentees to seek, welcome, receive and utilize input from mentors, often within psychologically testing environments. Some related research by David Clutterbuck on coaching relationships found that the way in which learners approached the coach had a major effect on the style of help that they received. Training coachees to prepare how they presented their issues to the coach made it much easier to get the appropriate response in style terms. Our view is therefore that mentee training is every bit as important and necessary as mentor preparation.

Who is responsible for organizing the training?

The onus of responsibility for organizing the training falls on the person who has been chosen to oversee the program. This is often the program co-ordinator, who is responsible for managing, maintaining and evaluating the program. Keeping the management of training in the program co-ordinator's hands further ensures that there is one overall point of contact for the whole program and its various elements. Since this individual will have had contact with virtually all participants, he or she is in a good position to determine who requires training and who should carry it out, and is additionally well placed to provide input into the training design – i.e. will be in the picture with regard to the possible training contents.

Who should conduct the training?

In Chapter 8 we touched on this topic when considering the different responsibilities of program co-ordinators, relationship supervisors and trainers. As you might remember, we then presented three options:

1. Your own in-house trainers.
2. A manager (from, for example, the HR department) who knows a lot about mentoring/mentoring schemes and who has either trained before and/or could be effectively trained by a trainer-trainer to conduct a training session – please note that this person might well be the program co-ordinator.
3. External professional trainers specializing in mentoring.

The latter two points mention the topic of trainer specialization. Naturally, employing a trainer who knows a particular subject very well is always likely to be much more effective. Such trainers are likely to be more flexible when it comes to training design, the materials and methods they will use tend to be more appropriate, and they are better equipped to deal with unforeseen situations during the training sessions. With regard to training for mentoring schemes, we therefore recommend that you choose specialist trainers. There are a variety of companies that offer this service, but when choosing between them be sure to inquire about their track record and ask for some client references. Specifically, you need to know that the trainer can demonstrate sustainability, a robust conceptual model, and practical lessons from previous schemes.

Training needs analysis

The optimal preparation for designing effective mentoring training involves:

- Understanding the roles and intentions of each party associated with the scheme.
- Identifying the knowledge, skills and attitudes that each trainee group needs in order to perform their role effectively.
- Assessing the different groups against these knowledge, skill and attitude requirements, i.e. conducting a training needs analysis (see Chapter 8 for a more detailed explanation of this topic).

Once you have carried out these three steps, you will be able to choose appropriate training objectives and design effective programs tailored to your trainees' needs. In this section, we will consider the topic of training needs analysis in more detail. When conducting a needs analysis for a mentoring scheme, it is vital to involve the people who will be receiving the training. By encouraging them to be active in diagnosing their own needs, their motivation to participate in the actual training sessions will be enhanced because they feel a sense of ownership over the program and perceive the contents as more relevant to them.

Among the methods that can be used to establish the training needs of mentoring scheme trainees are:

- Interviews and/or questionnaires to identify the areas in which training is needed; using this method, you can assess deficits in knowledge, skill and attitude.
- Role plays or case studies for participants in which they can demonstrate the skills and attitudes required for their role.
- If possible, assessing the evaluation data of previous mentoring schemes/mentoring relationships: what did participants want more of and less of? What specific skill and knowledge gaps did the majority of mentors/mentees/relationship supervisors display?

Who should be trained with whom?

Deciding which trainee group should be trained together, and indeed whether this should happen at all, will depend on a variety of factors, such as:

- Your budget.
- Your training philosophy.
- The organization of your program – for example, if the relationship supervisors are part of your implementation team, they will need their briefings to happen much earlier than mentors and mentees do; this means that you cannot therefore brief these three groups jointly on the scheme facts.
- The size of your scheme – the larger your scheme the more people require training, and the more people require training the more groups you will tend to have, because training group sizes need to be managed to ensure the effectiveness of the training. Variations in training needs are likely to be more pronounced in larger schemes, too. With regard to mentors and mentees, you might want to accommodate diverging training needs by grouping together those requiring more and those requiring less support – for example, separate novice mentors from experienced mentors

on counts such as the practical skills training. However, do train them jointly on other topics since novice mentors can learn substantially from discussions with their more experienced counterparts. Remember, though, that while every mentor's skills might theoretically need refreshing, you should never force people to take part in such training. Make it optional so that mentors do not feel disenchanted with the scheme before it has even started.

You might remember that this latter approach was adopted by David Megginson and Paul Stokes of Sheffield Hallam University (see Case study 3.1). All of their mentors were seasoned managing directors who had mentored throughout their careers and did not perceive it as appropriate to engage in formal skills training. They were, however, happy to discuss their skills and share experiences.

Naturally, there are diverging opinions between organizations as well as consultants as to the right approach to pairing decisions. There are those that advocate training groups together on some aspects but not on others. Apart from the example of Sheffield Hallam University, the Leadership Consortium (in association with British Telecom) also ran a combined induction for mentors and mentees. This induction included the background to the schemes in BT, information on what mentoring is, what was expected of mentors, and where to get support. Mentors and mentees were also encouraged to talk about prior mentoring experiences (see Case study 3.3).

On the other hand, there are companies and consultants that tend to keep trainee groups, particularly mentors and mentees, strictly separate. For some, such as the Yellowbrick Consultancy (Yellowbrick Consulting, 2000), this seems to be a matter of principle:

> Generally it is better that the mentors and protégés have individual forums to allow wide-ranging discussions regarding their respective roles (which might be inhibited in each other's presence).

(Note that the inhibition is a consequence of the power–distance aspect of sponsorship mentoring, and is less of an issue for developmental mentoring relationships.) For others, training separately seems to be a matter of practicality. This is the case at Allianz Insurance (see Case study 3.8) where, as you will remember, mentoring for employees is one facet of an international management training program. Since the participants need induction to the whole of the training program, Allianz incorporated the mentee training into this overall induction. Separating mentor and mentee training was therefore a logistical decision.

In general, we believe that some combination of trainee groups is advantageous. What are these advantages?

- Training mentors and mentees jointly on some aspects enables them to get to know each other, and this enhanced familiarity will aid the matching process. As the participants in Megginson and Stokes' scheme said, it helps them to understand much better what the scheme is all about.
- Holding joint briefing sessions with all the parties involved in the scheme also fosters trust in the scheme and provides people with an opportunity to get to know the individuals they will be in close contact with (e.g. the program co-ordinator and the relationship supervisors).
- Combined training allows participants to explore mentoring from the other person's perspective. They can even practice being the other person!
- Pairing trainee groups takes some of the pressure off the training administrator and is a more cost-efficient way of running training programs.

On the basis of the above, Table 9.2 shows our suggested approach to the pairing of trainee groups.

When it comes to *skills* training, you may want to split mentors and mentees further into novice and experienced groups. As pointed out earlier, some of the highly experienced mentors might view it as an affront to be asked to partake in practical exercises on, for example, their listening skills.

The contents of training programs

As with all training, the training for mentoring schemes can be split into three behavioural components: knowledge, skills and attitudes. With regard to the first two, we mentioned earlier that training for mentoring schemes should mainly consist of conveying factual knowledge about the scheme and the roles of individuals by way of presentations and discussions, and helping people to master the skills they need for their roles by engaging them in practical exercises. The matter is not quite as straightforward as far as the attitude component is concerned. As every trainer will know, it is very difficult to attend to attitudes effectively – i.e. to change them purposefully during

Table 9.2 Pairing trainee groups

Training need	Trainee groups to be joined
Briefing on scheme facts	All: mentors, mentees, relationship supervisors, line managers, senior management/ external clients, and support staff
	(This list does not include the program co-ordinator since we are assuming that s/he might actually conduct the briefing. If s/he is not conducting it, s/he should nevertheless be present in order to ensure that s/he begins to form a positive relationship with the scheme's participants)
Expectation management ('Attitudes' can be omitted)	Mentors and mentees – but the following general rule should be adhered to:
	✓ If mentors and/or mentees are graduates or otherwise inexperienced with work life, train them *separately*
	✓ If mentors and mentees are experienced employees such as managers and/or professionals, train them *together*
	Again, if the program co-ordinator is not conducting this part of the training anyway, s/he should still attend it. This is because
	✓ It will provide useful information for his/ her efforts to match mentors and mentees. Thus, they are given the opportunity to listen to the expectations of mentors and mentees and to observe the chemistry between them. This will help to prevent mismatches
	✓ Mentors, mentees and program co-ordinators can begin to establish a relationship
Skills training: conflict management and counselling	Relationship supervisors and program co-ordinators (if appropriate)

a short training session. This is because attitudes are caused and changed by so many different factors unique to the individual – a situation that is not helped by the fact that the attitudes of different people are also extremely diverse.

Perhaps the best way of ensuring that participants gain awareness of attitudinal requirements is to:

- First, talk to your trainees about the attitudes expected of them; ask them what attitudes they hold and what attitudes they think they should hold.
- Secondly, define what type of attitude you would like to see associated with each role (e.g. with that of a mentor: openness towards the mentee; being committed to the mentee and having his or her best interests at heart). Explain to trainees why the attitudes you expect them to hold are actually important.

In a moment we will look at the content of mentoring training sessions for each trainee group, which is summarized in Table 9.3.

However, prior to considering the content of mentoring training, we would like to emphasize a few points. First, the *quality* of training is by far more important than its quantity. In no training session will it be possible, or indeed desirable, to attend to the full range of competencies (defined here as behaviours necessary for effective job performance) required by mentoring program trainees. Reasons for this include budgetary limitations, limitations in the extent to which people *can* be trained on certain competencies, limitations in time and, very importantly, limitations in the trainees' concentration span.

It is therefore important to align the training contents to your pool of trainees wherever possible. Naturally you cannot tailor training to the needs of every individual trainee, but you should research the needs of the majority and use these as a baseline. In this chapter we will address what we perceive as being the most essential components of mentoring training programs – yet they should only be included in your program if they are really needed by your trainees.

Secondly, when you design your own training program it is important that you understand precisely what the roles of your trainees entail. Only then can you conduct a meaningful training needs analysis as well as create an effective training program.

Thirdly, mentoring training, like all other training, should never result in an imposing process such as talking *at* trainees for several hours without considering their views and allowing

Table 9.3 Mentoring trainee groups and training agendas

	Mentors	Mentees	Relationship supervisors	Program co-ordinator(s)	Line managers	Sponsors and clients	Administration staff
Knowledge component	Briefing on scheme facts	Briefing on scheme facts	Briefing on role and scheme facts	Briefing on role and scheme facts	Briefing on role and scheme facts	Briefing on scheme	Briefing on role and scheme facts
	Behaviours to avoid	Behaviours to avoid					
	The mentoring process	The mentoring process					
	Mentor competencies	Benefiting from mentoring					
	Career management basics						
Skill component	Active listening	Active listening	Conflict handling	Conflict handling			
	Questioning	Receiving feedback	Counselling	Counselling			
	Giving feedback	Conflict handling; constructive challenge					
	Building rapport						
	Counselling						
	Coaching techniques						
	Conflict handling; constructive challenge						
Attitude component	Expectation management	Expectation management					

them to interact. There are several reasons underlying this suggestion, including that:

- Individuals have different learning styles and, in order to ensure that all trainees learn as much as possible, different methods should be applied.
- People tend to have fairly different conceptions of mentoring, and if they are not given a chance to voice these you will not be able to manage these different views in an attempt to ensure that their concepts approximate yours (i.e. those of the organization).
- Trainees might become angry and distressed if they are made to feel that their views do not count.

On the basis of the above, we recommend that you intersperse your 'lecturing' with as much interactivity as possible – provide plenty of space for trainees to ask questions, discuss topics and engage in role-plays. Remember that they can learn as much or more from each other as from the trainer!

Training content for mentors

There follows an outline of a possible training agenda for mentors. You do not have to include all of the components into your training session; which ones to include and to what extent will entirely depend on your trainee's level of knowledge, skills and attitudes prior to training.

Briefing on scheme facts

This briefing can be used for all trainee groups, and may include:

- The purpose/objective of the scheme, including who it is currently open to (the mentee target group).
- The expected benefits of mentoring for mentors/mentees/the organization (alternatively, you could leave this to be an interactive discussion later on in the training).
- Who is behind the scheme – i.e. whose brainchild it is, who sponsors it and who is in charge of it?
- The scope of the scheme – how many people are involved in running the scheme? Who are these people and what roles do they occupy? How many participants (mentors and mentees) will be involved in the scheme? Who else will have an impact on the scheme (e.g. line managers and sponsors)?

- Where are the mentors drawn from?
- Time frames – when is it supposed to commence? How long is it supposed to run for? How long are the mentoring relationships meant to last for on a formal basis?
- The organization of the scheme – how are mentors and mentees being selected and matched? What administrative duties do mentors and mentees have to fulfil? (e.g. are mentoring agreements obligatory? Are PDPs expected? Progress reviews? If yes, what is the procedure for any one of these?)
- Involvement of third parties – how do others, such as scheme co-ordinators, relationship supervisors and line managers, feature in the mentoring relationships?
- How and when will the scheme be evaluated?

Expectation management – the mentor's role, the mentee's role and what the organization expects

As you will remember from our conclusions in Chapter 3, virtually all companies that contributed case studies to our book incorporated expectation management into their training sessions. If you want to ensure that your program runs as planned, then keeping with this tradition is of great importance. It is also vital to have sufficient time in the training program for this issue.

Expectation management really consists of three parts, as depicted in Figure 9.1.

The first part entails asking the mentors about their views with regard to the following subjects: how do they view their role? What do they expect from the organization/the mentoring scheme? This is a good way of finding out whether there are any significant discrepancies between the perceptions of mentors and those of the organization. If you have provided sufficient information prior to training (for example, an information pack), you will typically find that there are no worrying differences in expectations. However, if there are, these need to be managed in order to avoid future problems. The best way to manage gaping differences in expectations is in a one-to-one setting outside the training context, and involving the program co-ordinator. This is particularly true if you suspect that a particular individual might not be able to remain on the program because the mismatch in expectations seems irreconcilable.

The second part involves you explaining to potential mentors how the *organization* views mentors and what they expect them to do. This might include the following points:

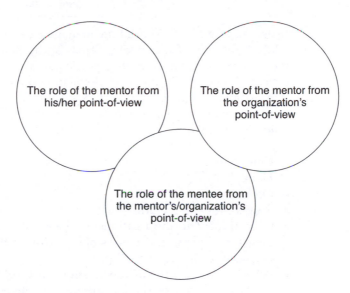

Figure 9.1 The three stages of expectation management for the mentor.

- The organization's preferred definition and model of mentoring (by 'model' we mean conceptions of mentoring, such as the 'integrating model' first introduced in Chapter 1).
- Supporting mentees in identifying career-related development needs, setting development goals and creating development plans in line with the objectives of the mentoring scheme.
- Helping mentees to balance personal objectives with the objectives of the mentoring scheme.
- Supporting mentees in decision-making and problem-solving through coaching, counselling, guarding, networking and facilitating.
- Enabling mentees to become independent thinkers through questioning, listening and feedback.
- Helping mentees to explore potential options and their outcomes.
- Providing a safe space without judgment or unsolicited criticism.
- Meeting with mentees (for example, once per month) and being contactable by telephone/e-mail throughout the rest of the month.
- Ensuring that any administration related to the mentoring sessions occurs – for example, the filling in of progress reviews (unless, of course, this is the sole responsibility of another person such as the relationship supervisor).
- Confidentiality.
- Honesty.
- Respect for the mentee.

In the final part of expectation management, you will have to address the role of the mentee. This can be done in two stages: the first stage involves asking participants to define what *they* expect of mentees. In the second stage, you could provide them with a brief insight into what the *organization* believes mentors can reasonably expect of mentees. This is likely to include the following points:

- Confidentiality.
- Honesty.
- Openness.
- Respect for the mentor.
- Commitment to the relationship, including keeping appointments, sticking to the actions agreed during the meetings and engaging in the relationship.
- Being proactive – the mentee taking charge of the relationship, e.g. setting an agenda for meetings, calling on the mentor when necessary, being active in identifying development needs and realizing the personal development plan.
- The desire to grow – wanting to learn and grow and accepting the mentor's help in doing so.
- Developing independence – mentees should learn how to help themselves and find their own solutions to problems rather than becoming dependent on the mentor (naturally, this process should be enabled by the mentor).

As you will see when reading about mentee training below, we suggest that you take a similar approach to their expectations regarding the role of the mentor – that is, ask them first about what they expect from mentors and then reflect back to them what the organization sees as the mentor's role. An alternative approach is that taken by David Megginson and Paul Stokes of Sheffield Hallam Business School (Case study 3.1). As you might remember, they are running a mentoring scheme for businesses wanting to diversify into the export market. As far as training was concerned, they provided mentors and mentees with a joint workshop session, during which they asked them to discuss their expectations of each other. Mentors, mentees as well as the program co-ordinators found this to be highly valuable in managing expectations.

Expectation management can either end here or proceed to include the following elements:

1. *What do mentors not do*: provide participants with information on what mentors do not do. This should list behaviours such as:

- Telling/directing.
- Providing mentees with solutions.
- Deciding for mentees.
- Getting mentees promoted.
- Solving conflicts for the mentees.
- Assuming responsibility for the mentee's career or personal development.

2. *Attitudes towards the mentee*: a discussion of attitudinal requirements with regard to the mentee could be as follows: mentors ought to:
   - Hold a genuine belief in the capabilities of mentees to make progress.
   - Have a sincere interest in mentees and have their best interests at heart.
   - Trust mentees.
   - Be fully committed to the relationship.
   - Be open towards mentees.
   - Be non-judgemental.
   - Be committed to both parties learning.

Skills training

Highly experienced mentors, particularly those stemming from top management levels, might be unwilling to partake in any lengthy training. Skills training in particular might be viewed as unnecessary. The trainer must be very sensitive to issues such as this during both training design and training delivery, and will have to strike a balance between what mentors need and what they want. In addition, highly experienced mentors might really not require skills training, and this might be revealed during the training needs analysis.

If you do decide to conduct skills training for mentors, please refer back to Table 9.3 for a listing of skills you might want to include in training for mentors (a later section, 'Training methods', will provide you with some practical suggestions regarding skills training exercises).

Handling problems in mentoring relationships – constructive challenge

This is an important point and should not be skipped. Mentors, particularly novice ones, must be aware of what could go wrong within mentoring relationships. This awareness can help them to pre-empt problems by adjusting their own behaviour. If problems do nevertheless occur, this training will at least have prepared them and provided them with guidance on how to deal with common difficulties. One method of conflict management that should be introduced to trainees is 'constructive challenge'.

However, a word of caution is required with regard to high-lighting problems in relationships: do by all means refrain from scaremongering. Although problems between mentors and mentees do occur, they are usually very minor and can be resolved without recourse to a third party. More serious issues rarely arise. It is probably best if you stick to describing two or three problem scenarios and then ask participants to discuss courses of action that could be taken to resolve the issues. BT and BitC used this approach for their mentor and mentee training for the Roots & Wings schools mentoring scheme (Case study 3.3).

In cases where relationship problems are serious and cannot be resolved between mentor and mentee, you might want to suggest that they should contact the relationship supervisor or program co-ordinator. (For more detail on problems in mentoring relationships, see Chapter 11.)

Undesirable mentor behaviours

Just as there are behaviours a mentor should demonstrate, there are also behaviours that should be avoided at all costs. These include:

- Telling – even if it might be comfortable for a mentee to be told what to do without having to think and decide, too much direction defeats the aims of mentoring. For example, if a mentor is too autocratic the mentee's growth towards self-reliance is not supported. Furthermore, mentors who push their own agenda do not actually focus on their mentees' needs, rendering mentoring worthless to them.
- Having preconceptions – preconceived ideas regarding mentees, their needs and their business obstructs the identi-fications of their real needs.
- Passing judgement – mentors ought to give feedback to their mentees but only as agreed. Thus, mentors should be tactful about feedback and ask mentees whether they would like to receive it. As mentioned previously, unexpected feedback can come as a major shock, particularly if negative. When giving feedback, the mentor should not be judgmental regarding the mentee's actions as this can cause great offence. What is more, at the end of the day it is the mentee who has to make decisions – the mentor's role is solely that of an objective sounding board.
- Defensiveness – when a mentee provides a mentor with

critical feedback, the mentor should react calmly, accepting the feedback and reflecting upon it. The latter are reactions mentors would expect to see in mentees, so they should set an example by acting in the same manner.

- Offensiveness – it is one of the tasks of a mentor to help mentees develop self-confidence and to grow by enabling them to accept and master certain challenges. However, the mentee might occasionally be apprehensive when it comes to pursuing challenging tasks. In such situations, mentors must refrain from being aggressive or sarcastic towards the anxieties and concerns voiced by their mentee.
- Emotional instability – displaying depressive, aggressive or simply moody behaviour is a taboo for mentors. They must learn how to manage their emotions so as to be capable of providing mentees with the calmness, patience and reflectivity that is required of them.
- Patronizing behaviour – even if a mentor has had more experience and acquired more knowledge than a mentee, there is no need to be patronizing or condescending. This will only serve to reinforce any potential insecurities that mentees might harbour, rather than help them build their self-confidence. In extreme cases, such behaviour might even lead to the premature break up of the relationship.
- Interrupting the mentee – the effect of interrupting mentees too early whilst they are attempting to solve a problem/make a decision has a similar effect to the one described above: it also hinders the process of building self-confidence as well as the development of a mentee's analytical and problem-solving skills.
- Disinterest – a mentoring relationship will suffer if enthusiasm for and interest in the mentee is blatantly absent. However, faked interest is no good either since the mentee is bound to notice – it really must be genuine. Sincere interest motivates, creates openness, and inspires self-confidence within mentees; it is also necessary in order to provide the level of support that they require.
- Limited time and effort – mentors should also refrain from making mentees feel that they are not prepared to invest appropriate time and effort into the mentees' development. This will be interpreted as lack of commitment and can, once again, compromise an otherwise healthy relationship.

Additional behaviours that mentors should avoid can be gauged from Chapter 5 by simply reversing the list of desirable characteristics. For example, one of the attributes a mentor should possess is patience: during your training session, mentors could be encouraged critically to evaluate themselves with regard to patience, as well as some of the other characteristics mentioned above and in Chapter 5. Using a short self-evaluation questionnaire might be a good way of dealing with this. Such an activity could either be seen as a way of stimulating mentor's self-awareness, or it could form the basis of a group discussion. Naturally, the content of the questionnaires should remain confidential – you should not try to force anyone to talk about their responses. Furthermore, the questionnaires should remain the property of the trainees.

Inexperienced mentors

When organizing training content for inexperienced mentors, include:

- Mentor competency (see Chapter 5).
- The mentoring process (Chapter 6).
- Career management basics.

The latter point typically concentrates on three different areas: clarifying responsibility for career management; establishing short-term and long-term goals and finding ways of achieving these; and having a good appreciation of the needs and interests of the individual (whose career requires managing) in relation to the needs and interests of the organization.

Training content for mentees

Whilst prospective mentees may already possess many of the capabilities needed for 'being a mentee', they will not necessarily know which ones to draw upon in mentoring relationships, or how to do this most effectively so as to maximize their gains. A good analogy is that of driving a car under varying circumstances. Drivers are usually adept at driving on a variety of roads, surfaces and under changing conditions, and even different vehicles do not tend to pose a problem to most drivers. Yet if these same drivers were put in a Formula 1 car under race conditions they would be expected to fail miserably, despite the fact that it is again only their ability to drive that is being called upon. Difficulties are likely to be caused by not having had driving experience specifically within Grand Prix racing environments – drivers would simply not know how to best use their capabilities. Mentees often claim that they are unsure of how they should behave within a mentoring relationship and how to get the most out of it. This signals that they do need some help to acquaint themselves with a mentoring situation, even though the behaviours they will be asked to use are not new to them.

In many respects, mentor and mentee training will tend to overlap not only with each other but also with the training (or rather the briefing) required by other people. In terms of mentee training, the greater the work experience of mentees, the more their training can overlap with that of mentors. This is because it is important for the mentee to appreciate the mentor's perspective. As a general rule remember:

- If mentees are graduates and younger, less experienced people, they are best trained separately from the mentors.
- If mentees are more experienced managers and professional personnel, they should be trained jointly with the mentors; this allows participants to swap roles for greater insights, and creates an opportunity for pairings to be organized at the training event.

Let us now proceed to looking at a potential mentee training agenda.

Briefing on scheme facts

See above under 'Training contents for mentors'.

Expectation management – the mentee's role and what the organization expects

This issue consists virtually of the same elements as the expectation management for mentors:

1. The role of the mentee from his or her viewpoint: ask mentees to describe their views regarding their role. Encourage them to articulate what they expect from the scheme and what they are hoping to gain from the mentoring relationships. The trainer can then manage these expectations by, for example, moving on to the bullet points below, which serves to advise mentees of realistic and unrealistic expectations.
2. The role of the mentee from an organizational viewpoint: provide your view on the role of mentees as well as a brief on what the organization expects of them. This is likely to feature the following elements:
   - Mentees are in charge of the relationship: for example, they are responsible for managing their own learning; they

should be active in identifying and achieving goals, setting an agenda for meetings, and utilizing the mentor.

- Commitment, including keeping appointments and sticking to agreed actions.
- Confidentiality.
- Honesty.
- Openness.
- Mutual respect between mentor and mentee.
- A desire to learn and grow and to accept the mentor's help in doing so (for example, by playing the 'question game' – this means not being defensive when the mentor asks reflective or probing questions, and rather seeing it as an opportunity to learn about a new way of solving problems).
- The development of independence – mentees should learn how to help themselves and find their own solutions to problems rather than becoming dependent on the mentor.

3. The role of the mentor: how do mentees see it and what does the organization believe mentees can expect of mentors? The answer to the latter part of the question has previously been provided in the section on mentor training. Here is a reminder of its content:

- The organization's preferred definition and model of mentoring.
- Supporting mentees in setting career-related development goals and creating development plans in line with the objectives of the mentoring scheme.
- Helping mentees to balance personal objectives with the objectives of the mentoring scheme.
- Supporting mentees in decision-making, problem-solving and goal achievement through coaching, counselling, guarding, networking and facilitating.
- Enabling mentees to become independent thinkers through questioning, listening and feedback.
- Helping mentees to explore potential options and their outcomes.
- Providing a safe space without judgment or unsolicited criticism.
- Meeting with mentees (for example once per month) and being contactable by telephone/e-mail throughout the rest of the month.
- Ensuring that any administration related to the mentoring sessions occurs, for example the filling in of progress reviews (unless, of course, this is the sole responsibility of another person such as the relationship supervisor).

- Confidentiality.
- Honesty.
- Mutual respect between mentor and mentee.

As with the mentor training, you might want to add a briefing on attitudinal requirements to the agenda point of expectation management. Desirable mentee attitudes include:

- Openness towards the mentor and his or her methods.
- Trust in the mentor.
- Being enthusiastic about the relationship.
- Commitment to the relationship.
- Not being arrogant.

How to gain the benefits from mentoring relationships

The importance of covering this topic both for mentees and for the overall success of the scheme cannot be overemphasized. A good way of ensuring that mentees know how to behave in mentoring relationships and how to gain the benefits is suggested in the following summary:

1. Engage in expectation management.
2. Help them to understand the basics of career management.
3. Bring in experienced mentees: they could be encouraged to share with the novice mentees how to achieve the greatest gains.
4. Recommend the following tactics to mentees:
   - Ask them to get stuck in, to take the relationship seriously, to be committed, open to change, and willing to learn.
   - Encourage them to ensure that they know what is expected of them and to fulfil this (for example by implementing the personal development plan, attending meetings etc.).
   - Remind them to be proactive; this includes preparing meetings and taking notes during the sessions, thinking about development needs, seeking and utilizing learning opportunities, asking for feedback, and asking the mentor to articulate his or her expectations.
   - Encourage them to listen carefully to feedback from the mentor and to useful messages 'hidden' in questions.
   - Impress the importance of involving their line managers.
   - Offer them a learning styles assessment and encourage them to utilize their knowledge about their most/least preferred styles (see Chapter 6).

Skills training

The previous agenda point could then be followed up with skills training that is linked to some of the recommendations you have made to mentees. Skills to be addressed include:

- Active listening.
- Receiving feedback.

There is an additional skill that is of importance to mentees but on which no real skills training (in the truest sense of the meaning of the word) can be conducted. This skill is 'personal development planning and the identification of development needs'. It would suffice to cover it by providing mentees with information on how to go about identifying their development needs and setting up a PDP. This information could be as follows.

Explain what a PDP consists of. This would typically include a section in which to write down development goals, one in which to stipulate how and when these are going to be achieved and a section for start and completion dates, review dates, and signatures. Furthermore, you might want to provide mentees with some ideas as to how to identify their development needs, which is something that can occasionally pose a problem, particularly for inexperienced mentees. Thus, you could suggest the following approaches:

- Filling out a self-assessment questionnaire such as the Myers–Briggs-Type Indicator. This personality inventory provides insights into a person's Jungian type, which has been found to be a useful basis for purposes such as self-development, career development and career counselling.
- Consulting with a line manager.
- Reflecting on work and/or personal life.

Handling problems in mentoring relationships – constructive challenge

Once again, do not scaremonger when tackling this point. It is wise to describe some potential problems (see Chapter 11), but it is equally necessary to emphasize that serious problems such as sexual harassment are very rare occurrences. Most problems encountered by mentoring participants are much more mundane, and include anxiety on the part of the mentee about 'taking the mentor's time', 'lack of depth in discussions', or 'meeting slippage'. Nevertheless, try to address the following issues: what problem situations could arise in a mentoring relationship? How do I deal with these? What do I do if I want to opt out of the relationship? As with mentor training, emphasize the importance of learning to challenge constructively in order to solve conflicts.

Behaviours to avoid

As with mentors, there is a range of behaviours that mentees should not display. You might want to remind mentees of these. As stated in Chapter 5, these entail:

- Emotional distance.
- Argumentativeness.
- Arrogance.
- Disinterest.
- Sloppiness.

The mentor's worst nightmare is the mentee who absorbs everything but never reacts and puts things into action – this kind of mentee is also often referred to as a 'black hole'.

What happens during mentoring meetings? – The mentoring process

Here you could provide a brief account of what mentees can expect to happen during the first and subsequent meetings (see Chapter 6).

Training content for relationship supervisors

Briefing on scheme facts

See above under 'Training contents for mentors'.

Briefing on the role of relationship supervisors

This involves advising relationship supervisors of their responsibilities and duties. The exact content will once again depend on your definition of this role. In Chapter 8, we described aspects that *can* be associated with it. These involve:

- Periodically monitoring the progress of the relationship.
- Acting as the first point of contact for mentors and mentees should there be any questions or problems; liaising with the program co-ordinator about problems; and potentially

- Attending the first meeting to help clarify any issues and to provide help with documentation. This, however is not very common and only occurs in a handful of schemes.

If one of the responsibilities of your relationship supervisors is to manage problems rather than referring mentor and mentee to the co-ordinator, they will need training on this subject.

Skills training

Whether skills training for relationship supervisors is necessary at all will depend on the nature of the role. Thus, if the relationship supervisor does need to become involved in managing relationship problems, you might want to provide training in the following two skills:

- Conflict management.
- Counselling.

Handling problems in mentoring relationships

As with the 'problem training' for mentors and mentees, you might want to start off by introducing the types of problems that could arise. In addition, point out which ones are more/less likely to occur. In the case of the relationship supervisor, it is probably advisable to address a wider range of problem scenarios than you did with mentors and mentees simply because you can then provide clearer guidelines as for how to deal with any one of these. This latter point is of course very important: whoever bears responsibility for managing problems in mentoring relationships requires clearly outlined procedures as to how to go about this. Thus, even if problem management is the duty of the program co-ordinator and he or she has been championing the scheme from the very start, it is important that time is taken to sit down and develop guidelines for potential scenarios. Although it is unlikely that something serious will happen, if it does the 'problem manager' is at least somewhat prepared, which helps to prevent the exacerbation of issues. (NB: if you will be running a mentoring scheme within one company only, mentors and mentees will probably be asked to adopt your existing disciplinary/grievance procedures if a serious offence occurs. However, if you are organizing a scheme for other parties, e.g. a range of individuals or companies, you should certainly think about establishing such procedures.)

Training content for the program co-ordinator

As mentioned in the introduction of this chapter, we are assuming that the program co-ordinator of your scheme does not require further briefing, either on the scheme or on the role. We are also assuming that he or she is familiar with mentoring and the implementation and maintenance of mentoring schemes. However, should this not apply in your case and your co-ordinator does require support on these aspects, you can use the materials previously provided in this book as guidelines:

1. For a description of the role of the program co-ordinator, see Chapter 8.
2. The contents of the briefing on scheme facts has been covered in this chapter under 'Training contents for mentors'.
3. To promote the program co-ordinator's knowledge of mentoring and the implementation and maintenance of mentoring schemes, you could do some or all of the following:
   - Ask the program co-ordinator to read up on the subject of mentoring and mentoring schemes.
   - Use the content of this book as a basis for creating either a presentation or an information pack on these subjects.
   - Encourage him or her to consult with colleagues in other organizations who have been involved in running mentoring programs.
   - Ask the program co-ordinator to speak to individuals in your or another organization about their mentoring experiences.
   - Employ a consultant specializing in mentoring and mentoring schemes with whom the co-ordinator can discuss ideas.

In general, a training agenda for the program co-ordinator could entail the following points.

Handling problems in mentoring relationships

Irrespective of whether your program employs relationship supervisors to deal with relationship problems or not, the co-ordinator will always have the final responsibility for managing difficult situations. Since the same principles apply to the program co-ordinator as to the relationship supervisor regarding this subject, you might want to structure the training in similar ways.

Skills training

There are unlikely to be many skills on which the co-ordinator requires training. This is because he or she should have been recruited on the strength of possessing the skills needed to carry out the role effectively. Skill requirements for the program co-ordinator include:

- Project (or program) management.
- General management.
- Presentation.
- Administration.
- Evaluation, measurement and quality assurance.

The skills on which you might want to provide training or, if you are the program co-ordinator, seek training, are as follows:

- Conflict management.
- Counselling.

Training content for line managers

As with the administration staff, line managers will only tend to require a briefing on the scheme as well as an explanation of their role. The latter should make clear to them:

- Whether and how they are expected to get involved in the mentoring relationships.
- Their importance in making the relationship work by, for example, being supportive and understanding, not being suspicious and not interfering in a destructive manner.
- The benefits they gain from having employees who receive developmental training through a mentor.

Training content for senior management and external clients

For senior management and external clients, a briefing on scheme facts will usually constitute the only form of training required. However, since you will already have consulted with either or both of these parties regarding the implementation of your scheme, they should already be very familiar with it. Their familiarity will have been underscored by your efforts to keep them in the picture throughout the design phase of the program. This means that they will already know about the scheme facts prior to the start of your scheme – which is when you would normally schedule the training sessions for all other parties bar the program co-ordinator.

However, there are still some benefits in thinking about conducting an additional briefing session for senior management and external clients:

- Even if the program's sponsors, such as senior management and external clients, are familiar with all aspects of the scheme, it is nevertheless a good idea to ask them to attend a briefing jointly with the other parties involved in the program. As you will remember, we made this point earlier and rationalized it by saying that this promotes the attractiveness of a program.
- Between the last time you informed them about the scheme and the time of the training sessions, some minor amendments may have been made to the scheme. This would necessitate an update of individuals' knowledge.

Overall, the briefing on scheme facts for this trainee group will be identical to the one for all the other scheme participants. However, if you do hold a briefing that involves the program's sponsors, you might want to consider emphasizing the scheme's benefits to the organization. For illustration purposes, you could add some case study examples of the evaluation results of schemes run in other organizations. Re-emphasizing the benefits of mentoring schemes will reinforce in their minds that this has been and will be a worthwhile investment.

Training content for administration staff

The role of the administration staff is primarily to assist with administering, collecting and organizing the paperwork associated with the mentoring program. This might include ensuring that evaluation forms are distributed and collated, that the pairs receive and sign mentoring agreements and contracts, and that the logistics are adequately planned, etc. Briefing on the scheme and on their role may thus suffice to meet the training needs of the administration staff.

The timing of training

The timing of the training session for each trainee group will again partly depend on the way you have organized your scheme. Thus, if the program co-ordinator needed any briefing at all, he or she would probably have been the first person to receive it and this would have occurred very early on in the life of the scheme. The latter would particularly be the case if the co-ordinator is also leading the design and implementation of the program. The relationship supervisors may need briefing very early on, too, if they are part of the implementation team. The *skills* training for both co-ordinator and supervisors should, however, be conducted nearer the start of the scheme.

Carrying out the training at a date that is neither too far away from nor too close to the start of the scheme (i.e. the time around which the majority of mentoring pairs are expected to meet for the first time) is the most crucial point in getting the timing 'right'. Thus 6 weeks prior to the start of the relationships would be considered too early, whilst just 1 or 2 days would be too close. Training people too far in advance may lead them to forget most of what has been learned, whereas training people too close to the event might mean that there is not sufficient time for the learning to have been consolidated. Ideally, training should take place between 1 and 2 weeks prior to the start of the relationships. However, if you want to use the training as a first step in matching mentors and mentees, you might have to train earlier – between 2 and 3 weeks prior to commencement of the relationships. In most cases, this should give you sufficient time to match people, receive their responses to your suggestions, and get them on track for their first meeting.

Regardless of how well you timed your training, people can forget and/or alter information and skills learned under your guidance. They may also feel that they need additional refinements and support. It is for these reasons that it is so important to have ongoing support facilities in place, particularly for mentors and mentees. Apart from providing a regular point of contact, such as the program co-ordinator, you should consider the following options:

- Initiating regular workshops and review meetings facilitated by the program co-ordinator.
- Promoting the formation of support networks – either where people can physically meet up or virtual ones where members of a particular group (e.g. mentors or relationship supervisors) have their own secure chatroom and noticeboard on the company intranet or on the Internet.
- Providing learning resources such as guides and books.

Training methods

As with all training, you will have to apply different methods in order to facilitate trainee learning most effectively. If you are familiar with training, you will already know that there is a very broad range of methods available, including:

- Lectures/presentations.
- Information packs, books, CD-roms.
- E-learning (including a course available from Clutterbuck Associates and the Hertfordshire Small Business Service).
- Videos.
- Practical exercises that promote the application of skills (for example role-plays).
- Case studies.
- Discussion groups.

Although useful tools, you do not need to utilize all of them when it comes to mentoring training. In fact, our overriding recommendation is to keep it simple and stimulating, and to involve participants as much as possible. The greatest benefit comes from participants sharing experiences, thoughts and concerns in a group. After all, mentoring is about dialogue!

Provide as many opportunities for input from learners as possible; this can be done using the methods described below.

Suggestions for training methods

The following methods are described in relation to the knowledge, skill and attitude components.

Knowledge component

This entails, for example, the briefing on scheme facts, which can best be addressed through a presentation interspersed with discussions and question-and-answer sessions. Knowledge should be disseminated through the distribution of an information pack prior to the training program. If we count the case of 'expectation management' for mentors and mentees as belonging to the knowledge category, the onus should be a lot more on the participants than on the trainer. This means that presentations take a back seat and participants are charged with discussing the issues. Time should also be provided for personal reflection.

Attitude component

This can be addressed by using a mixture of presentation, discussion and reflection.

Skills component

As you will know, there is a huge market offering off-the-shelf skills training exercises on topics such as conflict management, active listening, and counselling. Hence you could theoretically pick and choose a different exercise for each of the skills that mentors, mentees and others need to acquire. However, this approach will make your training session too lengthy an affair. As aforementioned, we strongly emphasize quality over quantity, and believe that the best way to address the skills component is to tailor the exercises to your trainees. You can do this by employing a combination of self-designed role-plays, (real-life) case studies, and discussions. We will consider examples of these in a moment.

These activities can then be supplemented by first providing some background information on the skills in question. This should explain to trainees in what ways these skills are useful within mentoring relationships, which will open them up to the actual skills training to follow, since they will now be able to understand its relevance.

Table 9.4 depicts two examples of skills and their associated background information.

Let us now take a look at the methods you could use for designing simple yet effective skills training exercises. To illustrate this, we will consider the following examples:

- Building rapport, active listening, questioning, and counselling – for *mentors.*
- Active listening – for *mentees.*
- Conflict management – for *all.*
- Counselling – for *relationship supervisors* and *program co-ordinators.*

Building rapport, active listening, questioning, and counselling – for mentors

PURPOSE AND DURATION

The aim of this exercise is to give all mentor trainees the opportunity to engage in a simulated mentoring session. During this simulation they can practise the skills that they will soon be using, as well as receive peer feedback afterwards regarding their performance. If trainees can be split up into groups of three, the approximate duration of this exercise is 90 minutes: 20 minutes of role-play plus 10 minutes of feedback per person. (Please note that this timeframe is only a guideline, which should be kept flexible.)

Table 9.4 Background information in skills training

Active listening	Questioning
✓ *Active listening*: active listening involves	✓ *Why is questioning important?*
✓ Really concentrating on what another person is saying; 'holding a space'	✓ It enables both mentor and mentee to clarify issues and to ascertain mutual understanding
✓ Non-verbal inputs: nodding, leaning forward, smiling, keeping eye-contact	✓ It helps mentees to see solutions to problems for themselves
✓ Verbal inputs: reflecting back content, emotions etc. summarizing or paraphrasing, asking clarifying questions, and acknowledging that one is listening (saying, for example, 'I see')	✓ It enables mentees to understand a different method of solving problems
✓ *Why is active listening important?*	✓ *Different types of questioning:*
✓ Most effective way of ensuring that understanding takes place	✓ Reflective
✓ Enables to clarify issues where the speaker has not provided enough information	✓ Hypothetical
✓ Is the prerequisite for being able to help another person by way of, for example, asking relevant questions or sharing useful experiences	✓ Justifying
✓ Makes the reception of feedback a meaningful activity that can be used constructively	✓ Probing
	✓ Checking

Prepare three different scenarios (A, B and C) in which you describe in detail the issues that a *fictive* mentee is facing at work (e.g. problems with boss/colleagues, persistent demotivation, the prospect of being made redundant). After having explained the purpose and nature of the exercise, divide the mentoring trainees into groups of three if possible; otherwise, pairs will suffice. Provide each group member with a scenario so that one of them will have a copy of A, the second person a copy of B, and the third person a copy of C. Ask them to read their copy carefully and to memorize the essence of the content. Now ask the groups to decide in which order they would like to play the following roles: mentor, mentee and observer.

In this exercise, it is the role of the 'mentor' to build rapport with the 'mentee', establish the mentee's issues, and counsel him or her – in other words, they should try and engage in a 'typical' mentoring session. Emphasize that this is intended to give the trainee an opportunity to practise skills such as active listening, questioning and so on.

The role of the 'mentee' is to provide the 'mentor' with a good environment in which to practise mentoring skills. This would involve knowing the content of the scenario, not being hostile, and generally trying to act as realistically as possible.

Lastly, it is the role of both the 'mentee' and the observer to:

- Pay attention to the 'mentor's' ability to build rapport, listen actively, question, and counsel.
- Give feedback to the 'mentor' once the role-play is completed.

After the first round of this simulation, 'mentor', 'mentee' and the observer swap roles. This is repeated one more time after that.

Active listening – for mentees

The aim of this exercise is to give all mentees the opportunity to engage in a role-play that enables them to practise their active listening skills. The exercise should be preceded by giving trainees general background information about active listening (see Table 9.4). If trainees can be split up into groups of three, the approximate duration of this exercise is 60 minutes: 15 minutes of role play and 5 minutes of feedback per person on active listening. (Please note that this timeframe is only a guideline, which should be kept flexible.)

CONTENT/DESIGN

Again, active listening could be practised in a simple role-play. Mentees could be asked in *advance* of the training to think about a topic that they are genuinely interested in and which they would be prepared to talk about to a stranger. During the session, split the trainee group into sub-groups of three once you have explained the purpose and nature of the exercise. Ask them to agree on who is to play which of the following three roles first: the speaker, the listener, and the observer. Explain that these roles will be swapped once the first round of the exercise is complete.

In this exercise it is the role of the speaker to talk to the listener about the subject of his or her choice. Consequently, the listener is tasked with engaging in active listening. The observer's role is simply to evaluate the listener's ability to listen actively. Once the speaker and listener have completed their conversation (after approximately 15 minutes), both the observer and speaker could give the listener feedback. Once this is done, listener, speaker and observer swap roles.

Conflict management – *for* all

PURPOSE AND DURATION

The aim of this exercise is for individuals to handle potential relationship problems in the most effective way. The duration of the exercise is highly variable, depending on how many scenarios you wish to discuss.

CONTENT/DESIGN

As aforementioned, the most effective way of helping individuals to manage potential relationship problems is to present them with scenarios (ideally real-life case studies) of incidents that could occur. Next, divide your trainee group into sub-groups of, for example, four people and ask them to discuss ways in which these issues could be managed. You could encourage the groups to make a note of their favoured strategies in relation to each scenario, which could then be shared with the other sub-groups in a plenary session. Ideally, this session should be facilitated by an experienced mentoring trainer, who could also provide some recommendations on handling each of the conflict situations. In addition, you might want to familiarize trainees with the use of constructive challenging in order to manage problems.

Counselling – for relationship supervisors *and* program co-ordinators
PURPOSE AND DURATION

> The aim of this exercise is to enable relationship supervisors and program co-ordinators to practise their counselling skills in a role-play setting. The approximate duration of this exercise is 30 minutes, with 20 minutes spent on the role-play and 10 minutes spent on feedback.

CONTENT/DESIGN

> Again, a role-play simulation would be ideal in order to practise counselling skills. Ideally, you would want to design the scenario based on the problems that could occur within mentoring relationships and for which counsel might be sought. This might include the mentor or mentee lacking commitment, the mentor and mentee failing to establish rapport, the mentor over-challenging the mentee etc.

Summary

> Apart from giving you tips for the design and delivery of your mentoring training, we hope that this chapter – and the case studies presented in Chapter 3 – have convinced you of the importance of training for mentors, mentees, and relevant third parties. If you must cut any corners in the implementation of your scheme, then don't do it here – far too much is at stake.
>
> When designing your training, *relevance* and *quality* are the two most important determinants of its content. During delivery these two factors can be promoted by involving your trainees, giving them lots of room for discussions and input. With regard to content, you have seen that each party involved with a scheme has its own training agenda. That said, many a part can be delivered to certain trainee groups simultaneously, and this may even be highly advantageous. Thus, try to brief mentors and mentees on the scheme with the program co-ordinator present. This ensures that a first bond can be forged between these parties. Furthermore, train career-experienced mentors and mentees together, and use these joint sessions as a first stage in matching individuals.
>
> What other important points with regard to training did we make in this chapter? The program co-ordinator, who is usually responsible for managing the training, should ensure that it is designed and delivered by a person who is both highly familiar with mentoring schemes and skilled at training; ideally, he or

she would be someone who specializes in mentoring training. Training design should be preceded by a thorough training needs analysis so that you can customize the sessions to the specific needs of your trainees.

With regard to training methods, knowledge and attitudes are best addressed through presentations, discussions and reflection, whilst discussions and practical exercises should be used to tackle skills deficits. To facilitate the practical application of skills, it is best to utilize role-plays simulating a mentoring setting. Bar certain exceptions, training for all (particularly *skills* training) should be scheduled for 1 or 2 weeks prior to the commencement of the scheme.

References

Clutterbuck, D. (1998). *Learning Alliances*. CIPD.

Corporate Mentoring Solutions Inc. (2001). CMSI's Mentoring Program Benchmark 2000 Survey. At: http://www.mentoring.ws

Gibson, C. (1999). Home-grown gurus: an insight into successful mentoring schemes. *Modern Management*, **Aug**, 8–9.

Yellowbrick Consulting (2000). The complete guide to mentoring and coaching. Chapter 5 at: http://www.mentoring-programs.com

Evaluating mentoring schemes

If the mentoring system you set up is not systematically evaluated, monitored and shown to be effective, it will be dropped by design or by default. No CEO, board of directors or shareholders who are doing their job properly will tolerate the implementation or continuation of a system that is not being monitored or cannot show its effectiveness. It will be of no use saying to your inquisitors: 'It is of double benefit to the organization: the (mentors) improve their people management and motivation skills; the (mentees) improve their productivity; the organization benefits from both.' Unless you can demonstrate the benefit in hard statistical terms, you'll sound like just another bleeding heart, or empty promise salesperson.

(MacLennan, 1995)

Despite this strong argument in favour of evaluation, it is often overlooked in training and development because it is difficult to do. The results can be bland or irrelevant for executives with short attention spans, especially when compared to the excitement of a new initiative. Evaluation will rarely get people's attention unless the measurement is tied to a business priority. Overall, there is really no good reason not to evaluate the mentoring program, and there are many excellent reasons why this should occur.

What is evaluation and why evaluate?

What is evaluation?

> Evaluation is the systematic collection of descriptive and judgmental information necessary to make effective training decisions related to the selection, adoption, value and modification of various instructional (developmental) activities.
>
> (Goldstein, 1993)

The evaluation of the mentoring program closes the loop with the original proposal for mentoring. Its main purpose is to assess whether the objectives of the scheme have been met and whether the scheme has generally had a positive impact on your organization. Effective evaluation clearly shows you whether the time and effort invested has been 'worth it', whether continuation of the program is desirable, and whether any aspects of the program design require changing. Figure 10.1 depicts the purpose of evaluation.

We strongly advocate the measurement of mentoring schemes because of the invaluable insights this provides. Yet few organizations treat evaluation as a value-adding activity. Most times, it is regarded as a *post hoc* audit to verify that activities took place according to plan, and that allocated funds have not been misappropriated. This type of audit is most common in situations where the mentoring program has been funded by a public body that must show due diligence in the allocation of money to 'worthwhile causes'. In this case, the funding body may have no interest in the future of the mentoring program, and so improvements to the mentoring scheme are seen as irrelevant. This view of evaluation totally disregards the potential opportunities for 'organizational learning'. That said, most of the companies who contributed case studies to this book (see Chapters 3 and 8) regarded evaluation as highly important and did use it as a valuable learning source.

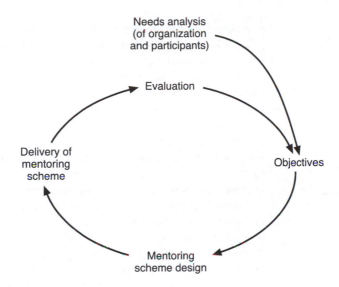

Figure 10.1 The evaluation loop.

Why evaluate?

In a wider sense, evaluation becomes an active and conscious appraisal of the ways in which the organization's systems and practices either facilitate or prohibit individual and team achievement. With these aims, the evaluation is geared towards making an analysis of the past and additionally making recommendations for the future.

At its simplest, then, evaluation helps us to reach conclusions about past events and/or to arrive at lessons for the future.

The main benefits to be drawn from an evaluation of the mentoring program are as follows:

- The evaluation provides information and insights to enable ongoing 'steering' of the mentoring program, and highlights specific problems and opportunities. As such, evaluation provides a focus for continuous improvement efforts (Conway, 1998).
- Evaluation is also about client orientation. This means ensuring that program sponsors and participants are satisfied, which, if true, increases the likelihood of future investment in the program (Boverie *et al.*, 1994).
- An often overlooked benefit of evaluation is that it can give positive reinforcement to the participants. This may be as simple as reminding mentors and mentees how much they have achieved and how many issues they have tackled. For mentors it will also be encouraging to hear that they are

perceived as competent, and they might find it beneficial to gain insight into their particular strengths. Lastly, the program co-ordinator will also appreciate the acknowledgement that his or her personal commitment to the scheme was worth all the effort (Conway, 1998).

- There are also good legal reasons for keeping tabs on the progress of the mentoring scheme. The main concerns are about discrimination and harassment (Segal, 2000). The program co-ordinator must ensure that all mentors adhere to the highest standards of professional conduct by tracking mentee responses to evaluation questions. Additionally, it is important to ensure that the mentoring scheme at least 'does no harm' – in other words, no group should do worse on the mentoring program than any other. For example, if all the dropouts from the mentoring program are men, or if all 'graduates' of the scheme are promoted within 24 months apart from those of Asian ethnic origin, then there are clearly problems with the scheme that must be explored and resolved.

All in all, evaluation is necessary in the same way that health check-ups are useful. They prevent small issues from becoming 'life threatening' to the whole scheme, and serve to motivate participants to maintain healthy mentoring relationships.

Is mentoring evaluation possible?

Whilst evaluation may be important in principle, it is notoriously difficult in practice! It is quite hard to evaluate, for example, the centrepiece of a mentoring scheme: the individual mentoring relationships. Many of the important functions of the mentor–mentee relationship (such as 'being supportive' or 'offering encouragement') defy universal standards and clinical examination.

Additionally, many mentoring outcomes are quite intangible. Mentoring is – most of the time – more about abstract qualities such as networking skills, enhancing potential or fostering independent learning. This presents quite a challenge to the evaluator of the mentoring scheme!

There are three main reasons why a generic evaluation method for mentoring is unlikely to appear in the near future (Wang, 2000):

1. First, different organizations have very different organizational goals as well as diverging training/human resource

development (HRD) functions. Therefore, mentoring schemes will also vary between organizations, including the measures and methods applied to evaluating them.

2. Secondly, evaluation in HRD (and mentoring) is a fairly recent concept and still needs to become better established. Theories and practise, particularly with regards to cost–benefit analyses, still need to be further developed.

3. Lastly, and most importantly, evaluation focuses on measuring human beings. The effectiveness of *any* learning method will vary greatly between individuals, being affected by internal and external factors. Internal factors include individual preferences in learning styles and attitudes. External factors include an organization's openness towards the application of new learning. Variations on all of these factors will cause variations in the results of a mentoring scheme evaluation. However, these are not necessarily a true reflection of the effectiveness of the program.

Confidentiality

In addition to the various problems outlined above when evaluating the mentoring program, there is the fundamental issue of confidentiality. Confidentiality is usually most pertinent to any appraisal of the mentoring *relationship* (as opposed to the evaluation of the program). However, confidentiality considerations are also vital at the program level. In order to establish what works well about the scheme, it will be necessary to judge whether mentees have benefited from the process. This may well involve an appraisal of their abilities before and after the mentoring program, plus an assessment of how the mentoring program specifically helped them.

If the mentoring program extends the right of confidentiality to both parties, then evaluation risks interfering with this and may cause disillusionment on the part of the mentee. Therefore, it is essential to ensure that the evaluation measures the relationship management aspects of the scheme, and not the progress of the mentee.

Confidentiality is a highly charged concern that must be balanced against the benefits to be obtained from evaluation. If the evaluation will itself compromise the outcomes of the program by damaging (or appearing to damage) the confidentiality of the mentoring relationships, then alternative forms of evaluation must be found. One approach would be to explain the benefits of evaluation, and then ask a sample group of mentees to suggest ways in which the program could be evaluated without compromising confidentiality.

Careful judgment is needed to ensure that an appropriate compromise is found between the costs of evaluation (e.g. staff time), its benefits (for learning) and its risks to mentoring relationships (e.g. in being exposed to scrutiny). Although a timely evaluation is of benefit to all concerned in the mentoring scheme, there is no need to rush into it, and a good deal of trouble may be avoided by taking the time to consult those involved before embarking on a great investigation.

Aside from the specific technical problems associated with choosing the right evaluation approach for your organization, there is the underlying issue of motivation. Few organizations really bother to conduct a thorough review of their HRD practices, blaming more urgent tasks, plus perhaps an unspoken concern that the appraisal may reveal flaws in the original scheme that will be embarrassing. The best way to prevent such resistance is to include the evaluation stage in the original implementation proposal. If the assessment criteria are formulated and shared at an early stage, then the evaluation is more likely to be conducted in accordance with the original aims of the mentoring program (Murray and Owen, 1991). For other reasons, too, it is advisable to include an outline of the evaluation strategy and format in your implementation proposal. Doing so allows you to collect the most uncontaminated, unbiased, and therefore most accurate data.

In the next section, we will explore ways of maximizing the value of evaluation in the face of the various challenges outlined above.

When and what to evaluate?

The timing of evaluation

There are two types of evaluation that can benefit the improvement and maintenance of mentoring programs: formative (ongoing) and summative (final). Formative evaluation is concerned with the implementation of measures that help you to evaluate how a program is currently doing. It is similar to a review that takes place on an ongoing basis – it is all about 'keeping an eye on the scheme'. In this sense, formative evaluation enables:

- The troubleshooting of relationships in order to maximize the chances of their success.

- Quality assurance for the program.
- The assessment of whether or not the desired outcomes are being achieved.

Summative evaluation, on the other hand, is much more formal and extensive, and is concerned with the implementation of measures that enable you to determine whether a scheme has ultimately achieved its objectives. It takes place once the scheme has been running for quite some time – perhaps after 1 or 2 years.

Formative evaluation involves the assessment of mentoring relationships and the mentoring scheme at *various points in time* whilst they are still 'running' rather than when they have come to a close. In principle, it is similar to a Formula One team pulling the car in for a pit stop during a motor race. An examination of the engine at this stage will not tell us whether we will win the race, but it will help us to keep the engine running smoothly so that winning (or at least finishing!) the race is more likely.

Formative evaluations help to keep the mentoring program healthy, and as such may rely on outside perspectives from consultants or trusted colleagues within the organization. This gives the benefit of an external perspective to calibrate or validate the views of mentors, mentees, relationship supervisors, and the program co-ordinator. For example, a third party experienced in mentoring might observe mentors whilst they are interacting with a mentee. That way, improvement opportunities can be spotted and amendments made immediately, benefiting both the mentor and the mentee in the subsequent meetings.

A good way to think of formative evaluation is as an extension of the original training activities associated with the launch of the mentoring program. The evaluation helps to keep the program on track with its objectives.

Summative evaluation is the term for the assessment of mentoring relationships and mentoring programs when they come to a close, or at least after a substantial amount of time has passed. Going back to the Formula One analogy, summative evaluation is more like a final assessment of where our car came on the finish line. How well did the car perform, and why/how? It is not enough to merely state that the program met its original aims. We must also discover why and how:

- What helped the program work well?
- What hindered the success of the program?

No evaluation can be complete without these insights, which then allow us scope to make more informed choices about mentoring programs in the future.

Table 10.1 summarizes the characteristics of formative and summative evaluation.

Deciding *exactly* when these evaluations should be undertaken is largely a matter of judgment based on the scale and duration of the total mentoring program. For example, a small organization with 10 mentoring relationships over 1 year may benefit from one formative evaluation at 6 months and one summative evaluation at 12 months. By contrast, a major organization with hundreds of mentoring relationships will probably require a summative evaluation of a *pilot* scheme (perhaps after only 6 months) before rolling out the full mentoring program that may then last for 10 years. In this case, each cohort of mentees may require a summative evaluation at the end of 2 years of mentoring.

In terms of deciding when and how often to conduct evaluation, its costs should be weighed against the potential gains in the application of learning for future mentoring.

The focus of measurement

In terms of *what* to assess, the simple answer is to revisit the original proposal for mentoring and pull out the objectives for the program to establish how well these have been met. The more clearly the objectives have been defined, the more confidence we can have in making an appraisal of the program. Consider the following quotation (Yellowbrick Consulting, 2000):

> Whether difficult or easy, it is vital to spend time refining and understanding the underlying issues prompting your mentoring program, because only by knowing the underlying issues your program is seeking to address can you set relevant objectives for the program; establish measurement criteria to judge whether or not the mentoring program is meeting its objectives; and brief people on their roles and expectations.

Having made the point that the evaluation should proceed from the original aims of the mentoring program, the appraisal should also be open to what has changed during the life of the mentoring scheme. The issue here is that unexpected events do happen, and these could relate to the following topics:

- How has a major strategic issue such as a merger or downsizing affected the mentoring program?

Table 10.1 Characteristics of formative and summative evaluation

Formative	Summative
✓ Is concerned with establishing how a scheme is *currently* progressing	✓ Concerned with determining whether a scheme has ultimately achieved its objectives
✓ Assesses mentor and mentee performance, the mentoring relationships and the mentoring scheme at regular intervals, starting early on (e.g. after the scheme has been running for one month)	✓ Assessment of mentor and mentee performance, the mentoring relationships and the mentoring scheme when they come to a close or when they have been running for a long period of time
✓ Evaluation measures include looking at the mentee's development reviews and having brief conversations with mentors, mentees, relationship supervisors and others as to their perceptions of the scheme	✓ More formal and extensive than formative evaluation: measures include intensive interviews with a range of individuals, the design and dissemination of questionnaires and, potentially, cost benefit analyses. Eventually, there will also be a write-up and presentation of an evaluation report
✓ Intended to keep the scheme healthy and to make minor amendments as it progresses	✓ Intended to inform decision makers about the overall outcomes of the program; provides input for substantial amendments to the scheme and a basis for deciding whether or not to continue the program at all

- How has the mentoring program linked in to other subsequent HR initiatives?
- How has mentoring affected attitudes to working life outside the formal aspects of the program?
- Did it enhance commitment to the organization and job satisfaction?.

The evaluation should therefore also be open to capturing the surprises and collateral outcomes that may never have been anticipated in the original proposal.

Measurement categories

In terms of what to evaluate, there are three main categories for organizing the information to be gathered:

1. *The program*: did the scheme achieve its overall objectives? If not, why not? How do you define the *successful* achievement of objectives? In addition to the overall objectives, do you expect the scheme to have had a positive impact on other factors too (e.g. turnover, skills, motivation, readiness for higher-level positions)? To what extent was the program well organized? Were the processes and systems helpful and efficient? Did the program co-ordinator do too much or too little? Can any of the forms be eliminated or edited? Should any new forms be introduced? How often should the mentor and mentee report on their progress (if at all)? What opportunities for cost savings can be found? What about areas in which we should invest more money? How competent were the relationship supervisors? Were they necessary at all, and were they sufficient in numbers? How did the involvement of line managers work?

2. *The relationship*: were the relationship objectives (as outlined in the PDP) achieved? How do you define successful achievement? Do mentors, mentees and line managers agree on the extent to which objectives have been achieved? Did the mentees benefit from the mentoring relationship? How? How can we be sure that the benefit is down to mentoring? How much value does mentoring add to a mentee? How does mentoring affect the mentor? Do mentors achieve more than non-mentors? How? How often did pairs meet? What helps to get the relationship started in the right way? What hinders effective mentoring relationships? How do we keep relationships productive? What are the common characteristics of effective mentors? What can mentees do to get the most from the mentoring program? How do relationships conclude? What

support do mentees need *after* mentoring? How many mentees can a mentor reasonably handle in a year? Can one mentor meet all the development goals of any given mentee?

3. *The organization*: how has the organization improved as a result of the mentoring program? How can we be sure? How have 'hard' measures changed (e.g. productivity, sales, staff turnover)? How have 'soft' measures changed (e.g. culture, overall performance, motivation, job satisfaction, etc.)? If nothing appears to have changed, what do we do with that knowledge? Continue/discontinue the program? Is the organization perceived differently (better/worse) as a result of the mentoring program by a) mentees, b) mentors, c) other staff, d) outside stakeholders (clients, suppliers, shareholders)?

As an alternative to the categorization system suggested above, the focus of evaluations can also be captured in the model shown in Table 10.2.

Evaluation should enable the organization to reach conclusions about how well the mentoring program achieved its original and specific aims (as set down in the mentoring proposal). Clearly, it is of little value to criticize a mentoring scheme for failing to improve the diversity of senior management if its original aim was to improve graduate retention. If the success of a mentoring scheme highlights other needs in the organization, then these other needs should be addressed on their own merit.

The evaluation should also help to answer questions about the evolution of mentoring in the organization. It will feed options and suggestions to the steering group and implementation team that can then form the basis for revising the program or starting new schemes.

Specifically, the evaluation should help you to make recommendations about the nature of the mentoring relationships in terms of:

- Aims – what problems/opportunities does mentoring address?
- Formality – how much structure is appropriate?
- Logistics – how often should pairs meet, and what organizational support do they need?
- Duration – how long should the mentoring relationship be, and how frequently should pairs meet?
- Confidentiality – what organizational commitments can we make to mentors and mentees about the confidentiality of the relationship?

Table 10.2 Evaluation of four aspects

	Relationships	Scheme
Process	The quality of relationship processes	The quality of the scheme's processes
Outputs	The quality of outputs for the individuals and the organization produced by the relationships	The quality of outputs for the individuals and the organization produced by the scheme

Evaluation methods

Having devoted our attention to the *why* and *what* of evaluation, it is now time to address the most appropriate methods of evaluation. Thus, the evaluation data can be collected using one or more of the following means:

- Self-report questionnaires containing a mixture of open and forced-choice questions. These could be distributed amongst mentors, mentees, relationship supervisors, line managers and program co-ordinators. In addition, you could also use this method to consult with peers, customers and/or suppliers – i.e. anyone who could provide you with valuable evaluation data. Make sure, however, that you customize the questions to the group of respondents you are addressing.
- Interviews with, for example, mentors, mentees, line managers and any of the other groups mentioned above. Interviews can be held individually as well as in groups (e.g. jointly interviewing a mentor and mentee pair).
- Assessing PDPs/learning plans against progress/development reviews: do the mentoring outcomes correspond to its objectives?
- Logs and diaries.
- Direct observation of the mentee's performance at work: this could be done by the line manager, since this person is in the best position to assess whether and how the employee's performance has changed and whether this could be as a result of the mentoring.
- Group discussions/focus groups.
- Statistical measures of changes in line with the mentoring objectives (e.g. alterations in productivity or staff turnover, cost–benefit analyses).

Notwithstanding the problem of confidentiality mentioned earlier, you should attempt to involve as many people as possible in the evaluation. That is, try to gather data from as many sources as possible so that the objectivity and generic applicability of your findings will be maximized. In addition, using multiple methods to collect data will further validate any findings and the conclusions you might draw on the basis of these.

Structuring the evaluation process

The most often cited framework for the evaluation of training programs (as opposed to pure mentoring) was proposed by Kirkpatrick (1979). His model outlined four levels of evaluation, which begin with the immediate reactions of participants and go through to the effects of the training on the organization as a whole. At each stage there is a quantum shift in the complexity of the measures to be evaluated, and hence a big step in terms of difficulty.

Level 1: Reactions

Level 1 evaluates the reactions of people to a training course – i.e. what people felt about the course. Typically participants are asked questions about the quality of the course and their satisfaction with it. This level can easily be applied to mentoring schemes, too. It taps into the immediate feelings about the content, process and outcomes of the learning experience. With regard to mentoring, you could therefore ask mentors and mentees, through interviews or questionnaires, how they 'feel' about the mentoring experience. Although this information is rather subjective, it can be very revealing indeed. Furthermore, it is also the most often used level in mentoring evaluation.

Level 2: Learning

The main question addressed by this level is whether the mentee has *theoretically* acquired the desired knowledge, skills or attitudes he or she was supposed to acquire. In most mentoring schemes, rigorously testing as to whether any of these have been picked up might not be appropriate as it can conflict with the mentoring culture. Thus, using exams or multiple choice tests to establish a mentee's achievements may seem a touch too formal. It might also be impossible to test for the acquisition of certain types of knowledge, skills and attitudes, given that a large number of mentoring learning objectives are rather abstract. Let us look at the example of a graduate mentoring scheme. In this, the overall objective might be to induce new recruits to their jobs and the organization. However, the objectives of any individual mentee might not only differ from those of other mentees; they might also be difficult to assess in pre- and post-mentoring terms. Consider, for instance, the following objectives:

- 'Getting to know and developing a better fit with the organizational culture'.
- 'Networking and building trust with colleagues.'

In contrast to these, other objectives can be more easily assessed at the learning level:

- 'Having gained knowledge of job procedures'.
- 'Having acquired relevant technical knowledge.'

Here, a pre- and post-appraisal, potentially involving the graduate's line manager, could be carried out to assess the extent to which these objectives have been achieved.

Hence, if it does seem appropriate formally to test whether and to what extent mentees have *learned*, one or more of the following methods could be used:

- Testing *knowledge* acquisition: interviews and/or the discussion of case studies can be conducted on a fairly informal, non-threatening basis. Whilst exams, open-book tests and multiple-choice tests are an option, they appear far too stringent within a mentoring context.
- Testing *skills* acquisition: observation, using simulations, role-plays or real-life exercises.
- Testing change in *attitude*: interviews, observation and valid psychological tests.

Level 3: Behavioural changes in the transfer setting

Level 3 explores the application of learning through changes in behaviour in the transfer setting (e.g. the workplace) as opposed to, say, the mentoring relationship. The evaluation aims to establish whether the knowledge, skills and attitudes learnt in a mentoring relationship or a training program are actually impacting on people's behaviour on the job. For example, the supervisor/manager might review the performance of a mentee

3 months after the start of a mentoring relationship to evaluate whether the mentee does his or her job better.

Level 4: Organizational benefits

Level 4 evaluates the effectiveness of mentoring (or training) on the results of the organization. This establishes not only whether the training helps the individual, but also whether it helps the business aims of the organization. For example, the review aims to work out whether the organization meets its business aims better or is more profitable because of the mentoring. As such, this level is similar to the third category suggested in our system in 'Measurement categories' above.

As you will perhaps already know from *training* evaluation, this level is by far the most difficult to establish. This is usually attributed to training having indirect, subtle and long-term effects rather than directly measurable short-term ones. The same applies to mentoring – i.e. outcomes are often abstract and not quantifiable, at least not over the short-term.

Furthermore, it is also difficult to conduct a Level 4 evaluation that truly distinguishes the impact of the training or mentoring from other factors. For example, if a new CEO is appointed to an organization during the mentoring program, then his or her influence on turnover, morale and organizational productivity will potentially be far greater than the impact of the mentoring scheme.

Additionally, Boverie *et al.* (1994) make the point that training as well as mentoring is often used for purposes *other than* achieving a measurable impact on the performance of the organization. For example, sometimes training is seen as a perquisite for performance that has already been judged successful, or as a cultural 'rite of passage' that all those hoping to advance must complete. In these cases, the value of the training is more symbolic than technical.

In order to receive the most complete and most accurate picture of your mentoring scheme, you should endeavour to collect data in relation to all four of these levels.

Who should carry out the evaluation and who should provide the data?

In response to the first part of the question, we are in agreement with Phillip-Jones (1998):

The planning/implementation group should collect at least some of the data internally. Examples include: numbers of mentors and mentees, participants' satisfaction with training they received, their satisfaction with the mentoring experience as a whole, whether or not planned activities actually occurred. Participants can turn in reports on what they did together, what they learned, and suggestions for improvements. You can also get short-term retention numbers (Do participants stay with your organization after they complete the program?).

In addition, we strongly advise you to get outside evaluation help. An outside source which specializes in mentoring evaluation and which guarantees confidentiality will ensure that your participants share more detailed and candid information. You and the team can strategize with the evaluators on data needed, items to be asked, procedures, and what you want the report(s) to cover.

With regard to the question of who should provide the evaluation data, the answer involves the following:

- Mentees.
- Mentors.
- Line managers.
- Relationship supervisors.
- Program co-ordinator.
- Program sponsors.

You could also consider involving the peers of mentees as well as customers and suppliers, particularly if you wish to assess whether the learning that has occurred in a mentoring association is being applied in the workplace.

Antheil and Casper (1986) emphasize the importance of collecting and presenting the information in a way that will be meaningful and relevant for the specific audience involved. They propose three steps to ensuring that the evaluation is meaningful:

1. Discuss the focus and goals of the evaluation study with the identified evaluation audience (this will include mentees, mentors, managers, the implementation team, etc.).
2. Design and implement data collection strategies aimed at tapping one or more levels of program effects. These strategies should reflect the audience's expressed needs for information.
3. Communicate evaluation results to the audience through a

process that enables people to learn from and use the results. Encourage joint interpretation of the data.

All in all, the literature is short of universal evaluation tools for training generally, and for mentoring in particular. However, most reviews emphasize the importance of external consultants in validating and verifying the mentoring program, and in drawing lessons and comparisons from best practices outside the organization.

Independent facilitators also have a role to play in conducting review sessions where groups of mentors (and sometimes mentees) meet together to consider the feedback. The sessions help participants to develop their mentoring competence, and gather suggestions for improvements to the program.

Summary

The aim of evaluation is to gather data for both measuring the effectiveness of an initiative and making future adjustments on the basis of the evaluation results. The key issue here is that the evaluation should not be a static *'post-mortem'* report, but should be a dynamic set of recommendations and actions to enhance the program further and build on the success of mentoring in the organization.

Mentoring evaluation should proceed from the original objectives of the scheme, measuring the extent to which they have been attained. It should provide explanations for why a scheme did or did not work well, so as to facilitate organizational learning. In order to gather the necessary information, aspects in addition to the program's objectives should be evaluated. Thus, mentoring evaluation typically concentrates on measuring the *program*, the *relationships* and the scheme's effect on the *organization*. When using this categorization system to evaluate your scheme, you will automatically tap into the 'four levels' suggested by Kirkpatrick's evaluation framework. You will find out about people's reactions to the mentoring, whether they learnt what they were supposed to learn and whether they apply this learning to the workplace, and the program's impact on the organization.

To obtain the most complete and accurate picture, both formative and summative evaluation should be carried out. Furthermore, as many people as possible should be consulted as part of the evaluation process, including mentors, mentees and line managers. Ideally, the measurement should be undertaken by an external agency specializing in mentoring evaluation.

The evaluation of mentoring schemes involves many challenges, and being clear about what you expect from it is vital for its effectiveness. To help you conduct an evaluation of your program, we have compiled the following checklist. This should assist you with addressing the many issues in advance, rendering the actual measurement process smoother.

Checklist for designing a mentoring scheme evaluation

1. What were our original objectives for a) the program; b) the relationships; c) the organization?
2. How do we define the successful achievement of objectives in these three categories?
3. What information do we need from mentors, mentees, line managers (etc.) in order to determine the extent to which objectives have been achieved?
4. What questions do we want to have answered through an evaluation? What information are we seeking?
5. Has anything external to the scheme affected its ability to achieve its objectives?
6. How can we ensure that we will receive the information we need?
7. How will we use the evaluation results?
8. When will we carry out the formative evaluations and when the summative one?
9. Who will be responsible for managing the evaluation?
10. Who should be involved in collecting the evaluation data?
11. Who should we gather data from with regard to a) the program; b) the relationships; and c) the organization?
12. What methods will we use to collect the data?
13. What strategy will we adopt for dealing with confidentiality issues? Will we use volunteers or partially remove confidentiality from all relationships so that evaluation is made possible?

References

Antheil, J. and Casper, I. (1986). Comprehensive evaluation model: a tool for the evaluation of non-traditional education programs. *Innov. Higher Ed.*, **11**, 55–64.

Boverie, P., Sanchez Mulcahy, D. and Zondlo, J. A. (1994). Evaluating the Effectiveness of Training Programs. At: http://hale.pepperdine.edu/~cscunha/Pages/KIRK.HTM

Conway, C. (1998). *Strategies for Mentoring*. Wiley.

Goldstein, I. L. (1993). *Training in Organisations*. Brooks/Cole Publishing.

Kirkpatrick, D. (1979). Techniques for evaluating training programs. *Training Dev. J.*, **33**, 78–92.

MacLennan, N. (1995). *Coaching and Mentoring*. Gower.

Murray, M. and Owen, M. A. (1991). *Beyond the Myths and Magic of Mentoring: How to Facilitate an Effective Mentoring Program*. Jossey-Bass.

Phillip-Jones, L. (1998). Time to Evaluate. At: http://www.mentoringgroup.com/01_99_PG/199ideas.htm

Segal, J. (2000). Mirror-image mentoring. *HR Magazine*, **45**, 157–62.

Wang, G. (2000). Some opinions on ROI. Discussion Forum of the American Society of Training and Development (ASTD). At: http://www.astd.org/virtual_community/forums/eval_ROI/eval_ROI.cgi?read=873

Yellowbrick Consulting (2000). The complete guide to mentoring and coaching. Chapter 5 at: http://www.mentoring-programs.com

CHAPTER 11

Problems with implementing and maintaining your scheme

During the implementation and maintenance phases of a mentoring scheme, mistakes can be made and problems arise. This is an often overlooked topic within the textbooks dealing with scheme implementation, perhaps because it is perceived as boring or unimportant. Be this as it may, maintenance and troubleshooting are vital to the success (or otherwise) of your scheme. Consider, for example, the following statistics: in well-planned and well-implemented schemes, successful mentoring relationships (i.e. those in which 'significant mutual learning takes place') constitute roughly 85 per cent of all pairs. Furthermore, 90 per cent or more of all participants state that they would be happy to enter into another mentoring relationship. These are encouraging figures but, since mistakes and problems do occur, these success rates *can* be substantially less. In poorly planned and implemented mentoring schemes, relationship success rates could be 30 per cent or less. It is therefore crucial to understand what to pay particular attention to when implementing a program, what can go wrong, and what to do if it does. This is the focus of this present chapter: we will consider the aspects involved in creating and maintaining a healthy program, which include:

- Introducing ways of dealing with certain problems.
- Identifying common pitfalls and mistakes associated with schemes.
- Drawing your attention to the support mechanisms that promote the development of a successful program.

Since formal mentoring in any organization takes place at two levels, we will consider the mistakes that can be made during implementation and any arising problems separately for:

- The program level and
- The relationship level.

Lastly, this chapter will also look at *mature* mentoring programs and what you can do to sustain them – if that is at all desirable.

Before we begin to look at the problems and pitfalls associated with mentoring schemes, we would like to put what is to follow into a realistic perspective. Concentrating on problem areas tends to exaggerate perceptions of their occurrence. In reality, problems are typically not as frequent and as severe as one might be inclined to think. Focusing on the pitfalls might also leave you with unwarranted concerns about the mentoring process. Yes, most mentoring pairs *do* experience some problems, but they are often both an essential part of the maturation process and easily resolvable without any outside help. Most people who experience mentoring (be this the mentor or the mentee) find it highly rewarding, if not exhilarating, from both an emotional and a developmental perspective. So, be aware of the problems – but there's no need to feel threatened or overwhelmed by them!

Mentoring programs – what to look out for

Carefully select and match mentors and mentees

An important feature of good selection is to have clear criteria of what makes a good mentor and what type of mentee you are looking for. With regard to mentors, this would include assurance that someone has the right attitude to mentoring, is capable of developing others, and possesses the experience needed for mentoring under your scheme's objective. Selecting mentees should mainly concentrate on recruiting those who fit the program's target group and who are able and willing to engage in a mentoring relationship. You should never use subtle or obvious coercion in the recruitment of mentors and mentees. Forcing people to take part in a scheme will impact on their motivation, rendering them at best non-committal and at worst plain disruptive.

With regard to matching, a commonly made mistake involves not considering the mentee's preferences. That said, more attention should be paid to preferences in relation to who the mentee does *not* want as a mentor rather than who he or she does want. This is because, when asked to describe their ideal mentor, mentees tend to paint an image of a person that nobody could live up to. Even if we are not dealing with imaginary choices but with preferences in relation to existing people, taking into account 'negative' preferences is also frequently more feasible than attending to who the mentee might want as a mentor. This is because, given a selection of mentors, every mentee may choose the one who seems most desirable. Unfortunately, since any one mentor only has limited capacity, he or she will not be able to take on all those mentees who might express such a preference.

Apart from preferences, another very helpful matching criterion is to assess the degree of fit between a mentee's needs and a mentor's knowledge and experience: can the mentor really support the mentee's development? Is he or she the best person for the particular mentee? A last point with regard to matching concerns the fact that mentor–mentee associations should never be enforced against the objection of either party, since these would be unlikely to work.

Provide appropriate training

In formal mentoring schemes, mentors and mentees are required to assume their new roles very rapidly and to adjust to them quickly. Training supports this process by, for example, helping them to understand their roles, providing them with relevant skills, and issuing guidelines on how to manage the relationship. As you know, training should also be provided for relevant third parties such as line managers. This prevents them from getting confused about how their role differs from that of the mentor, which in turn pre-empts other unpleasant consequences such as the manager resenting the mentor and interfering with the relationship. So skipping this vital preparation phase is certainly not recommended. Another important issue concerning training is that it must be *relevant* to your trainee group as well as sensitively delivered. Remember that quality is more important than quantity – otherwise the experience may prove boring and unproductive.

Clarify the mentor's role

In Chapter 1 we spent a long time elaborating on the tasks of mentoring and how the mentor differs from other developmental roles. A clear understanding helps you to explain the role better to the mentors in your scheme, as well as to other relevant parties who need to appreciate what a mentor does (these other 'relevant parties' include mentees, their colleagues and, again, their line managers). If mentors are not clear about their role, their developmental efforts may lack focus, they may take the wrong approach, and they may well after all stray into the line manager's territory.

If line managers become mentors, this can also reduce the clarity of roles. In fact, most mentoring schemes that tried this approach to providing mentors had to pull back because the line boss was unable to cope with the ambiguity of roles. Being an objective confidante on the one hand and having to appraise the employee on the other proves too difficult to reconcile.

Take time to prepare

When planning a mentoring scheme you need to consider a vast range of issues, the main ones of which were addressed in Chapters 7 and 8. To name a few, you need to ensure whether there is a true need for mentoring in your organization, the program's objective must be clearly defined, management support assessed, and its likely popularity with the mentoring participants evaluated. Poor planning and preparation will lead to a badly implemented scheme, the consequences of which include its complete rejection and/or a failure to achieve its objectives. What is more, once employees have experienced a poorly implemented scheme the implementation of another scheme, even a well-designed one, may be prevented for years afterwards. So, investing sufficient time and resources at the preparation stage is vital.

Involve the line manager

Throughout this book we have emphasized that involving the line manager is vital – an aspect that is fortunately recognized by most mentoring scheme co-ordinators. In case there is any question regarding how to involve the line manager constructively, this means:

- Making sure that the line manager understands the purpose of the relationship.
- Encouraging the line manager to support the mentee.

Some schemes do not formally inform the line manager who the mentor is, and the mentee decides whether or not to do so. The key issue here is avoiding resentment or distrust on the part of the line manager, who can be kept in the loop by inclusion in discussions about the future of the scheme and in regular communications.

This information should be supplemented by both advising the line manager of the benefits they will incur from having an employee who is being mentored, and explaining to them how their role differs from that of a mentor. As has been mentioned, confusion about roles is often the root cause of a the line manager's fear that the mentor might invade their territory and render them less powerful. Benefits for the line manager include:

- A reinforcing second opinion.
- Better relationship with the mentee and between the mentee and the team.
- Shared responsibility for developing the mentee.

Table 11.1 summarizes the complementary and differential aspects of the mentor's and line manager's roles.

Set objectives, and define and measure outcomes

What is the purpose of the scheme? What are we hoping to achieve? How are we going to establish whether the scheme is achieving the desired results? Precisely defining overall and subsidiary objectives is necessary to focus a scheme and to give people a reason to participate in it. Objectives rationalize the existence of a scheme and motivate people to partake. However, setting objectives without building in measures to assess whether or not these are being achieved will not suffice either. As emphasized throughout Chapter 10, both formative and summative evaluation measures contribute to the success of your scheme by giving you clues as to what is working well and what is not. Thus evaluation enables you to assess whether

Table 11.1 Complementary and differential aspects of the mentor's and line-manager's roles

Line manager		Shared		Mentor	
✓	Performance appraisal	✓	Encouragement, motivation to learn	✓	Help learner develop insights into causes of poor performance
✓	Agreed developmental goals within learner's current job	✓	Shape goals beyond current job	✓	Help learner manage the integration of job, career and personal goals
✓	Help learner build relationships within the team	✓	Help learner build relationships outside team	✓	Help learner build relationships with line manager
✓	Find opportunities to stretch learner's performance	✓	Find opportunities to stretch learner's thinking	✓	Challenging learners' thinking and assumptions
✓	Give constructive feedback through observation	✓	Help learner develop skills of intrinsic observation	✓	Help learner accept and manage feedback constructively
✓	Role model for task fulfilment and growth	✓	Role model of general behaviour	✓	Role model for personal achievement and growth

relationships are working out, whether they are on track, and whether the overall running of the scheme works as intended. This is important for many a reason, not least to justify the continued investment and enthusiasm of top management.

Establish a clear system for managing relationships that come to an end

In mentoring schemes, relationships come to an end for a variety of reasons. These include:

- Relationships that do not work out.
- Relationships that come to a natural end because the mentee's learning under a particular mentor has been completed.

Relationships that do not work out

For many a reason, mentors and/or mentees could become disenchanted with a particular relationship, wanting to terminate it early. This could happen because of a failure to build rapport, because of limited commitment by either party, or the mentee feeling that this particular mentor is unable to meet his or her needs. Whatever the reason, schemes should always operate a 'no-fault opt-out' clause, which entitles pairs to separate without there being any penalty. The existence of this policy should be emphasized from the very start of the program so that all those involved know what to expect. In fact, we even recommend that program co-ordinators promote it by monitoring relationships unobtrusively and encouraging pairs that do not seem to build rapport to rethink whether a different pairing would better suit the mentee's needs. After all, rapport is the key driver in mentoring relationships; it implies that there is trust and mutual confidence, which is the necessary basis for a successful association.

That said, it is of course necessary also to emphasize that relationships should not be terminated as soon as any problem arises because the likelihood of this happening is quite high. However, the likelihood of this problem being anything serious that could not be resolved between a mentor and their mentee is very small. Hence mentoring pairs should be encouraged to assess their decision to terminate a relationship carefully, and perhaps to seek the counsel of the relationship supervisor/program co-ordinator to subject the problem to a 'reality check'. If a decision to break up has been confirmed, we suggest that closure procedures (see below) are used to follow up on a relationship that has come to an end.

Relationships that come to a natural end because the mentee's learning under a particular mentor has been completed

Mentoring relationships are not eternal bonds, and the point will come at which they must disband. In most cases this happens because the mentor's ability to develop the mentee has come to an end. When this is the case, both mentor and mentee must be honest both to themselves and to one another: the fledgling has to leave the nest. A failure to part at that stage is likely to result in resentment and even enmity.

When relationships come to an end, you might want to follow them up with an official closure procedure. This serves a variety of functions, including:

- Helping the parties involved to ascertain whether a relationship really has come to a close.
- Enabling mentors and mentees to part on good terms, which contributes to ensuring the long-term benefit of a mentoring experience.
- Helping to retain mentors on the program.
- Reinforcing learning.
- Adding overall credibility to a mentoring program.
- Providing valuable data for the evaluation of the scheme.
- Recruiting mentees as potential mentors.

Closure steps could include the following:

- Private and confidential exit interviews, to debrief the mentoring relationship, between the mentee and staff, the mentor and staff, and the mentor and mentee without staff.
- A clear agreement regarding future contacts between mentor and mentee.
- Assistance for participants in defining their next steps for achieving personal/career goals.

Support for mentors and mentees

The type of support we are talking about here goes beyond the initial training to prepare participants for their roles. In addition to that, programs should offer *ongoing* support and development for mentors and mentees. In Chapter 9, we suggested the following options for providing this type of backing:

- Initiating regular workshops and review meetings facilitated by the program co-ordinator.
- Promoting the formation of support networks, with either physical or virtual meetings – members of a particular group (e.g. mentors or relationship supervisors) could have their own secure chat-room and notice board on the company intranet or on the Internet. To ensure that network meetings really take place, the scheme co-ordinator might want to make it his or her responsibility to schedule them and even, perhaps, facilitate them.
- Providing learning resources such as guides and books.

These measures are vital steps towards helping participants to feel less isolated, to develop further, and to create highly effective relationships.

Balance formality and informality

Too much bureaucracy can kill a mentoring program; for instance, requiring mentors and mentees to fill out a detailed report following each meeting may sour the mentoring experience. On the other hand, *a little bit* of formality within a scheme serves many positive purposes: asking mentees to fill out a personal development plan focuses the efforts of mentor and mentee. In addition, concise development reviews (see Figure 6.4) are a good way of establishing whether relationships are on track. They can be used to evaluate the program as it goes along (formative evaluation), enabling you to troubleshoot problems early. The golden rule appears to be: a small dose of formality in the scheme and a large dose of informality in the individual relationships.

Furthermore, the rules and policies originally established for the program will need thoughtful reconsideration after the scheme has been running for a while. A living mentoring program will embrace the need for changes in the rules as a sign of evolution and progress. The impetus and direction for such revisions could come from a formative evaluation, but also from informal feedback and reflections on the scheme.

Mentoring relationships – what to look out for

Ensure relationships are neither over- nor under-managed

Throughout this book we have emphasized that within *developmental* mentoring the main responsibility for the relationships lies with the mentee. Mentees should drive the association, set meetings and define the agenda. Even so, some mentors still tend to be overbearing, wanting to control the course of events. Naturally, this approach defeats the object of the relationship – to create independent learners, who gain strength and efficiency from knowing how to manage their own development. This is why it is so important to ensure that mentors really understand their role and its boundaries – managing the mentee is not an aspect of it! That said, it would be equally devastating to have a mentor who does not invest any thought into the relationship and does not think about and prepare for the mentee's needs in *any* manner. Again, the key lies in the balance: leaving most of the control with the mentee whilst providing gentle guidance.

Mentoring relationships can be over- or under-managed in other respects as well. For example, constantly having the program co-ordinator look over your shoulder may feel like extreme interference and be very disruptive. Within the framework of a formal scheme, the individual mentoring pairs should be granted as much freedom as possible. Yet external parties must be available to mentors and mentees if they require their help.

Take action to forestall breaches of confidentiality

Although extremely rare in formal schemes, breaches of confidentiality are a catastrophe when they happen. They damage the trust and confidence in all mentoring relationships within a program, not just the immediate one. In our experience, proper training of mentors and mentees goes a very long way towards ensuring that confidential information will not be leaked.

Avoid problems involving third parties

Problems from other people typically emanate from one or more of the following parties: line managers, colleagues or spouses. Each of these parties can get the wrong idea of the nature of a mentoring relationship. They can feel threatened (line managers), envious (colleagues) or jealous (spouses – particularly with cross-gender relationships).

Fortunately, there are ways in which you can minimize the occurrence of such feelings. As aforementioned, the whole organization (but colleagues and managers of mentees in particular) should be briefed on the nature and purpose of mentoring. The same should be done with spouses, this being the personal responsibility of mentors and mentees. In addition, it is important to make very clear why some employees but not others were afforded to enter the program. If the scheme is exclusive for any other reason, this must be put to others in the most rational and attractive way possible. Lastly, certain problems with third parties can also be minimized by encouraging mentoring pairs to hold their meetings in visible places, in which they can perhaps be seen but not heard.

Prompt mentor and mentee to establish the purpose of their association and to clarify their mutual expectations

'Why are we here? What are we trying to achieve? How are we going to relate to each other?' The success or otherwise of a mentoring relationship depends on the mentor and mentee answering these questions; it depends on defining the purpose of the relationship, the nature of the learning, and the roles that will be adopted by each party. Only with a clear focus will discussions be meaningful, motivation maintained and results achieved. What is more, having a particular goal to work towards (i.e. the mentee's specific learning, support or career needs) also provides a substantial boost to the rapport-building process.

Emphasize the importance of committing sufficient time

Not being able to commit the necessary time is a frequent problem on the part of both mentor and mentee. If the lack of time becomes pronounced, relationships tend to stagnate, not least because the person who makes more time available will begin to question the other party's commitment.

During mentor and mentee selection, a person's 'willingness and ability to invest time' should feature as an important criterion. The vitality of this can be further emphasized during the participant preparation when the issue of 'commitment' is being discussed.

Pre-empt cases of sexual/racial/disability discrimination

Discrimination can take many forms, but, as pointed out in Chapter 4, *all* types are likely to be the result of stereotypical thinking and behaviour present in organizations coupled with institutional discrimination. Variations of sexual, racial or disability discrimination within mentoring programs include the following:

1. People might be subtly or overtly prevented from having access to the program.

2. People might be given less support by the program's staff – this might pertain to help with finding a mentor and/or with the relationship in general.

3. People might be subjected to discriminatory behaviour on part of their mentor or mentee, and two types of relationships are most vulnerable to this occurring:

   - *Cross-gender dyads*: in principle, cross-gender mentoring has many merits: if the mentee is a woman and the mentor a senior (white) man, it provides her with an enhanced possibility to break the glass ceiling. (Male senior mentors seem generally more capable of providing mentees with economic advantages, but there is evidence that this effect is pronounced with *white* men. Naturally, this seems to be the result of situational factors, such as institutional discrimination, which marginalize the male black mentor in the first place, granting him less access to powerful positions than white men.) A male mentee will gain a lot in terms of learning how to interact with high-potential women or, indeed, women in general. The latter example was demonstrated in Case study 3.11, where senior managers were mentored by younger women in order to build a more woman-friendly work environment. Bearing in mind the increasing efforts of organizations to diversify at all levels, such an experience is invaluable! Unfortunately most organizations are still unable to provide sufficient numbers of female senior mentors who could mentor men, owing to the limited number of women in senior positions. Regardless of whether the mentor or the mentee is the man or woman, cross-gender relationships constitute a great opportunity for both parties to acquire different perspectives on issues.

   - *Cross-race dyads*: cross-race dyads can also bring enormous benefits to its members. Both parties are challenged to learn by being forced to venture outside their comfort zone and build their skill repertory.

In the rare cases where sexual, racial or disability discrimination occur, this needs to be dealt with swiftly for ethical reasons as well as the sake of the mentoring scheme's reputation. There are various penalties that can be applied to such offences, ranging from warnings of dismissal from the program to dismissal from the company. As with all disciplinary or grievance cases, the penalty should be appropriate to the offence and thorough procedures should have been carried out to verify any allegations.

To ensure that discrimination does not take place within your scheme, you can take the following measures:

- Inform everyone involved with the program about the company's position with regard to discrimination. Explain that a zero-tolerance policy is in operation, and that any such incidents will be taken very seriously, potentially leading to dismissal from the organization.
- Provide behavioural guidelines outlining ways in which ambiguities can be avoided. For example, encourage mentoring pairs to hold their meetings in fairly public places, such as company offices during work hours.
- Ensure that your reasons for excluding any one individual are related to factors other than race, gender or disability.
- Verify whether minority group mentees require additional help with finding a mentor, and if yes, respond to that need.

Mature mentoring schemes

There are many organizations running mentoring schemes that were initiated many years ago. Clearly, these organizations (and their people) will have changed significantly during this period – hopefully for the better as a result of implementing mentoring schemes!

The key issue with mature mentoring programs is not the wholesale 'preservation' of the original formula, but the appropriate evolution of the scheme. In other words, the steering committee must review (ideally annually) the effectiveness of the mentoring program to establish what changes are appropriate and economic. A total revamp each year would be stressful, confusing and un-economic; on the other hand, no changes over a 10-year period would be unwise and intensely boring (not least for the program coordinator!).

The foundations for a successful long-term mentoring program are the same as for any mature organization. The need for change must be balanced against the need for consistency and integrity of core values. Although people and situations change each year, the principles of personal growth and development with integrity are relatively stable. Therefore, the program coordinator and the steering committee must be alive to the opportunities for improvement revealed, but must exercise care and judgment when making any changes. Although the changes to the mentoring program following a formal evaluation were considered in detail in Chapter 10, some useful triggers for change are:

- *Feedback*: whether gained formally or informally, the views and suggestions of mentors and mentees over the long term will help to enhance both the effectiveness and the 'enjoyableness' of the scheme.
- *Benchmarking*: comparisons with other organizations can also help to keep the mentoring program valid. This is especially relevant when the organization is seeking to tackle a new challenge by using mentoring – contrasting it with an established scheme can be very valuable.
- *Expert contribution*: finally, external advisors will often come with fresh eyes to the organization, and bring experience of very different mentoring environments and processes to bear on the existing program.

The techniques of continuous improvement are critical in keeping the mentoring program fresh and relevant. Continuous improvement calls for many small enhancements to be made on an almost daily basis, ensuring that emerging problems and inefficiencies are identified and removed before they become ingrained.

The end of a scheme

Yes, all schemes should be evaluated and changes may need to be introduced to keep them effective. However, even the most successful schemes can come to a final close. This is quite natural, and reflects the fact that the goal for which the program was implemented has been achieved. A scheme can thus be terminated, or replaced by an alternative one that focuses on a different objective.

Summary

Many things could theoretically go wrong in a mentoring scheme – for example, there may be too little or too much formality, relationships that come to an end may do this without the necessary follow-up, or mentors and mentees may receive too little support throughout the scheme. Yet most of the pitfalls and problems that we have considered in this chapter are perfectly avoidable by planning, designing and implementing your scheme thoroughly. Planning for a mentoring scheme is a little bit like revising for exams – the chances of success are slim without forethought. Hopefully this chapter, and indeed this entire book, will help you to design a high-quality scheme.

Other challenges, such as mentor and mentee incompatibility, cannot be avoided, no matter how great the amount of planning. These types of problems are simply subject to risk-minimization. Again, this chapter should have given you some useful pointers as to how to do this. You also need an element of flexibility when running a mentoring scheme – as in all walks of life, things rarely go 100 per cent according to plan. Therefore you must be prepared to troubleshoot and to deal with issues as they arise, rather than panic when something goes 'wrong'. At some point, 'being flexible' might also mean allowing a program to come to an honourable finale.

Index